PELICAN BOOKS

A717

ON JUSTICE IN SOCIETY

MORRIS GINSBERG

Morris Ginsberg was born in 1889 and was educated at University College, London, where he was a Martin White and J. S. Mill Scholar. From 1914–23 he was assistant and lecturer in the Department of Philosophy and in 1926 he was elected a Fellow of the College. For several years he taught both at University College and the London School of Economics and in 1929 he succeeded L. T. Hobhouse as Martin White Professor of Sociology at the L.S.E. and was Head of the Department of Sociology for twenty-five years. Thousands of students will recall his lectures on Sociology, Social Psychology, and Social Philosophy. He has been Visiting Professor in several universities overseas. In 1954 the University of London conferred upon him the title of Emeritus Professor of Sociology. He is an Honorary Doctor of Laws of Glasgow and Nottingham Universities and was President of the Aristotelian Society in 1942–3. In 1953 he was elected a Fellow of the British Academy.

Among Professor Ginsberg's publications are: *The Material Culture and Social Institutions of the Simpler Peoples*, 1915 (joint-author); *The Psychology of Society*, 1921 (ninth edition 1964); *Sociology*, 1934; *Reason and Unreason in Society*, 1947; *On the Diversity of Morals*, 1956; *Evolution and Progress*, 1961; *Nationalism: A Reappraisal*, 1961.

MORRIS GINSBERG

On Justice in Society

*

PENGUIN BOOKS
in association with William Heinemann

Penguin Books Ltd, Harmondsworth, Middlesex, England
Penguin Books Inc., 3300 Clipper Mill Road, Baltimore 11, Md, U.S.A.
Penguin Books Pty Ltd, Ringwood, Victoria, Australia

—

First published simultaneously by Penguin Books and Heinemann 1965

—

—

Made and Printed in Great Britain
by Hazell Watson & Viney Ltd, Aylesbury, Bucks
Set in Linotype Baskerville

Contents

Introduction

'INJUSTICE arises when equals are treated unequally, and also when unequals are treated equally.'[1] What is the connexion between justice and equality and what sort of differences justify differential treatment? These are the principal problems which I set out to explore in this book.

I find it necessary to distinguish between formal and substantive justice. Formally, justice consists in the ordering of human relations in accordance with general principles impartially applied. But, as critics of Kantian ethics have taught us, we cannot deduce from the formal character of a rule or norm what the rule should be. The statement that equals should be treated equally and unequals unequally throws no light on what is to be done by, to, or for equals and unequals. To answer these questions we have to take into consideration the ends or purposes of action and the claims and obligations connected with them. In other words, in order to discover the content or substance of justice it is necessary to establish a body of rights and duties and to examine them in the light of the formal principle of equality, the aim being to exclude every form of discrimination not justified by relevant differences.

In developing my argument I have adopted the following procedure. In the first chapter I set out briefly the ethical theory which is to form the basis of my discussion. In this I have been guided by the rationalist tradition in ethics. In other words, I take moral judgements to be neither expletives, nor commands, nor irrational commitments, but genuine judgements in the sense that they are capable of being true or false and that, like other judgements, they are subject to rational tests, such as consistency and coherence.

1. Aristotle, following Plato, *Laws*, bk VI, p. 757.

In order to confine my discussion within a manageable compass I have tried to avoid all general treatment of the relations between ethics, social philosophy, and jurisprudence. My aim has been to clarify the concept of justice and to show its bearing on the social problems of our age. In this task I have derived most help from the writings of my teacher, friend, and colleague, L. T. Hobhouse (1864–1929). I have also been guided and stimulated throughout by the works of Henry Sidgwick, especially by the *Methods of Ethics* which I consider to be among the greatest treatises on ethics in the English language. My indebtedness to more recent writers will, I hope, be abundantly clear from my references.

Sidgwick was among the first thinkers to establish that value and obligation, good and right, are terms not further reducible or analysable into each other or into terms not implying them. He showed further that moral judgements have conative force, that is, that they are capable of supplying a motive to action, or of inhibiting and controlling action. Whether his theory of general happiness as the ultimate end and standard of conduct is to be accepted is another and independent question. In my view, moral experience discloses a plurality of values of varying importance and a plurality of obligations of varying stringency. The moral problem is to estimate the comparative worth of the different values and to arbitrate between the claims of the various norms or obligations they carry with them.

Hobhouse has, I think, given the best modern exposition of the doctrine that goes back to Aristotle of rational appetition or desire and he has used the doctrine effectively in the studies he devoted to the ethical evaluation and reconstruction of social and political institutions.[1]

The function of reason, in Hobhouse's view, is the progressive interpretation and guidance of life and experience. The 'practical reason' is not to be conceived as a

1. See *The Rational Good*, 1921, and *The Elements of Social Justice*, 1922.

faculty concerned with abstract truths deducible from first principles that have nothing to do with feelings and desires, but as operating within them and transforming them. We have not to choose between Hume's view of reason as the slave of the passions and Kant's view of it as independent of them and overriding them. We may conceive of it rather as that within our personality which strives for integration, deeper than conscious thought, but the more effective the more it uses thought, working within and through the basic impulses and interests and deriving its energy from them.

I follow Hobhouse further in stressing the fact that so far from dominating the moral code, reason, in its articulate forms, is a late comer in the field. Even the highly developed codes contain inconsistent elements, fail to apply the rules they enjoin universally or impartially, and vary greatly in their openness to criticism and reconstruction. The method of the practical reason is to bring the inconsistencies to light, to disentangle the rational elements that have established themselves, and to generalize them. In carrying out this work of reconstruction, there are, Hobhouse warns us, two dangers to guard against. The first of these is the fanaticism of abstract right, the fanaticism that sees one wrong and sees it so big that it overshadows all else, or that seizes upon one right and would wreck society to vindicate it. The other is the worship of the established order conceived not only as greater than any individual, but as something in which the individual is lost. I have tried in my own way to follow the procedure developed by Hobhouse in the effort to avoid both these dangers.

The task of ethics I take to be twofold: to bring out what is involved in the notion of a principle or norm of action, and to survey the major or dominant goods that we discover in seeking to satisfy our needs and capacities. Value and obligation are, I think, combined in the notion of an ideal of action. Ideals at once attract and constrain. They stand before us as something desirable, though not necessarily desired, something which makes demands on us, which we cannot attain without tension and struggle, but which none the less is also a fulfilment of our nature. Ideals are built up by a process of constructive imagination out of the experiences of successes and failures that we go through in seeking to satisfy our basic needs. Hence a survey of these needs affords a clue to the major or dominant goods. In this way, for example, the ideal of health is related to the needs of body and mind, the ideal of love to the need to seek a response from others and to respond to them, the ideal of truth to the need to know, to construct, to appreciate. Ideals serve as a source of inspiration pointing beyond what has so far been attained and capable of evoking potentialities hitherto unsuspected. They also serve as agencies of guidance and control. Truth, love, bodily and mental health have their own norms and impose their own demands. They provide what may be called the middle principles of morality and thus give content to the formal principle implicit in morality as such, the principle that there are principles applicable impartially to all cases coming under them.

In Chapter II I pass to the concept of justice. The core of justice I take to be the exclusion of arbitrariness. Hence the great importance of the growth of legality, or the rule of law, which is slowly seen to carry with it the implication that no one can be a judge of his own cause and that the conditions and methods under which society may apply coercion should in their turn be defined and limited by law. The just can up to a point be identified, as Aristotle said, with the lawful. But, of course, laws may themselves be unjust or unjustly administered. Justice therefore requires that the law-makers should themselves be subject to the law and that the laws should be not only impartially administered but free from arbitrariness or ungrounded discrimination. Broadly, justice consists in (i) the exclusion of arbitrariness, more particularly of arbitrary power, whether exercised by individuals on each other, or by society on its members; (ii) principles governing the distribution of the conditions of well-being; (iii) provisions to ensure remedies or compensation for losses or injuries.

The further definition of justice involves a survey of the main rights and duties now generally recognized as essential conditions of full membership of a democratic society. It is necessary to distinguish between moral and legal rights and duties. Morally, a person's rights consist of the claims that he can justly make to the conditions of well-being: his duties consist of what he can justly be expected to contribute to well-being. Legal rights and duties – that is, claims and obligations enforceable at law – may or may not be fully in harmony with prevalent moral opinion, or with what critical revaluation might establish as necessary conditions of well-being. The general principle governing rights and duties is that of equality. This asserts that like cases should be treated in like manner and that differential treatment requires justification by reference to differences in the persons concerned or in their circumstances. In this context Aristotle's distinction between arithmetical and proportionate equality is important. But for his principle of 'proportion to merit' we must substitute 'proportion to relevant resemblances and differences'. When this is done, it becomes clear that the criteria of relevance vary with the rights and duties under consideration. Thus what is relevant in dealing with political rights may not be equally relevant in dealing with economic or educational rights. The problems thus arising are central to my inquiry and they form the substance of Chapters III–IX.

In Chapter X I return to the part of justice concerned with the exclusion of arbitrary power and consider its bearing on the principles of the criminal law. My main concern is with the ethical basis of punishment. In dealing with it, I try to look at punishment in relation to the broad aims of the legal system which I take to be the definition, maintenance, and adjustment of rights and duties. In existing societies the use of penal methods is probably unavoidable, but it is argued that we must look forward to a time when dangerous criminals will be segregated and for the rest society will concentrate on removing the conditions favouring crime and on encouraging the growth of a widely diffused sense of responsibility increasingly independent of punishment or the threat of punishment.

In Chapter XI I discuss some of the problems of moral and legal justice among states. My aim in doing so has been to inquire how far the general account I have given of justice within states applies to the relations between states. The first principle that emerges is, as was already pointed out by Kant, that states have a duty to establish the rule of law. This entails that they must abandon their claims to be judges in their own cause and that they are under an obligation to create an international authority with power to enforce its decisions. Next, in passing from the formal requirements of justice to its substance or content, it becomes necessary to examine the body of rights and duties, moral and legal, recognized as binding or demonstrably necessary as conditions of general well-being. But here there is an important difference between justice within states and justice between them. For international justice and morality are still in what may be called the *laissez faire* or individualist stage. Justice is conceived as concerned mainly with the negative injunction not to hurt or interfere with others. It is only just beginning to concern itself with the positive task of determining what can be done to secure an equitable distribution of the conditions of well-being for all concerned. The rights of states are still interpreted as inhering in each state independently of the rest, instead of defining the conditions in which states can live together and co-operate in the service of a good common to them all. Neither in regard to economic matters such as access to markets or raw materials, or the movements of population, nor in reference to political rights, such as representation on international organs, have the principles of distributive justice been defined either from the legal or ethical point of view. The conceptions underlying the 'welfare state' have hardly begun to be seriously applied to the society of states.

The rights and duties of states are very imperfectly defined. The most commonly recognized in international law and opinion include, so far as I can see, the right of security and territorial integrity, the right of independence or self-determination, the right to conclude agreements and alliances, the right to a share in the making of international law. I have discussed these briefly in relation to the governing principle of equality. Some writers on international law have dismissed the 'equality of states' as redundant or misleading.[1] But the objections to it are based on a notion of equality which I do not wish to defend. Equality does not mean that states are in fact equal, nor that they ought always to be treated as though they were. It asserts that they are all entitled to equal consideration and that differential treatment requires justification in terms of relevant differences between them or in the circumstances. The distinction between what Aristotle called 'arithmetical' and 'proportionate' equality is of importance in this context. Thus, for example, in dealing with political rights, if a privileged position is given to the Great Powers, this requires justification on some relevant ground of differentiation, by showing, for example, that their exceptional voting rights are likely to increase the capacity of the international organization in question to discharge its functions effectively.

In a world divided into power *blocs*, facing each other in fear and suspicion, the prospect of establishing a world authority with inclusive powers of legislation and enforcement must seem utopian. Nor is even an authority restricted to the sole function of preventing war within sight. The most that we can hope for in the near future is that the two Super Powers, Russia and America, might be induced by the fear of self-destruction to agree to some measure of nuclear arms control. Even then there would

1. Cf. J. L. Brierly, *The Law of Nations*, ch. IV.

remain the danger arising from the desire of other major powers to develop or retain their own nuclear deterrents and of local non-nuclear wars precipitating a war involving the Super Powers. Possibly, the threat of annihilation may lead the rival groups of powers to work for the establishment of neutral zones and to accept a measure of international control of armaments generally. Granted the removal or mitigation of the fear of war, states would be more willing to accept limitations on national sovereignty and to increase the strength and widen the scope of existing international institutions, governmental and non-governmental. It would seem that, while the maintenance of peace can only be assured in the long run by a world-wide organization, other purposes may be served better by regional groups of like-minded states or functional groups cutting across state boundaries.

Throughout the previous chapters the question had repeatedly to be raised of the relation of law to morals. To this I return in Chapter XII. I deal first of all with the attempts made by Kant and his followers on the one hand, and the Utilitarians on the other, to define the principles of legislation and also with the recent discussions in connexion with the *Report on Homosexuality and Prostitution.*

I try to show that the tendency of liberal as contrasted with totalitarian societies has been to avoid both the separation and the fusion of law and morality. No single principle has emerged for determining what may be safely left to individuals and what justifies coercion. In general, restraint is considered just if shown to be necessary to equalize freedom or to assure greater freedom on the whole. The individualist formula that coercion is rightly used to limit coercion retains its importance, especially if interpreted to include not only the prevention of interference with one another by the use of physical force but also by the subtler abuses of unequal power. Nevertheless, it is now recognized that the formula fails to cover adequately the coercive powers of the law in promoting positive ends. With the growth of the idea of social responsibility, it has come to be realized that there are certain ends which are best secured by inclusive units with compulsory powers. The extent to which these powers are rightly used clearly depends on the level of social development. For what can be achieved by individuals acting independently or by voluntary agreement, and what requires collective action involving legislative control, depends on the degree of social differentiation and the diffusion of power and responsibility. What *ought to be done* by the various agencies thus partly turns upon what they *can do* consistently with the ends they seek to attain. Finally, free societies attach particular importance to freedom in the sphere of self-development and self-expression. They do so not because self-regarding acts are considered as falling outside the region of common concern, but because they value individual judgement and character and realize that these cannot be built up by coercion.

On the whole, while law and morals are increasingly interdependent, in the sense that changes in the law come to be influenced more and more by conceptions of well-being, care is taken in liberal societies to avoid their complete fusion. How the line is drawn depends partly on the limitations inherent in the machinery of the law, partly on the nature of the ends to which social policy is directed.

CHAPTER I

Ethical Foundations

Types of Ethical Theory

A HUNDRED years ago Whewell in his *Lectures on the History of Moral Philosophy* classified ethical theories as Dependent and Independent. In the Independent theories there is no explicit reference to the end to be attained by conduct; the quality of an action is taken to be known by direct intuition (Butler) or else a rule is obtained by reflection upon the nature of the case (Clarke and the *Jus Naturale*). In Dependent systems the quality of an action or its rule or maxim is considered as deducible from what is taken to be the end or chief good (Bentham). In our own time much the same point is made by classifying ethical theories as mainly Deontological in which the emphasis is placed on the notion of duty, obligation, rule or command, and Teleological in which the starting point is found in the notion of end or good. The distinction must not be drawn too sharply, for in some theories both methods of determining right conduct are recognized. Thus the Kantian ethics is perhaps the nearest approach to an ethic of duty. But even Kant does not discard the notion of end and he sums up the general content of duty in the injunction to seek one's own perfection and the happiness of others. And Aristotle, who held that the task of ethics was to define the good or chief end of human striving, maintained nevertheless that the virtuous act could be known directly by the wise and experienced man. However, the classification into Deontological and Teleological theories is useful as indicating serious differences of emphasis.

Both types of theory can be further subdivided as Reductive or Non-reductive. According to the reductive theories the notions of good and right are not ultimate, but can be interpreted psychologically or sociologically. 'X is right' is taken to express a psychological fact, namely that I like X and would like you to like it. Or else 'X is right' may be interpreted sociologically, namely, as asserting that X belongs to a class of acts which, in a given society, tend to arouse general liking or approval. Both the notions of 'good' and of 'right' can be thus analysed. 'Good' is shown to be related to desire, satisfaction, fulfilment; obligation to some form of constraint, whether considered as the pressure exerted by some part of the mind on others, or by society on individuals. The distinction I have in mind has been expressed in recent writings by the terms 'naturalistic' and 'non-naturalistic'. But these words are very confusing. 'Non-naturalistic' suggests something extra-natural or supernatural. But morality is 'natural' to man in the sense that desire, purpose, and the rational consideration of purposes and reflection on conduct are part of his nature. 'Naturalism', in its turn, suggests 'materialism'. If this highly ambiguous word is taken to exclude reason and purpose, it is difficult to see how notions like good or right can arise at all. The main point of the distinction, namely whether ethical terms are or are not analysable into terms which do not imply them, is then better expressed by the terms Reductive or Non-reductive.

The resulting classification may be shown in the following scheme:

Deontological Theories	Teleological Theories
(a) Reductive	(a) Reductive
(b) Non-reductive	(b) Non-reductive

In recent decades the 'Non-reductive' theories have concentrated mainly on the closer analysis of the notions of right and good, and their relations to each other.[1] On the

1. John Laird, *A Study in Moral Theory*, 1926.
   W. D. Ross, *The Right and the Good*, 1930.
   E. F. Carritt, *The Theory of Morals*, 1930; *Morals and Politics*, 1935; *Ethical and Political Thinking*, 1947.
   H. W. B. Joseph, *Some Problems in Ethics*, 1931.
   C. D. Broad, *Five Types of Ethical Theory*, 1930.

Reductive side the fullest account is still that of Westermarck, who has sought to support his theory of the emotional basis of moral judgements by showing its value in interpreting both the differences and similarities found to exist in the moral codes of different societies. The psychological approach may be illustrated by some of the works of Bertrand Russell, and by the 'emotivist' theories favoured for a time by some of the analytical or linguistic philosophers.

It is not my object here to examine these highly intricate movements of thought in any detail. But before proceeding to a statement of my own views some comment on the main issues seems desirable.

On the analysis of 'good' and 'right' I doubt whether anything of radical importance has been contributed since Sidgwick's meticulous discussion in the *Methods of Ethics.* He made the essential point that values could not be reduced to non-values. But he showed better sense than Moore in not stressing their indefinability. They could not indeed be defined in the sense of being analysed in terms which do not imply them. But they could be clarified, he thought, by examining their relations to other notions with which they are liable to be confused. 'Good', for example, though not analysable into more elementary notions, could be clarified by discussing its relations to the 'desirable', by showing that what is desirable is what I should desire if my impulses were in harmony with reason.[1] Similarly 'ought', 'right', are logically ultimate, though something might perhaps be said about the way these notions arise in the human mind.[2] Sidgwick argued further that if good and right could not be reduced to non-ethical terms, neither could they be reduced to each other. More consistently than Moore, he showed that right could not be defined as meaning 'best fitted to a given end or good' since right is used not only with reference to means but also to ends: we consider it right

1. Book I, ch. IX, 3. 2. Book I, ch. III, 3.

to adopt certain ends and to reject others, or to prefer a greater to a lesser good.

With all this I should agree but, in view of later discussions of the relation between the notions of good and right, I should add that, though different or distinguishable, these notions are not separable elements of the moral. The notion of value, excellence, or goodness carries within it the notion of worthwhileness, passing into obligatoriness. In recognizing anything as excellent we at the same time recognize it as worth having, worth doing, worth being or pursuing, as imposing an imperative of action or of respect and admiration. What particular kind of response is called for varies with the kind of goodness and its relative importance in the scale of excellence. Not all values have equal claims; the moral problem often consists in the grading of values and in making the choice that is most fitting.

The choice depends upon an appreciation of the proportionate objective values of ends and is at once cognitive and affective. It is not purely emotive but depends upon insight and judgement. This, also, Sidgwick saw clearly and thus disposed in advance of the 'emotive' interpretations of moral experience, favoured by some of the analytic philosophers in our own day. Moral judgements, he argued, cannot be fairly interpreted as meaning no more than that the acts judged evoke in the person judging a specific emotion or attitude favourable or unfavourable. Moral conviction does indeed contain feeling components, but these are inseparably bound up with beliefs, explicit or implicit, that the conduct in question is objectively right or wrong in the sense that it cannot without error be judged otherwise by any other mind. This of course does not imply that moral judgements are infallible. The claim to truth in this as in other contexts is not self-validating. What is asserted is that moral judgements are genuine judgements and unlike feelings are susceptible of being true or false. To take Sidgwick's example, it is absurd to say that when I assert that 'truth ought to be spoken' I mean no more than that the idea of truth-speaking arouses in my mind a feeling of approbation strengthened by the knowledge that people in my group generally sympathize with this feeling. For, if this were the case, it would follow that another man's disapprobation might equally be expressed by saying that 'truth ought not to be spoken'. We should then have two coexistent facts stated in two mutually contradictory propositions. Again, if I realize that an act which evokes in me a feeling of revulsion or disgust is not morally wrong and that I ought not to condemn it, the change in my moral opinion obviously does not mean that my feeling has changed, nor can a judgement that 'this action is right' mean that it is generally approved in my society. A moral innovator or rebel may well say: I know that this is generally approved but I think it wrong – *Athanasius contra mundum.* It is hard to believe that the opinions of the innovator have no moral significance until he gains wide approval for them.

Emotive Theories of Ethics

These arguments would perhaps not be disputed by those analytical philosophers who defend emotive theories of ethics. They agree that, in making moral judgements, people believe themselves to be talking not about their feelings but about the quality of the acts to which they refer. Nevertheless, it is maintained that in this they must be mistaken, since there is no evidence that there are such qualities nor any indication how they can be known. All that we can say, they maintain, is that in every community there are attitudes favouring certain classes of acts and not favouring others. In saying that such and such an act is right I am appealing to these attitudes. My object is not to state a fact but to direct, prescribe, or persuade. Why people respond favourably to certain facts and unfavourably to others is a question left to the sociologist, though nothing further is said about the kind of explanation which the sociologist might offer.[1] Ayer suggests that the Utilitarians have gone some way towards answering this question. But since the psychological basis of Utilitarianism is the weakest part of it, and since many forms of Utilitarianism repudiate 'reductivism', Ayer's suggestion is not very helpful.

If reductivism is to be accepted then moral experience must be profoundly delusive. People making moral judgements clearly take themselves to be making statements about acts or persons and not about how they feel about them. On what grounds is it maintained that in this they are mistaken?

In the early phases of logical positivism, appeal was made to the so-called principle of verification. According to this, statements have meaning only when they are either analytic or empirically verifiable. Since, in the view of the Positivists, ethical statements belong to neither of these types, in other words, since they are not tautologies and can be neither verified nor confuted by sense experience, they are not judgements, and, in making them, nothing whatever is asserted. As I can see no reason for accepting the verification principle, or for limiting experience to sense experience, I do not consider this argument impressive.

What other reasons are there for rejecting non-reductivist interpretations? So far as I can see, three lines of argument have been followed. The first two go back to Hume and relate to the notion of good. Thus A. Ross argues as against Moore that from the knowledge that an object O has the quality X (good) nothing whatever follows as regards effort or action; the mere recognition of an object by itself carries with it no injunction or command to bring it into being.[2] Similarly, Ayer argues that even supposing that good could be apprehended by a form of intuition other than sense perception, nothing whatever would follow as regards conduct. This echoes Hume's

1. Cf. Ayer, *Horizon*, vol. XX, September 1949, pp. 176–7.
2. Cf. *Kritik der sogenannten praktischen Erkenntnis*, 1933, p. 78.

argument: even if moral relations could be shown to exist, they would have no power to produce action: they could not be proved to be 'universally forcible and obligatory'.[1] Ayer's version of this is: to say that a situation has a certain property does not entail that it is preferable to other situations, or that it is anyone's duty to bring it into existence.[2] To this the reply is that an argument of this sort might have some validity as against those who take good to be a simple quality, analogous to the quality apprehended in sense perception. But it has no application to the view outlined above. For, according to this, the notion of excellence carries with it the notion of worthwhileness. It does not make sense to ask why it is worthwhile to pursue what is worthwhile. Furthermore, the apprehension of value is psychologically effective; it can exercise an important, if not necessarily a determinative, influence on our actions.

The other line of argument is clearly developed by Hume.[3] If you ask anyone why he does anything he will say it is because it is the means to a desired end. If you persist and ask why he desires this end he will refer to a further end until he reaches an end which is desired for its own sake. This ultimate end can have no further 'reason for it' other than its 'accord with human sentiment and affection'. In a similar way Ayer argues that when we ask why we value anything we should eventually come to the point where we would have to say: 'I value it, because I value it.' But the fact that in reasoning about our actions we discover that there are certain ends which are desirable for their own sake throws no doubt on the rationality of our choice. Consider the analogous case of reasoning in other fields. In examining our beliefs we may also reach a point where no further evidence is required, and we rely on direct intuition. If such direct intuitions are challenged we examine them further by comparing them with other intuitions or by inquiring

1. *Treatise*, Book III, part 1, p. 466.
2. *Horizon*, vol. XX, pp. 177–8.
3. *Enquiry*, app. 1, v.

whether they can be shown to be implicit in the generally accepted framework of knowledge in the relevant field. So in matters of choice if we ask if the thing we regard as having intrinsic value is really valuable, we have to consider whether we know enough about its nature and relations to other values, and whether it is implicit in the general scheme of valuation. Neither Hume's nor Ayer's arguments come in any way near showing that we do not reflect on our valuations or that such reflection is confined to means.

There is a further line of argument on which Russell in his earlier writings laid great stress. This is based on the diversity of opinions on moral matters:

> If we all agreed, we might hold that we know values by intuition. We cannot *prove* to a colour-blind man that grass is green and not red. But there are various ways of proving to him that he lacks a power of discrimination which most men possess, whereas in the case of values there are no such ways and disagreements are much more frequent than in the case of colours. Since no way can be even imagined for deciding a difference as to value, the conclusion is forced upon us that the difference is one of tastes, not one as to any objective truth.[1]

This was written in 1935. He does not proceed to inquire into the nature of moral disagreements and the conclusions he draws from the fact that there are disagreements are somewhat hastily formulated. Thus he argues that punishment cannot be justified on the ground that the criminal has done a 'wrong' act but only on the ground that he has behaved in a way which others wish to discourage. 'Hell, as a place of punishment for sinners, becomes quite irrational.' Why 'irrational'? All that follows is that the idea of Hell is one that Russell does not like.

It is worth while pointing out that in his earlier writings Russell gave an effective reply to the arguments based on the variability of moral judgements.

1. *Science and Religion*, 1935, p. 238.

The view [he argued] that good is subjective and variable is rendered plausible by the divergencies of opinion as to what is good or bad and by the difficulty of finding arguments to persuade people who differ from us on such a question. But difficulty in discovering the truth does not prove that there is no truth to be discovered.[1]

To this early view Russell to some extent returns in his latest work on ethics.[2] He expresses himself dissatisfied with the view that moral judgements merely express personal tastes. It is difficult to believe that when the Nazis say that to torture Jews is good and we say that it is bad the difference is analogous to the difference between those who say that oysters are good and those who say that they are nasty. This feeling of difference, though not decisive, says Russell, 'deserves respect and should make us reluctant to accept at all readily that all ethical judgements are wholly subjective'.[3] This leads him to inquire how people in fact differ about moral matters and he concludes that as to ends there is wide agreement. Most differences arise from different views about the effects of action and can be resolved with fuller knowledge. In other cases there is unreasoning submission to traditional taboos. These appear to believers as self-evident and unshakeable. Yet people can be made aware by a training in anthropology and history that while taken as certain in some communities they are rejected by others and that even in the same communities they are liable to change in the course of time. They can be induced to inquire into the *rationale* of the prohibitions and in the end to ask whether the prohibited acts do any harm other than evoking disgust. Russell gives very few instances of divergence of views about intrinsic values and in this claims far more than would be claimed by other rationalists. It is probable that even if agreement could be reached on matters of fact there might remain differences of opinion

1. *Philosophical Essays*, 1910, p. 10.
2. *Human Society in Ethics and Politics*, 1954.
3. op. cit., p. 26.

about the comparative worth of goods or their priority. The important point to stress from the point of view of the rationalist is not that there are no differences of opinion, but that such differences should not shake our belief that there is a true opinion to be discovered, and that in fact in the history of mankind some progress has been made towards moral truth as towards truth in other spheres of belief.

The arguments adduced by the 'reductivists' against their opponents are thus not very convincing despite the assurance with which they have been expounded. We may next ask whether the alternatives they offer are inherently consistent. To do this it would be necessary to inquire how far their general analysis is helpful in interpreting existing moral codes. The nearest approach is to be found in the massive work of Westermarck, who is not content with a theoretical analysis of concepts but tries to test their value by applying them to a wide range of facts. Less systematic but of great interest is the work of Russell, who again has not confined himself to the logical analysis of ethical terms, but has written extensively on the ethical aspects of social and political institutions.

As we have seen, Russell is not satisfied with the position he had adopted at an earlier period that moral judgements were expressions of wishes to which the distinction of true and false could not apply. In his most recent work he tries hard to justify the feeling that morality is more than a matter of individual taste. His new position, which is strikingly similar to Hume's, may be briefly summed up thus. (i) Good is defined as the property of arousing in the spectator an emotion of approval, bad as that which arouses disapproval. (ii) A survey of acts which arouse these emotions shows that on the whole those acts are approved which are likely to bring happiness or pleasure, while opposite effects are expected from acts that are disapproved of. (iii) Right conduct is then defined as an act which, on the available evidence, is likely to produce better effects than any other act that is possible in the circumstances; any other act is 'wrong'. What we ought to do is the act which is right. According to Russell, then, 'good' is the fundamental category of ethics, 'right' being defined as conduct which promotes what is good. The reason for this preference is that in his view there is more agreement as to what effects of action are thought desirable than as to what is thought right or wrong. These definitions and propositions, Russell claims, 'provide a coherent body of propositions which are as true (or false) in the same sense as if they were propositions of science'. With this may be compared Hume's summary of his own procedure:

> The hypothesis which we embrace is plain. It maintains that morality is maintained by sentiment. It defines virtue to be whatever mental action or quality gives to a spectator a pleasing sentiment of approbation; and vice the contrary. We then proceed to examine a plain matter of fact, to wit, what actions have this influence; we consider all the circumstances, in which these actions agree; and thence endeavour to extract some general observations with regard to these sentiments.[1]

How far does this attempt to build an objectivist ethic on a subjectivist basis succeed? Difficulties at once present themselves.

Firstly, in defining good or intrinsic value as that which satisfies desire it is at once added that this implies that the satisfaction of one person's desire is as good as another person's, provided the two desires are of equal intensity. It seems to me that this can only mean that it is Russell's desire that everyone should recognize that other people's desires are as good as theirs: it is certainly not the case that everybody, in fact, desires this. In Russell's view it is the business of wise institutions to encourage what he calls impersonal desires and to induce the belief that there need be no real conflict between self-interest and the interests of society. He invents a new emotion, called the emotion of impartiality, to this end. But to say that

1. *An Enquiry Concerning the Principles of Morals*, appendix I, 'Concerning Moral Sentiment'.

this is right or what ought to be done can mean no more than that it is Russell's desire that other people's desires should harmonize with his desires. Objectivity has not been attained. In the second place, in analysing desire Russell explicitly rejects the theory of psychological hedonism. What people desire is not pleasure but the various objects the attainment of which gives pleasure. If further it is agreed that pleasure is not the nearest that we can come to the common quality of the great majority of approved actions . . . that we do not in fact value pleasures in proportion to their intensity and that some pleasures seem to us inherently preferable to others[1] we seem to be led back to a theory analogous to that of Moore or of some Ideal Utilitarians which at one time Russell supported.

The difficulties of Russell's views, it seems to me, arise from the vagueness of his theory of human motives. In the Preface to his book he explains that those critics have misunderstood him who have accused him of overestimating the part of reason in human affairs. The trouble does not lie here but rather in his enormous over-simplification of the relations between inclination and will, reason and impulse. He quotes with approval Hume's assertion that 'Reason is and ought only to be the slave of the passions.' But he gives no very convincing arguments in support of this very quaint survival of faculty psychology. That reason 'by itself' is no cause of action no rationalist need be concerned to deny, since reason never works in an emotional or impulsive vacuum. Russell repeats Hume's assertion that reason is concerned only with means and never with the ends of actions, and he seems to think that this is obvious. But is it? The ends that people set themselves are complex and variable. They cannot be regarded as simply given and, in any case, means and ends are often intimately interwoven. Beliefs about ends and about the principles of conduct are far from being emotionally neutral. To say that they have no effect on action is con-

1. op. cit., p. 117.

trary to plain facts. Men have died for them. The whole theory of motivation thus needs re-examination. Impulse is no doubt needed to incite thought, but thought in turn can inspire or transform impulse. Reason has not only a regulative but a constitutive function in relation to the ends of action. A rational ethic must assume that there is such a thing as rational action, that intelligence has a part to play not only in cognition but in volition. It plays this part not merely by serving the natural inclinations or by overriding them and impelling them to conform to a law independent of the desires. It does so by bringing the ends of endeavour into consciousness and by clarifying and systematizing them in such a way as to make them serve the deeper needs of the personality. The function of the practical reason is thus misstated if it is confined to deliberation about means. It is concerned also with the relative worth of the different ends in relation to the cost involved in attaining them, and this task it cannot fulfil adequately without inquiry into the basic human needs and the grounds of our preferences and choices.

At heart Russell is an inveterate rationalist. 'The power of thought,' he once wrote, 'in the long run, is greater than any other human power.' [1] But he is hampered by an undue emphasis on the distinction between ends and means and an oversharp separation of impulse and will. He explains that reason can help us by taking into consideration all relevant desires and not merely those that happen to be strongest at the moment, and thus to realize our desires 'on the whole'. In our dealing with others, he says, reason enjoins impartiality, requires us to use persuasion rather than force and in persuasion to appeal to arguments which we believe to be valid. Is this because Russell believes that impartiality and intellectual integrity are more efficient than force or because they are valued for their own sake? That the former is the case has certainly not been shown. Russell himself has maintained that 'Conquest by force of arms has had more to do with

1. *Principles of Social Reconstruction*, p. 226.

the spread of civilization than any other single agency.'[1] If, however, impartiality and intellectual integrity are desired for their own sake, I do not see how such desires can be described as non-rational. It has to be added that in dealing with particular problems Russell repeatedly appeals to reason. Thus in his discussion of sexual morality he says that 'whatever sexual ethic may ultimately be accepted must be free from superstition and must have recognizable and demonstrable grounds in its favour.' ... 'There has to be consistency in life; there has to be continuous effort directed to ends that are not immediately beneficial and not at every moment attractive; there has to be consideration for others; and there should be certain standards of rectitude.'[2] It is hard to reconcile all this with the sharp separation of desire and reason, feeling and thought which his argument elsewhere implies and to believe that we can ever attain to 'a sane and balanced view of our relations to our neighbours and to the world' if the fundamental values lie outside the scope of reason.

Similar difficulties are involved in Westermarck's analysis of moral judgement.[3] His account is by far the most impressive of those who find the roots of morality in the emotional nature of man, backed as it is by a very wide survey of moral codes and social institutions. Yet in the end he allows to reason functions critical and constitutive to a degree which is inconsistent with his insistence on the emotional basis of moral judgements. Moral judgements are, in his view, ultimately to be traced to what, following Adam Smith, he calls the retributive emotions, gratitude and resentment, made 'disinterested' through sympathy and generalized through social agencies. What the moral judgement expresses, however, is not the emotions felt by individuals, but rather the tendency of certain acts to call forth emotions generally in a given society.

1. *Power*, p. 39. 2. *Marriage and Morals*, p. 243.
3. *Origin and Development of the Moral Ideas*, 2nd ed. 1917; *Ethical Relativity*, 1932.

Though he stresses the emotional origin of moral judgements, Westermarck is far from minimizing the part that has been played by reflective thought in the growth of morals. Reflection cannot change emotions but it can alter their direction in a manner which is socially extremely important. It can reveal more fully the character of the objects which normally evoke them and thus replace some emotions by others. Second, it can dissipate superstitious beliefs which tend to endow acts with qualities which do not really belong to them. Finally, by a critical examination of current morality it can often disclose the ways in which the emotions of approval and disapproval have come to be attached to given forms of conduct. Following this line of thought Westermarck shows with many illustrations that in the course of history moral attitudes have become more 'enlightened' and that there is good ground for believing that this growth of enlightenment will continue in the future.

In his account of the part played by reflection in morals Westermarck was no doubt again influenced by Adam Smith, who showed that approval and disapproval were not, as had been previously held by moralists, simple emotions but contain an element of judgement. Approval, in Adam Smith's view, involved not only a perception of the agreement of our feelings with the feelings of others, but also a recognition of the appropriateness or fitness of the feeling to its object. Westermarck tries to show how in various ways we discover by reflection that certain acts are not 'the proper objects of moral censure or blame'. As in Adam Smith's analysis, the notion of propriety or impropriety conceals a certain ambiguity. By 'proper' Westermarck sometimes means 'biologically primary or original', as when he says that gratitude is 'properly' felt towards what is a cause of pleasure and resentment towards anything that is the cause of pain. But at other times 'proper' is given a meaning analogous to the ethical use of the term 'fitting', as when we are told that we ought not 'properly' to condemn anything which, though it evokes aversion, in fact does no harm. In this way he thinks that certain sexual acts which are now morally condemned will come to be considered as morally indifferent, save in so far as they may involve injury to others. It would seem then that moral reflection has the important function of examining and criticizing existing tendencies to approval or disapproval in the light of a conception of what is 'fitting': that is, deserving of approval or disapproval.[1]

Linguistic Moralists and the place of reason in morals

Unlike Westermarck, who sought to test his definitions by showing their relevance in interpreting moral codes past and present, the analytic philosophers, who supported emotivism in the thirties and later, confine themselves mainly to a survey of verbal usage. I do not feel able to follow them in detail or to add anything to my previous comments on them. The pure emotivists appear to have talked themselves out, and, more recently, the linguistic moralists have sought in various ways to find a place for reason in moral judgements. The work of Mr Hare and Mr Toulmin is of great interest in this context, and I propose to comment on them very briefly.

Mr Toulmin's analysis of the functions of reason in morals is very elaborate.[2] It is conceived in a very generous spirit and his exposition makes a powerful appeal. Nevertheless I find it difficult to decide what his final position amounts to. He rejects the view that moral arguments are merely hortatory, persuasive, or imperative. We distinguish, he argues, between those approvals, recommendations, or commands for which there are valid reasons and those for which there are not. On the other hand, he also rejects the doctrine that moral assertions express judgements to the effect that certain actions or dispositions have

1. For fuller discussion compare my *Reason and Unreason in Society*, ch. III.

2. S. E. Toulmin, *The Place of Reason in Ethics*, 1950.

objective properties indicated by the words right or good. What then is expressed by moral judgements? His answer seems to resemble closely that given by Brentano. 'We call anything true,' says Brentano, 'when the recognition related to it is right. We call something good when the love related to it is right. That which can be loved with a right love, that which is worthy of love is good in the widest sense of the word.'[1] Toulmin puts the matter thus: to say that X is right is to say that X is worthy of approval, and this in turn seems to be regarded as equivalent to 'there is a valid reason for approving X'. In this, he says, moral judgements resemble logically valid statements. To say that an argument is valid does not mean that someone accepts it, but that it is worthy of acceptance. Similarly to say that an object is beautiful is to say that it is one which is worthy to be admired. 'These concepts – logical, ethical, and aesthetic alike – we can class together as gerundives, thereby opposing them to such logical categories, as properties or subjective relations (e.g. attractive). They can all be analysed as worthy of something or other.'[2]

There are two difficulties which I find in this analysis. Firstly, if 'X is right' is equivalent to 'X is worthy of approval' does not this imply that we are able to recognize X as something to which approval is appropriate? If so, do we not come back to the objective interpretation of moral assertions which Mr Toulmin has rejected? If 'X is worthy of approval' is taken as equivalent to 'there are valid reasons for approving X' the question arises what 'it' is for which there are valid reasons. The reasons given for a conclusion are surely not identical with the conclusion, and the latter may be true though the reasons given for it are invalid.

My second point relates to the account given by Mr Toulmin of the kind of valid reasons that may be given for accepting a moral assertion as true or rejecting it as false. His answer is (*a*) that there is a valid reason for

1. *Origin of the Knowledge of Right and Wrong*, English transl., p. 16. 2. op. cit., p. 71.

doing X when it can be shown to accord with rules or maxims accepted in our society while possible alternatives can be shown to conflict with such rules. (*b*) When the action under consideration is in conformity with some rules, but in conflict with others, or again, when the rules traditionally accepted are challenged, we consider it reasonable to appeal to an 'overall' principle, the principle namely that 'preventable suffering shall be averted'.[1] He explains that the avoidance of misery or frustration is the primary principle of morals, but that we also appeal to the positive principle of promoting fulfilment and happiness. 'The notions of "obligation", "right", "justice", "duty", and "ethics" apply in the first place when our actions and institutions may lead to avoidable misery for others; but it is a natural and familiar extension to use them also when the issue concerns the chance of deeper happiness for others and even for ourselves.'[2]

This is of course not a new doctrine but a return to rational utilitarianism of the type advocated by Sidgwick. With the form in which it is here put I have much sympathy. It is certainly important to judge actions or policies by their tendency to diminish or avert misery and to promote fulfilment and happiness. It is equally important to study the conditions, economic, political, and social, in which these ends can be attained. Toulmin's account leaves entirely untouched the question how we judge between different kinds of happiness, or rather between the different activities or modes of living in which happiness may be found, or how it is that we rate some activities as of higher value than others even though they do not differ in the amount of happiness associated with them. Nor does his discussion throw any light on the principles in accordance with which the means of happiness ought to be distributed, or on the question to what extent, if any, these principles are independent of utilitarian considerations. These are problems with which critics of utilitarianism are familiar. But apart from hints here and there

1. ibid., p. 69. 2. ibid., p. 160.

Mr Toulmin makes no serious attempt to deal with them.[1]

Mr Hare agrees that moral sentences are not merely expressions of approval or disapproval – not just interjections or expletives. They are commands. 'X is wrong' means 'do not do X', 'Good' is a term of commendation and to 'commend is to guide choice'. We do not use the term unless some decision is to be made; for example, to continue looking in the case of a good picture, to try to become like him in the case of a good man.

But commands may have reasons. The question is therefore what is the nature of these reasons?

To this Hare answers that the reasons are to be found in the effects the action is likely to produce, the principle which it observes, and the effects of observing the principle. If pressed further we should have to refer to a way of life of which the principle in question is a part:

> A complete justification of a decision would consist of a complete account of its effects, together with a complete account of the principles which it observed and the effects of observing those principles. Thus if pressed to justify a decision completely, we have to give a complete specification of the way of life of which it is a part. This complete specification it is impossible in practice to give. The nearest attempts are those given by the great religions, especially those which can point to historical persons who carried out the way of life in practice. If the inquirer still goes on asking: But why *should* I live like that, then there is no further answer to give him because we have *ex hypothesi* said everything that could be included in this further answer. We can only ask him to make up his own mind which way he ought to live; for in the end everything rests upon such a decision of principle. He has to decide whether to accept that way of life or not; if he accepts it then we can justify the decisions that rest upon it; if he does not accept it, then let him accept some other, and try to live by it.[2]

1. For further criticism see C. D. Broad, *Mind*, vol. 61, 1952; and Blanshard, *Reason and Goodness*, 1961, ch. IX.
2. R. M. Hare, *The Language of Morals*, 1952, p. 69.

This seems to assume that a way of life is a coherent system which you must accept or reject as a whole. But no existing society has such a coherent system. For example, within the 'Christian way of life' there are divergent and contradictory attitudes to divorce, birth control, war, capital punishment. Rational inquiry brings out these contradictions and this leads further to a re-examination of the accepted principles. This in turn passes to an evaluation of the content of the principles in terms of the ends they are supposed to serve and not merely in terms of their coherence with other principles. Thus Mr Hare's account ignores growth or change in moral outlook and throws no light at all on the way such change is to be directed or guided. How do you criticize the laws of divorce? Reference to a Christian way of life will not take you very far; for there are divergent answers which all claim to be Christian. Rational inquiry begins by considering the effects of the laws on the stability of the family; stability is itself shown to be necessary to secure the well-being of the children and to heighten the parental ties by a common interest in the well-being of the children. Even more general questions are involved, for example as to the attitudes to be taken to long term contracts which do not provide for abrogation in changed circumstances. We do not in fact argue about the way of life as a whole. We criticize the 'system' indirectly by challenging its constituent principles. Thus morality is never static; it is always in the making. For the philosophical critic it is not a case of 'Take it or leave it'.

Ideal Utilitarianism and the New Intuitionists

I cannot here attempt to deal even in outline with the highly intricate and subtle discussions that have been devoted, in the thirties, to the problem of the relations between the right and the good. By now the clouds of battle have dispersed, but it is hard to see what remains. The importance of what Moore called the 'naturalistic fallacy' appears to have been vastly exaggerated. It has very little application to those types of ethical theory which seek to find the nature of the good in rational appetition. It is possible but futile to ask whether it is good to desire what after due consideration of the nature of the object desired and its relations to other objects of desire you have judged to be worthy of desire. Nor does the method of deciding what things are intrinsically good by the ideal experiment of asking whether we should still think them good if they existed by themselves in absolute isolation seem to be as easily followed as Moore apparently supposed. I have always found it hard to share the excitement which these arguments aroused. More difficult is the problem whether the various goods enumerated by the Ideal Utilitarians or the duties singled out by the Deontologists form a 'disconnected heap', or are somehow united by a common principle. This, of course, is no new problem, but is one upon which philosophers have been engaged since the beginning of ethical theory. Recent discussions seem to me, however, to have suffered from an excessive reliance on the method of isolation and a failure to consider the relations of the various values and obligations to the basic needs of men and the social framework in which they seek satisfaction. The values of bodily and mental health, for example, cannot be isolated from the values of knowledge, insight, and constructive imagination, nor from the values of personal affections and group attachments. Moreover, if these values are to be assured for all, the problem of justice arises, the problem, that is, of assuring an equitable distribution of the means or conditions without which none of the major values can be attained. As we shall see each of the ideals has its own norms and they are therefore in a sense autonomous. But they are all limited by the constitution of the human mind and the conditions of life in society and are subject to the formal principles of morality; that is, universality and impartiality. The search for 'unity' means little unless it leads to a study of the ways in which the various ideals are in fact related and about the conditions, physical and social, in which they can be made to support one another or at least not to obstruct each other; by inquiring, for example, how mental is related to bodily health and how both these are related to the advance of morality and to improvements in social organization.

The result of my survey is to confirm my adherence to the rationalist tradition in ethics and particularly to the conclusion reached by Sidgwick that (*a*) moral judgements are genuine judgements and not expletives, commands, or irrational commitments, and that (*b*) the predicates they employ, good and right, are not further reducible or analysable into each other or into terms not implying them.

Thus goodness does not consist in being desired or in satisfying desire, or in evoking approval, though it may arouse desire, give satisfaction, or call forth appreciation. Similarly, obligation may be experienced as constraint or pressure, whether coming from within or without, but obligations subsist whether the pressure is felt or not. We discover values in the course of pursuing our purposes, spurred on by success and disappointment and guided by insight and constructive imagination. We may be wrong about them. What appears good may on reflection be seen to be not really good, and actions once tabooed may come to be seen as morally indifferent.

The simple judgements of value, such as those implied in the enjoyment of warmth or affection, resemble judgements of perception. They are direct, require no special training, and are very nearly universal. The more complicated valuations are built up slowly with the formation of complex purposes and involve comparative judgements of values and insight into means–ends relationships. The predicates good and right are the forms or categories which we use in making these judgements. In this they resemble the categories of perceptual judgement, such as quality or relation, but they are not reducible to them.

The way of being a value or good is different from the way of being a quality or relation. There are different ways of being a value just as there are different ways of being a quality. The goodness of wisdom, as Aristotle explained, is not the same as the goodness of pleasure or honour. Aristotle adds that, though what is good is different in different actions, it is in each case that for the sake of which an action is undertaken. Ends differ, but they are always something for the sake of which an action is done.[1] This confines value to end-seeking processes. Perhaps we ought to say that what values have in common is that they are considered to be worth having, doing (including contemplating), or being. This applies to goods or values generally. Moral values presuppose other values. They pertain to actions or dispositions to bring other values about, or to refrain from actions which bring about disvalues. This brings us to the notion of obligation; that is, the recognition that something ought to be done or avoided. 'Ought' is, as we have seen, irreducible. But *what* ought to be done is the production of a value. The ought is implicit in the value. The major values or goods have each their own norms. Health, truth, or love have their own canons and impose their own demands. Moral obligation is the recognition and acceptance of these canons and the discipline they impose. The norms are inherent in the values and vary with them. In other words, different values give rise to different claims and moral choice consists in estimating their comparative importance and defining the appropriate response.

Implicit in moral obligation is the recognition of and commitment to the principle that there are principles of action; that is, rules applicable impartially to all cases of a class of acts. What the rules enjoin cannot be deduced from the notion of rule as such and can only be determined by reference to particular values and the norms governing them. Obligation is experienced in the early phases of moral development in the respect for custom as

1. *Nicomachean Ethics*, Book I, VII, 1, Peters' translation.

custom, though there may also be some recognition of the values served by particular customs. As morality becomes more reflective the *rationale* of customs is challenged, and efforts are then made to disentangle the values involved and to reconsider the appropriateness of the norms supposed to be necessary to sustain them.

The task of ethics is then (a) to bring out what is implied in the notion of a norm or principle of action, and (b) to survey the major or dominant goods or values and the norms or injunctions they entail. In dealing with (a) we seek to define the formal character of morality; in (b) we are concerned with its content. The most important attempt to show what is implied in there being such a thing as morality at all is that made by Kant. Leaving aside those points in his analysis which depend on his metaphysical theory of the distinction between the noumenal and phenomenal self, and his views on the relation between will and desire, the notion of a principle of action carries with it as it seems to me the following implications:

(a) A law or principle is by its nature general. It asserts that something is to be done or omitted by like persons in like circumstances.

(b) In acting in accordance with the rule we may have to overcome immediate impulse or desire.

(c) The recognition or acceptance of the rule is capable of supplying a motive to action.

(d) The generality of a rule implies impartiality as between different persons. What constitutes 'like' persons and 'like' circumstances has to be ascertained objectively: that is, by criteria which define the class of acts to which the rule applies. This impartiality has to be learnt. It is easy for anyone to believe that he is an exception to the rule, or that the circumstances in which he finds himself are different from the circumstances contemplated in the rule.

(e) The notion of rule or law is sometimes taken as implying a relationship of command–obedience, and the moral law is then interpreted as a self-imposed command – a command of the 'higher' part of our nature over the 'lower'. From the psychological and sociological points of view there is truth in this. The rules come to the individual from without and are imposed upon him. But I think that even in early stages it is dimly recognized that for commands there are reasons, though the reasons given may be wrong reasons. If the command is interpreted as coming from God it may nevertheless be seen that the will of God is not arbitrary, that God wills the right because it is right, and that what is right is so, not merely because he wills it. Perhaps there is a realization of this in Abraham's intercession for Sodom: 'Shall not the judge of all the earth do right.' [1]

The notion of rule or law as a command is, however, important because it is in reference to the administration of justice by judges or other authorities that the notion of impartiality was first clearly formulated. Thus already in ancient Egypt judges were instructed: Regard him thou knowest as him whom thou knowest not. In Deuteronomy we are told 'Ye shall not respect persons in judgement but ye shall hear the small as well as the great'; [2] and, it may be noted, this is said to apply to the stranger within the gate. In Greek jurisprudence the principle of the equal application of the laws among the citizens is clearly recognized. Indeed it is taken as axiomatic in all legal systems.

These points have been brought out in various ways by philosophers. The most important is the Kantian Categorical Imperative: 'Act on principles which you would see universally adopted.' With this may be compared Sidgwick's Axiom of Justice: 'Whatever action any of us judges to be right for himself, he implicitly judges to be right for all similar persons in similar circumstances.' A corresponding proposition stating what ought to be done *to*, not by, different individuals is Clarke's Rule of Equity: 'Whatever I judge reasonable or unreasonable

1. Genesis, xviii. 25. 1. Deut., i. 17.

that another should do for me: that by the same judgement I declare reasonable or unreasonable that I should *in the like case* do for him.' These principles are more precise than the Golden Rule. For, as this is usually stated, it ignores the possibility that there may be differences in the circumstances, or in the natures of two individuals A and B which would make it wrong for A to treat B in the way in which it is right for B to treat A. Furthermore, the 'other' may not be satisfied with what we would want in his place and what he wants may not be good for him or for the world. It might perhaps be thought that the qualifications introduced by Sidgwick and Clarke – 'similar persons', 'in the like case' – make the principles trivial. But this is a mistake. The idea that like cases should be treated alike has been and is of the greatest importance as a weapon against injustice. It challenges those who wish to treat individuals differently to show cause for differential treatment, and the growth of justice has consisted very largely in the realization that certain differences such as those of sex, race, religion are no adequate ground for discrimination.

The formal principles, as we have seen, are implied in every rule but they cannot determine which rule – if any – is applicable in any particular case, or with what limitations. Sidgwick thought that particular duties were deducible from the principle of general happiness. But happiness, as critics of utilitarianism have shown, is too wide a term for this purpose. To be serviceable it has to be related to the activities in which it is found, to what Sidgwick himself calls the sources of happiness. 'We are happy in something and the something must be worthwhile. Take from it its intrinsic value and our happiness becomes an illusion.'[1] If we separate happiness from the experience which it tones or qualifies, it becomes difficult to distinguish kinds of happiness – a distinction which in developed moral experience we certainly make. Once this separation is avoided, we are led to admit a plurality of

1. Hobhouse, *Elements of Social Justice*, p. 18.

ends which are worthwhile and to realize that worthwhileness or goodness is not exhausted in pleasureableness or hedonic tone. The vacillations or variations of customary morality are, I think, more intelligible on the hypothesis of a plurality of goods than on that of a single or all-inclusive good. Granted a variety of goods, differences in moral codes can be linked in part with differences of view regarding their comparative worth or order of priority, different ways of resolving conflicts between them, and differences in the conditions, physical and social, in which they can be obtained. That the only differences which are important are differences in simple pleasurableness or hedonic tone has not been shown and is far from being self-evident.

But perhaps Utilitarianism has suffered unduly from its association with psychological hedonism. If happiness is interpreted not in terms of simple pleasureableness but as a more pervasive feeling indicating healthy functioning of basic impulses and absence of frustration, then the injunction to promote happiness is clearly of great moral importance. Perhaps the contribution of Utilitarianism can be seen more clearly in what it excludes than in what it enjoins. The elimination or mitigation of misery, suffering, and pain is surely a task sufficiently definite whatever may be thought of the difficulty of defining positive good. It has indeed been suggested that instead of the general happiness of the greatest number it would be more practicable to aim at the least pain of the smallest number.[1] Next, Utilitarianism deserves credit for the stress it lays on impartiality. Sidgwick's principle of justice has already been cited above. But with whatever consistency, earlier Utilitarians are no less emphatic. 'The happiness of the most helpless pauper constitutes as large a portion of the universal happiness as that of the most opulent member of the community.'[2] 'Everyone is to count as one and nobody for more than one,' Bentham tells us. 'Between

1. Goldscheid, *Zur Ethik der Gesamtheit*, p. 383.
2. Bentham, *Constitutional Code*, I, XV, 7.

his own happiness and that of any other human being the utilitarian theory requires a man to be rigidly impartial,' says J. S. Mill.

It remains that Utilitarianism did not do justice to the variety of values and disyalues and that it did not give a consistent account of the basis of obligations to others. We have to assume a plurality of values. Of these there is no generally accepted classification. A clue to them may perhaps be found by considering the basic or root-interests which underlie the major departments of behaviour. These fall into fairly well defined groups. There is, first of all, the interest in self-maintenance, under which the care of the body and all its appetites must be ranged. Secondly, there is the interest in other beings, to seek and give response, which includes among its specific modifications and developments the capacity for sympathy, the feeling for and with others, affection, the sex and parental impulses, and the generalized sentiment for the group as a whole. There is, thirdly, the interest in the environment around us, physical and social, the impulse to understand, to construct, to make and remake things. Whether the aesthetic impulse should be regarded as an independent interest is disputed, and according to some it is to be regarded rather as a fusion of the constructive and other emotional tendencies. All these interests or needs have a hereditary basis, but they are continually shaped and reshaped with the growing complexity of human relations and some, for example, the constructive and the aesthetic, are unevenly distributed and are more readily atrophied than others. These interests, interwoven in various ways, underlie the mass of feeling and impulse-shaping behaviour. The important thing from the ethical point of view is that in the course of seeking to satisfy them the leading elements of value (and disvalue) are discovered and ideals emerge which serve as a source of inspiration, but also of guidance and control. Each ideal generates its own norms and makes its own demands. Thus in relation to the bodily needs and appetites the ideal of health forbids self-neglect and enjoins temperance and self-control.[1] In regard to the social needs there arise the ideals of friendship and love at their best and these have their own norms, enjoining sincerity, steadfastness, selflessness, patience. In group life we come to appreciate the virtues of generosity, sympathy, sensitiveness to suffering, loyalty, self-respect, respect for others, justice and equity in dealing with the claims of others. In pursuing the cognitive and constructive interests we discover the ideal of truth which again has its own requirements, disinterestedness or detachment, self-knowledge, freedom from self deception, intellectual integrity, the resolute facing of the world as it is, the avoidance of make-believe. We also discover the importance of moral wisdom, the power of discriminating between different kinds of excellence and of moral strength, the power of pursuing steadily the values so discriminated. We may further learn to appreciate the virtues of toleration and of adventurousness in the search of new values.

On the view here adopted the connexion between desire and value is that it is in the process of satisfying desires that we discover values, that is, what is worth desiring, and the standards or norms which the various values involve. Values do not consist in satisfaction or fulfilment, but inhere in the experiences worth taking satisfaction in, or finding fulfilment in. The worth of the experiences is not measured by the degree of satisfaction. The grading of the various ideals is in fact never unitary or self-consistent and there are always different ways of life within a general framework difficult to define. This is no doubt due to the fact that moral development is not unitary but follows different lines of growth, often traceable to different sources. Thus many of the ideals of a community may be due mainly to its religion, while the law and the working moral code may have different roots; philosophical reflection may have still different affilia-

1. 'Self-love, my liege, is not so vile a sin as self-neglecting.' *Henry V*, II, iv.

tions; and the four may stand to each other in varying relations of juxtaposition, synthesis, or conflict. What is called the Western way of life, for example, obviously contains many, partly conflicting ways of life. There is, nevertheless, in every society a general framework the maintenance or furtherance of which comes to be conceived as an overriding obligation, though this may come into conflict with the demands of particular ideals. In all this it is not implied that the ideals arise first, and that the way of life is constructed out of their relations to each other. The general form of life and its constituent ideals and norms grow up together and influence each other, without being, it seems, ever in harmony.

The concept of an ideal seems to me to be central in moral experience. For in it value and obligation are combined and both are related to the fundamental human needs or interests. The ideals are rooted in these needs, the need for a life in common, the need to know, construct, and understand, the need to be at home in the world, but as they develop the ideals make demands which transform and control the original drives. These demands are not arbitrary but immanent in the structure of the needs and the ideals and, so to say, necessitated by the structure. Each ideal as we have seen generates its own norms. They appeal and constrain in varying degrees but, in all cases, they stand before us as something desirable, though not necessarily desired, as something which may involve abnegation or renunciation, but which, if we could but rise to it would be not repressive but liberative. Perhaps we can in this way overcome the difficulty that has frequently been urged against teleological ethics that goods or values provide no basis for obligation and, at the same time, the difficulty confronting the deontologists that out of the notion of law or principle we cannot get to any actual end to be pursued.

Utilitarian and self-realization theories are generally recognized as having failed to deal satisfactorily with the problem of the transition from what is good for self to the good of all, from the good as my happiness to the happiness of all, from the good of self fulfilment to the fulfilment of all selves. Bentham admitted the difficulty openly: 'When I say the greatest happiness of the whole community ought to be the end or object of pursuit ... what is it that I express? This and no more, namely, that it is my wish, my desire to see it taken for such.'[1] Others have tried to resolve the difficulty by emphasizing the social impulses in man or by pointing to the dependence of the individual for his happiness or self fulfilment on the society of which he is a member. On the view here advocated the problem hardly arises. We have seen that it is implicit in there being such a thing as morality at all that there are principles of action or rules applicable impartially to all coming under them. What these rules are we discover by analysing the norms governing the major divisions of value, and these norms again are general and independent of individual likes and dislikes. What is good is good as such wherever and in whomsoever it is found.

This is not to say that values are necessarily harmonious or that a partial good may not conflict with a wider good, but that the conflicts that arise are not necessarily due to a clash between individual and general good. Consider the ethics of knowledge. The pursuit of knowledge is intrinsically good and this as we have seen imposes its own norms. But knowledge gives power and can be used for good and evil. Are nuclear atomic physicists right in pursuing investigations which may result in the death of millions of innocent people? Even the beneficent powers of science raise similar problems. Thus the advances made in medicine and public health have resulted in the reduction of infant mortality and the prolongation of the span of life. But these beneficent activities have been accompanied by an increase of population which may well lead to increasing deprivation and social disturbance and to an over-use of natural resources ending in permanent and perhaps irretrievable loss. Again, free and open discus-

1. Bentham, *Constitutional Code*, Introduction, *Works*, IX, p. 4.

sion has generally been regarded as an elementary principle of the ethics of the scientist. But here again the question can hardly be avoided whether it is really right to insist that all scientific knowledge should immediately be disclosed, without any reservation of any kind. In the case of nuclear physics the problem is peculiarly vicious, but it is not new and has appeared in many forms. There have always been people who have felt that the wide dissemination of knowledge and the mental habits which it inculcates tend to weaken ancient beliefs, institutions, and traditions and that there are certain subjects which had better not be investigated or, at any rate, not widely taught or discussed. I am not suggesting that these are conflicts which cannot be resolved, but that they do not arise out of a clash between individual and general good but rather between a partial and a wider good or between immediate good and the good or evil of the foreseeable indirect consequences of action. Similarly, the norms of sex love may clash with the norms of family love and those of family love with the wider loyalty to nation or mankind. In general, the moral problem is to arbitrate between the claims of the different ideals and with the conflicts that may arise even within each of the major divisions of value. Furthermore, we often have to choose not only between values but also between lesser or greater disvalues, in particular, we are confronted with the problem of the limits of repression and renunciation. The problem is largely practical, that is to assure an equitable distribution of the means or conditions without which none of the values can be attained and to reduce or eliminate the occasions that make for misery, conflict, and frustration.

The part of morality which can be stated in the form of rules, whether negative or positive, relates to the minimum conditions required for the attainment of values. But morality is more than conformity to rules. It is true that in some cases the virtues consist in enduring dispositions or habits of obedience to rules. Thus veracity is the habit of telling the truth. But intellectual integrity involves more than truth-telling, and in many other cases the virtues consist rather in a certain strain of fineness shown not in conformity to rules but in a sensitive and differentiated response to the needs of a situation: for example, kindliness, compassion, respect, considerateness. In general, the virtues are features of larger patterns of conduct and they have to be judged in relation to the ends or values they serve or qualify. Rules are for general guidance, but insight is required in following them. It may be doubted whether any rule is such that it should be followed on every occasion. As we have been told: the sabbath was made for man, and not man for the sabbath.

CHAPTER II

The Concept of Justice[1]

SINCE the war there has been a revival of interest in the idea of justice and its relation to law. The main contributions have come from the side of jurisprudence among which may be mentioned Sir Carleton Kemp Allen, *Aspects of Justice* (1958); Potter, *The Quest of Justice* (1951); Friedmann, *Legal Theory* (1944); Stone, *Province and Function of Law* (1947); Paton, *Textbook of Jurisprudence* (1946); Goodhart, *English Law and the Moral Law* (1953); H.A.L. Hart, *The Concept of Law* (1962); E. Dowrick, *Justice According to the English Common Lawyers* (1961). There have also appeared English translations of important continental contributions, such as the translation by Campbell of del Vecchio's *Justice* (1935); by C. D. Broad of Axel Hägerström's *Inquiries into the Nature of Law and Morals* (1953), and the work by Alf Ross *On Law and Justice* (1958).[2] Perhaps this revived interest in the problem of the relation of law to morals is best seen in the work of the International Commission of Jurists whose avowed aim is 'the support and advancement of those principles of justice which constitute the basis of the Rule of Law' and by the Rule of Law they mean not merely formal legality assuring regularity and consistency in the enforcement of order but substantive justice based on the recognition of the supreme value of the human personality and of institutions providing the framework for its fullest expression.[3]

It is not my intention here to examine this movement

1. This chapter first appeared as an article in *Philosophy*, April 1963. I wish to thank the Editor for permission to reproduce it here.

2. A work which I found very helpful is: *Grundzüge der Rechtsphilosophie*, by Helmut Coing (1950).

3. Cf. *The Rule of Law in a Free Society: Report on the International Congress of Jurists*, New Delhi, 1959, pp. 187–97.

of thought in any detail but before proceeding to my own analysis I should like to comment briefly on two approaches to the theory of justice which are typical of the differences which in the past have divided and still continue to divide schools of jurisprudence. I have in mind the writings of G. del Vecchio,[1] who deals with the problem in the light of philosophical idealism, and Alf Ross[2] who writes in the spirit of the analytical philosophers and already in 1933 committed himself to an 'emotive' theory of moral assertions. Del Vecchio's approach is epistemological. He argues after the manner of the philosophical idealists that consciousness of self implies consciousness of others and this, he thinks, means the awareness of others not merely as objects but as subjects, as selves. This notion of 'otherness', *alteritas*, leads to the notion of several selves linked by intersubjective intercourse. From this he thinks there follows the notion of reciprocity and equality between selves, imposing a series of bilateral and reciprocal obligations, so that to rights or claims there correspond equivalent duties and to duties claims. Furthermore, this recognition of the relation of the self to other selves is not purely cognitive. It also generates a feeling and provides a motive to action, or an ideal to guide action. This ideal may be best expressed as the recognition of the autonomy of each person and it is one, he thinks, which has inspired critics of existing law in all ages. 'Immanent in our consciousness and ever reborn, this idea of justice is found in all law but not exhausted in any.'[3]

Despite the great wealth of learning which del Vecchio displays in his illuminating survey of the history of the idea of justice, and despite my sympathy with his views of the values of the human personality, I cannot but think that his metaphysical deduction of justice from the concept of self-consciousness is delusive. From the proposition

1. My references are to the French version, *Justice, Droit, État, Études de Philosophie Juridique*, 1938.

2. op. cit. 3. op. cit., p. 73.

that self-consciousness depends upon or implies intersubjective intercourse, nothing whatever follows as to the moral quality of such intercourse. The cognition of others does not necessarily imply respect for them as persons. There is needed the additional proposition that persons have capacities for good and as such are worthy of respect. Still less can we deduce from the bare idea of self-consciousness the principle that 'a subject cannot act in a given way towards others without rendering lawful or just a like acting in the same circumstances of others with regard to himself'. This which recalls Sidgwick's axiom of justice is indeed implicit in the notion of a rational morality, the notion namely that human action is subject to general principles and is in this sense *a priori*, but it is not deducible from the general necessity of intersubjective intercourse. Individuals can certainly enter into relations with each other in societies full of inequalities. Equality of consideration, respect for persons as 'ends in themselves' are not necessities of intersubjective relations in the sense that without them no society can exist, but desiderata, ideals to be aimed at. It is arguable that these ideas are inherent in a rational morality; they cannot be derived from the conditions of self-consciousness or awareness of self as dependent upon awareness of others. We are aware of others when we hate, fear, or are suspicious of them, just as much as when we love them, sympathize with them, or respect them. That the latter attitudes or conditions are morally good and the former bad cannot be deduced from the bare idea of self-consciousness.

By contrast, Professor Ross begins by rejecting as completely futile any attempt to base either morality or law on metaphysical speculations. He is interested in what he calls a 'scientific' approach and nothing is scientific which is not ultimately verifiable by observation and experiment. There can be no such thing as rational appetition or practical reason, no such thing as a specific normative knowledge. Norms, legal or moral, are a species of social fact: they are to be interpreted not as *ought* propositions but as *is* propositions. The idea of an *a priori* principle of justice as a guide for legislation is an empty idea, and legal politics has therefore to be discussed in a relativistic spirit, that is, in relation to hypothetical values in fact accepted on emotional grounds by influential groups in a society. The values themselves cannot be rationally justified: they express emotions or attitudes and as such are incapable of being true or false. If it be asked how it is that we experience the need to 'justify' or give reasons for our actions in terms of general principles, an answer can be given. The cause is fear. We are afraid of having to make decisions on our own responsibility. We therefore look for principles outside ourselves, whether God-given or apprehended by a mysterious *a priori* reasoning of our own, but in any case eternal and immutable and independent of our choice.

How far will this tough realism, reducing all moral distinctions to illusion, carry us in the analysis of the idea of justice and its relation to law?

Professor Ross accepts what may be called the formal principles of justice as a basis of law. The notion of a legal order implies that decisions shall be made not arbitrarily but in accordance with general rules, and that these general rules (whatever they are) shall be correctly (that is, what moralists call impartially) applied; that is, by criteria defining the class of cases coming under the rule, and not affected by the subjective reactions of the judge. Justice then is conformity with existing law. But there is no scientific way of deciding whether the existing law is 'right law'. The only scientific criterion of a 'good' or 'right' law is its efficiency in attaining its purpose whatever that purpose may be. Granted equal efficiency, the laws of Hitlerian Germany are as good as the laws of the democracies, though he allows that the power given to judges in totalitarian societies to disregard fixed rules and decide according to the 'sound legal consciousness of the people' or 'the interests of the proletariat' involves a rejection of the very idea of law. Along similar lines, Ross argues that the idea of equality widely regarded as the core of justice is of no avail in determining what is right law. That like cases should be treated in like manner is implied in the very idea of a rule. But the formal idea of equality tells us nothing about the rule itself, for it throws no light in what respect the qualities in which individuals are alike or different are relevant in the framing of rules: they cannot, for example, help us in determining what constitutes a 'just' wage or a 'just' system of taxation or a 'just' penalty for the infringement of a law. Anyone who says that a particular legal order is just or unjust 'provides no reason for his attitude but merely gives it an emotional expression. . . . To invoke justice is the same thing as banging on the table: an emotional expression which turns one's demand into an absolute postulate.'[1]

The 'emotive' theory of moral judgements upon which Professor Ross's analysis of justice is based has moved a good deal since the appearance of his book *Kritik der sogenannten praktischen Erkenntnis* (1933). In any case I find it completely inacceptable. That morality must have a basis in experience is true, but it is sheer dogma to confine experience to what is acquired through the senses. There is such a thing as moral experience. Men not only make choices but they reflect on them and there is no reason for believing that reflection is confined to means. Whether such reflection is called 'scientific' or not seems to be of little importance, so long as it is orderly, clear-sighted, and self-critical.

Leaving this larger issue aside we may consider Ross's theory of justice from the point of view of inner consistency. I find it difficult to understand why Ross attaches a sort of priority to certain values such as predictability, regularity, consistency in behaviour, over all others. 'Objective regularity,' he says, 'as opposed to subjective arbitrariness is experienced as a value in itself.'[2] In another passage we are told that these are valued because they

1. op. cit., p. 274. 2. op. cit., p. 281.

are the conditions of security and calculability in the affairs of community life. But security means freedom from the fear of losing or being deprived of the conditions necessary for the attainment of basic values. The demand for a minimum of rationality, we are told, results from 'the character of law as a social institutional order as opposed to individual moral phenomena'. But this dichotomy begs the question. Would we really value institutions if they served no good purpose? And does not the demand for a minimum of rationality for 'the rule of law rather than the rule of men' and for impartiality in applying the rules imply a minimum of morality? Furthermore, does it really make sense to say that while the formal principle of justice, namely that there must be rules governing action, can be rationally defended, the rules themselves never can be? Can it really be the case that we are more certain about the desirability of regularity and predictability than, say, about the rules which forbid men to kill or hurt one another? A theory which leads to such conclusions must surely rest on insecure foundations.

I have, of course, only given the barest outlines of these opposed theories of justice. I am not suggesting that the works in which they are elaborated can be lightly dismissed as of no importance. To do them justice an elaborate treatise would be required. I have drawn attention to them because they exemplify a divergence which in different forms reappears in the history of philosophical jurisprudence, dividing those who try to find a basis for justice in some form of natural law, and the positivists who claim autonomy for law and maintain that justice is not inherent in the notion of law. The former proceed on the assumption that there are *a priori* principles defining not only the formal principles but yielding also the substance of justice, the body of rights and duties, moral and legal. The positivists, on the other hand, maintain generally that no such derivation is warranted, and those among them who are influenced by the analytical or linguistic philosophers add that the substantive rules of justice as distinguished from the formal principle cannot be rationally defended at all, but are based on emotions or attitudes predominant in a group to which the distinction between true and false does not apply.

The emotive theory of moral judgements is, as we have seen, inacceptable. Approvals and disapprovals are not mere likes and dislikes: they contain judgements which are subject to rational tests of clarity, consistency, and coherence. *Ought* statements are not reducible to *is* statements: the moral cannot be deduced from the non-moral. On the other hand, I do not think that moral judgements have no 'empirical' basis. On the contrary, it is a fact of experience that human activity involves choices and preferences and these have from the very beginning a cognitive element serving to guide and control them. Thus even in rudimentary moral experience there is an implicit distinction between what is desired and what ought to be desired. The development of morality consists in the widening of human sympathies, the progressive clarification of human needs and purposes, and a fuller grasp of the obligations or norms which they carry with them. Natural or rather ideal morality is not something which is, so to say, there at the beginning from which specific rights and duties are deducible, but emerges slowly and develops as men grapple with the problems of human relations and find ways of reconciling conflicting interests. Following this line of thought, what I wish to maintain is that, though from the idea or concept of justice as such we cannot deduce the whole body of rights and duties, the latter have a rational basis of their own. The problem is to define how formal and substantive justice are related.

Justice in the broadest sense consists in the ordering of human relations in accordance with general principles impartially applied. As Aristotle explained, the just is a form of the 'equal'; that is, it involves the principle that like cases should be treated in like manner and different cases differently. Justice is thus opposed to (a) lawlessness, anomie, to capricious, uncertain, unpredictable decisions, not bound by rules; (b) partiality in the application of rules, and (c) rules which are themselves partial or arbitrary, involving ungrounded discrimination; that is, discrimination based on irrelevant differences. It is clear that from the formal character of justice we cannot deduce the content of justice. The bare idea of equal treatment of like cases throws no light on what is to be done by, to, or for, equals or whether and on what grounds persons who are not alike or who are in different circumstances are to be treated differently. There is a similar difficulty in deducing the content of justice from the general idea of freedom or liberty. For if by freedom is meant the right to do what one likes without interference by others, the question arises what constitutes interference and indeed whether interference is never justified, and this cannot be answered without some conception of the ends or purposes which individuals set themselves and their relations to each other. The best known attempts at deducing the fundamental principles of justice from the idea of liberty are those made by Kant and Spencer. These have not stood the test of criticism.[1] In any case they are not purely formal. Spencer's formula: 'Every man is free to do what he wills provided that he infringes not the equal freedom of any other man' is subject as he himself explains to the general principle of maximizing happiness.[2] The formula is not to be taken, for example, as justifying A in knocking down B so long as B is given equal liberty to knock down A. It is intended to convey that, in carrying on activities which are conducive to life and its maintenance, a person shall not be interfered with save as it is necessary that others are to carry on similar activities. The ultimate appeal is therefore to the principle of the greatest sum of happiness. There is a similar difficulty in the Kantian formula: 'Legal right is the sum of the conditions under which a

1. For a criticism of Spencer, see Maitland, *Collective Papers*, vol. I, pp. 267–303, and Hobhouse, *Elements of Social Justice*, ch. IV.

2. *Principles of Ethics*, Vol. II, p. 46.

man's freedom of action can be combined with the freedom of action of others according to a universal law of freedom.'[1] This principle is not purely formal since it rests on the notion that individuals are ends in themselves and ought never to be treated as means merely. To decide whether a particular action involves treating an individual as a means merely for example, whether non-marital sexual relations are of this character it is necessary to know a good deal about the effects of sex relations on the individual and about the nature and limitations of reciprocity in sex relationships. In general, it seems to me that formal principles of justice are never purely formal. They imply at least that in evaluating an action the individual has to consider others and that arbitrary power by one person over others is to be excluded. The problem is what sort of consideration and what constitutes arbitrariness.

In dealing with this problem it is necessary, first of all, to establish a body of rights and duties and then to inquire in what sense the principle of equality applies to them. It will then be found that, in reference to certain rights such as those concerned with the security of the person, what Aristotle called arithmetical equality applies, all alike being entitled to protection irrespective of any differences. In the case of other rights, on the other hand, such as the right to education or the payment for services, proportionate equality may have to be considered, the relevant differences being, for example, differences in needs or capacities or weight of responsibility, and perhaps also differences in the incentives that have to be appealed to in order to secure the best results. The theory of justice thus involves an examination of the body of rights and duties accepted in a society in the light of the formal principles of equality, the aim being to rid it of arbitrary elements; that is, discrimination not grounded on relevant differences.

1. *Einleitung in die Rechtslehre*. Werke. Cassirer edition: Band VII, p. 31.

What then is the ethical basis of rights? For the Utilitarians the standard adopted was conduciveness to general happiness. Leaving aside the difficulties arising from the 'individualist' interpretation of this principle, there can be no doubt that in its day it exercised an important influence on legislation. But, as critics of Utilitarianism have shown, happiness is too elusive a concept to serve as a basis for the whole body of rights and duties. Bentham's dictum that 'what happiness is every man knows' is, to put it mildly, anything but self-evident. Happiness is a feeling that accompanies or tones the satisfaction of the enduring and pervasive needs of personality, and these vary widely with changing conditions. The deeper needs are no doubt interrelated but not always harmoniously. In any given situation the claims to which they give rise may come into conflict. Problems of adjustment then arise involving a comparative evaluation of the various goods and evils involved and inquiry into the conditions in which conflicts may be resolved. They cannot be resolved by appealing to a single, or supreme, good. We have to accept a plurality of goods, possibly conflicting. Justice is concerned with problems of balance and adjustment. Hence rights and duties have to be defined and redefined as we obtain fuller knowledge of the constituents and conditions of well-being.

It is not to be inferred from the above account that justice is here taken as including the whole of righteousness. We should not ordinarily include under justice the norms inherent in the ideals of love, truth, or beauty, though problems of distributive justice may arise in connexion with these ideals. In any event there is much in morality that is not reducible to rule. Mill seems to have thought that justice should be confined to duties of 'perfect obligation', that is, duties to which there correspond specific rights. This would exclude, for example, the duties of beneficence or generosity which confer no specific rights on particular individuals. More illuminating is his insistence that justice is a name for certain classes of moral rules, namely, those which concern the essentials of social life, such as security. Upon it depends not only immunity from evil but all values going beyond immediate satisfaction. Hence, he thinks, the peculiar intensity of the feeling of justice:

> The moral rules which forbid men to hurt one another (including wrongful interference with each other's freedom) are more vital to human well-being than any maxims, however important, which point out the best mode of managing some department of human affairs; they determine the social feeling needed to preserve peace, they are indispensable conditions of all other goods.

On this view, the concern of justice is to protect the elementary goods and in this way to provide the conditions for the higher or subtler values.[1]

Both Mill and Sidgwick claimed that an essential element in the idea of justice, in so far as this imports more than equality or impartiality, is the notion of requital of desert – good for good, evil for evil. But closer examination of their writings shows that on this they had serious misgivings. Thus as to good for good Mill thinks the principle is real though not 'obvious'. 'Whoever accepts a benefit and denies a return when needed inflicts a real hurt by disappointing a natural expectation and one which he must have tacitly encouraged: otherwise the benefits would seldom have been conferred.'[2] But to help the needy and not to disappoint natural expectations are hardly the same as 'good for good'. Sidgwick discusses the principle in connexion with the problem of reward for services. But his treatment is very inconclusive. He cannot find any standards for estimating the intrinsic value of labour or for determining what is a fair or equitable reward for services and, in the end, he has to admit that common-sense morality can offer no clear guidance on

1. Compare Hartmann, *Ethics*, II, 237: 'The lower goods as being the minimum conditions of the higher need a stronger weapon of defence. The good will, so easily deficient, is not an adequate security.'

2. J. S. Mill, *Utilitarianism*, ch. v.

these matters. As to evil for evil, both Mill and Sidgwick discuss the matter with references to punishment, and here their misgiving and hesitations are even more marked. Sidgwick doubts whether pain ought to be inflicted on a man even if no benefit results either to him or to others from the pain, and he thinks that, though still widely held, this view is 'gradually passing away from the moral consciousness of educated persons in the most advanced communities'.[1] In the *Elements of Politics*[2] he is more explicit. As far as legislation is concerned he tells us that 'it is evidently necessary to take as the primary end of punishment the prevention of mischief and not the retribution of wickedness; and to decide on this principle any doubtful question as to the allotment of punishments.' Mill suggests that the belief in an inherent connexion between wrong-doing and punishment, such that inherently and irrespective of consequences wrong-doing merits retribution, is the product of a long association of the two in social practice – for which there have been intelligible reasons of expediency. The guilty conscience is thus a synthetic product.[3] In the end, both Mill and Sidgwick rely not on retribution as such, but, in the case of reward, on the importance of providing a stimulus to effort and instruments to those who can use them effectively; and, in the case of punishment, on the need to prevent crime in the interests of general security.

Among later moralists some Utilitarians and Intuitionists also reject the view that there is a fundamental or underived duty to reward the virtuous and punish the vicious. This, if I understand him aright, is the position adopted by Sir David Ross.[4] The duty of reward and punishment can, in his view, be subsumed under the duty of producing as much good as we can, if we can assume, as he thinks we can, that a combination of moral worth and

1. Sidgwick, *Methods*, Book III, ch. v.
2. Sidgwick, *Elements of Politics*, p. 114.
3. J. S. Mill, *Examination of Hamilton*, p. 508.
4. *The Right and the Good*, 1930, p. 58.

happiness is a greater good than either by itself, and a combination of wrong-doing and pain inflicted as punishment a lesser evil than wrong-doing unpunished. But the grounds for this latter belief are somewhat obscure. Rashdall has argued that the combination of goodness and happiness is to be preferred because the kind of happiness of which the virtuous are capable possesses higher value than the happiness of the non-virtuous.[1] So it might be argued that wrong-doing punished is a lesser evil than wrong-doing unpunished, because in some way the pain will make the sufferer better or because it will satisfy his own need for punishment. In either case we seem to have left the principle of retribution far behind. Furthermore, this sort of argument seems to have little relevance to human justice, since we are not in a position to review the merits and happiness of all the members of a society and to apportion the means of happiness and moral worth accordingly. In the end, so far as I can see, all that Sir David Ross retains of the notion of retributive punishment is the argument that in failing to respect the rights of others a person forfeits his own rights and the state is then entitled to deal with him 'as a consideration of the good of the community and his own good requires'. We are thus thrown back to the question whether punishment achieves any good other than dealing with the offender according to his desert. It is sometimes argued that the infliction of pain is necessary in order to make the offender realize the degree of moral condemnation that his conduct has evoked and thus to help him to amend.[2] If this argument is applied to punishment as administered through the criminal law, it would have to be shown that the methods used attain or are likely to

1. *Theory of Good and Evil*, 1924, I, p. 257.

2. For a Christian view see O. C. Quick, *Christianity and Justice* (pp. 9–10): 'It cannot be *due* to a man to injure him. But punishment, ideally and in its essential nature, is not an injury at all. Punishment recognized as just awakens the wrong-doer's conscience to the fact that he has done wrong and also enables him to feel that he has purged his offence.'

attain this end. In the case of most adult offenders this is, to put it mildly, very doubtful.

Despite the strong appeal which the notion of merit has to the ordinary man, I doubt whether it can form the basis of justice as administered by men. When we say an action has merit we mean either that it has intrinsic worth or value, in which case there seems to be no necessary connexion between it and an external reward; or we may mean that it is one that the average man would not do without the extra stimulus of a reward, in which case again the notion of an inherent connexion disappears. As to ill-desert the belief that there is an intrinsic fitness in the sequence between penalty and wrong-doing is very deep-rooted, and despite repeated attacks on it the retributive theory of punishment still has powerful defenders. But the theory is full of ambiguities and as a basis for legal justice it is liable to very insidious forms of self-deception. In most cases those who defend the retributive theory believe that in some way the infliction of pain on the wrong-doer, if recognized by him as coming from a just authority, will induce repentance. But this ignores the difficulty of moral assessment and of apportioning punishment to guilt. In any event the notion of criminal justice as an effort to balance good and evil and administer a sort of moral tit-for-tat breaks down completely when confronted with what in fact is or could be attempted in the administration of justice in the courts of law and the prison system.

The central core of the idea of justice is not the requital of desert but the exclusion of arbitrariness and more particularly the exclusion of arbitrary power. Hence the enormous importance of the growth of legality, the emergence of the notion that persons are under the rule of law and not of men.[1] The rule of law is slowly seen to carry with it certain implications: (i) that no one can be judge

1. Cf. Aristotle, *Nichomachean Ethics*, Book V, VI, 5. 'We do not allow an individual to rule over us, but reason or law: for an individual is apt to take more for himself and to become a tyrant.'

of his own cause; (ii) that methods are provided for settling disputes without the use of force by the parties concerned; (iii) that the coercive powers which the law must necessarily have at its command are not unlimited, that those who make the law are themselves subject to law, and that there are ways of preventing them from abusing their power. In large measure the history of justice has consisted in movements of protest against the law's delays, against arbitrary application of the law, and against the iniquity of the laws themselves.

The notion of justice is perhaps first explicitly recognized in the injunction given to judges, such as we find in ancient Egypt or in early Hebrew law, to administer the law impartially, to 'hear the small as well as the great'.[1] Thereafter development can be traced mainly along the following lines. First, it is recognized that laws which are impartially applied may themselves be unequal. There arises the notion that differential treatment requires justification in terms of relevant differences. In this way laws come to be changed so as to remove arbitrary discrimination, such as those based on race, colour, religion, sex. Next, the notion of impartiality is extended by applying it to a wider range of rights and duties: there is a movement from equality in political rights to equality in social and economic rights. Accompanying this transition there is a shift of emphasis from 'commutative' justice as a sort of equivalence of exchange or balance of claims and counter claims between individuals, to distributive justice as a social responsibility assuring to all at least the minimum conditions of physical and mental well-being. Thirdly, the conception of justice is recognized as applicable to the relations between states. There is a growing effort to get states to abandon their claims to be judges in their own cause and to resort to force in maintaining what they take to be their rights. There are the beginnings of some notion of distributive justice, for example, in controlling the world resources and the movements of

1. Deut., i, 17.

populations. Finally, in Western civilization there are deliberate efforts to define the limits of coercion, to mark out spheres which should be left to the free choice of individuals, for example, the spheres of thought and its expression, religious belief and worship. In all these ways the notion of justice according to law is gradually pervaded by the notion of justice in the law.

We may next deal with the question whether the principles of justice are independent or whether they can be subsumed under the duty of doing as much good as we can. Sidgwick was of the opinion that, in considering two modes of distributing a given quantum of happiness, it was important to ask whether one way of distribution might be better than another, though the total would remain the same. He concluded that the principle of the greatest happiness has to be supplemented by some principle of a just distribution, and according to him the principle to be followed was that of equality. He added,[1] however, that equality in apportioning the means of happiness was likely to produce more happiness on the whole. The reason for this is not only that men have an aversion to unreason but that they resent inferiority to others, especially when there seems no reasonable ground for discrimination. Russell seems to follow Sidgwick in this latter contention; an uneven distribution causes envy and hatred in the less fortunate and fear and hatred in the more fortunate. Unlike Sidgwick, however, he does not think that justice in distribution is an independent principle.[2] Broad concludes that where justice (in the sense of equality) has neither utility nor disutility, as in the case of the shipwrecked sailors with a single biscuit which is not enough to keep even one of them alive, we 'approve of a just distribution and disapprove of a bestial scramble for it'.[3]

I cannot feel very sure about this. It seems to me that

1. *Methods of Ethics*, Book IV, chs. I and III.
2. *Human Society in Ethics and Politics*, p. 133.
3. *Five Types of Ethical Theory*, p. 58.

we must distinguish between the formal principles of justice and their application to specific claims. The principles that everyone involved has to be considered, that no one's claims shall be ignored or overridden, that like cases must be treated in like manner and different cases differently, contain no reference to specific goods or values. On the other hand specific claims are claims to conditions or powers needed to realize a good or interest. To weigh claims impartially, to decide what differences between the claimants are relevant or irrelevant, it is necessary to take into consideration differences in needs, capacities, and circumstances. In dealing with them we need in addition to the formal principles of justice secondary or mediating principles based as we have seen on the nature of the major or dominant goods and the conditions in which they can be realized.

I must now try to bring this discussion into relation with older views of the nature of justice. Most of these can be traced back to Aristotle. Aristotle distinguishes two kinds of justice, 'general' and 'particular'. The former he identifies with the whole of righteousness, 'complete virtue', and, since in his view law covered the whole range of human activity, the just could be considered as identical with what is lawful. He does not in this context raise the question how law is related to morals, though, of course, he was well aware that in some states the law may fall short of what it ought to be. Particular justice he subdivides into distributive and corrective or remedial. Here he introduces the important principle of proportionate equality. In distributing such things as honours and office the state must take account of differences in individuals. It is as unjust to treat unequals equally as to treat equals unequally. The problem is to decide what differences are relevant. The analogy of the arts shows that certain differences are seen to be irrelevant. If you are distributing flutes among flute players, complexion or stature would not be important. In athletic contests the swift will get the reward. In the political sphere the differences that are relevant are those which affect the existence and well-being of the state. In the *Politics* he indicates wealth and free birth but also the temper of justice and martial habit as relevant.[1] In a later book he mentions free birth, wealth, culture, and good descent.[2] In the *Nichomachean Ethics* the basis for distributive justice is taken to be merit. He explains that what constitutes merit is differently interpreted in different states: in a democracy all free men are deemed equal; in an oligarchy wealth or noble birth counts; in an aristocracy, virtue. Whatever quality is taken as a basis, awards must be proportionate to it. Corrective justice is concerned with restoring a violated equality. It applies both to voluntary transactions, for example, selling or lending, and involuntary transactions, for example, fraud or theft. It thus corresponds roughly to contract and tort in English law. In both cases, the injury is done to an individual and the judge's object is not to punish but to give redress. The involuntary transactions are crimes as well, but Aristotle treats them here as what we should call civil actions. Regarded as crimes, that is, as offences against the state and not only against individuals, they would come under 'general' not under 'particular' justice.[3] Here Aristotle thinks the principle is arithmetical proportion. 'It makes no difference whether a good man defrauds a bad man, or a bad man a good one . . . the law looks only to the difference created by the injury, treating the parties themselves as equal.'[4] There is a third kind of justice which later comes to be called 'commutative'. This aims at a fair exchange which takes into account the skill of the parties and the corresponding worth of their products.

In the writings of the Schoolmen, if I have understood them correctly, Aristotle's 'general' justice appears in what is called *legal* or social justice. Its business is to

1. III. XII. 2. IV. XII.
3. Cf. Sir D. Ross, *Aristotle*, p. 211.
4. *Nichomachean Ethics*, V. IV. 3.

direct action towards the common good. I take it that this means that its function is to define the general principles of social organization. Particular justice is concerned with partial or specific operations within the general framework and is divided into commutative justice concerned with the relations of individuals to each other, and distributive justice which deals with the relations of society as a whole to its members.[1] The precise delimitation of the three kinds of justice is a very difficult matter. For example, I take it that in mediaeval theory the 'just wage' is determined by commutative justice as a sort of equivalence between the pay and the value of the product or of the productive capacity. This, however, was qualified by a second principle that normally the pay should be sufficient to enable the worker and his family to maintain the standard of life customary in his social grade or status. The two principles are distinct and might conflict. If they are to satisfy the requirements of the common good, that is of social justice, it would be necessary to show that the prevailing status or class structure is just and that the economy as a whole is organized in such a way that the wage as estimated by the value of the product or productive capacity will not be unfair from the point of view of needs. This inquiry, however, was not undertaken by the medieval thinkers. The justice of the status system was not questioned and there was no systematic effort to determine the conditions in which the rate of pay based on needs was likely to correspond with the rate based on

1. 'Particular justice is directed to private individuals, whose relation to society is analogous to that of parts to a whole. Now every part admits of a twofold relationship. There is first the relationship of one individual to another. This order of relations is directed by commutative justice, which is concerned with mutual dealings between two persons. Second is the relationship of the whole to its parts, and to this corresponds that of the society with each of its members. This second order of relations is directed by distributive justice, which is concerned with distributing common goods proportionately.' *Summa Theologica*, Part II, 2, Qu. 61 (cited: *The Church and Social Justice*, J. Y. Calvez, J. Perrin, p. 158).

the value of the product of work or of productive capacity. Recent scholastic writers, aided by Papal Encyclicals, are acutely aware of these difficulties.[1] How far they succeed in meeting them I will not here inquire. It seems, however, that, just as the mediaeval thinkers took the prevalent status system for granted, so the modern scholastics begin by assuming the justice of the system of free enterprise based on private property. This leads them, I think, to sanction a greater degree of inequality in property and income than might be warranted by a more thorough examination of the principles of distributive justice and its relation to social justice.

Aristotle's theory of justice has been and continues to be widely influential but it requires revision at several points. What he calls 'general' justice, which he identifies with the whole of righteousness, is too wide a term to be serviceable. Nor can we accept his identification of general justice with conformity to law; for clearly we distinguish between just and unjust laws. If we use the term in a general sense all that we mean is that in dealing with claims justice requires us to ensure that all involved have been considered and that none are given preference on irrelevant grounds. This implies equal satisfaction of equal claims. But equality requires further specification, for people may be treated equally yet wrongfully. If all of a given class are condemned to be tortured the iniquity is not lessened because no exceptions are made.[2] Equality, in short, has to be considered in relation to the grounds on which the claims are made. It then means arithmetical equality for equal claims, proportionate equality when there are relevant grounds for differentiation. Similar remarks apply to the notion of fairness, for what is fair

1. Cf. J. Y. Calvez and J. Perrin, *The Church and Social Justice*, 1961, and M. Fogarty, *The Just Wage*, 1961, especially the appendix on 'The Scholastic Theory of the Just Wage'.

2. Cf. Ihering, Zweck im Recht, I, 287: *'Welchen Wert hat die Gleichheit unabhängig von jeder inhaltlichen Bestimmung derselben. Gleichheit kann auch Gleichheit des Elends sein.'*

as between individuals cannot be determined without reference to the grounds on which their claims are based.

While the central idea of justice is the exclusion of arbitrary inequalities, historically there is one kind of arbitrariness which has been of the greatest importance in the struggle against injustice. This is arbitrary power, the power of man over man, whether exercised directly over persons or indirectly through power over things. Justice has therefore been mainly concerned with the control of aggression and of domination made possible by natural inequalities or by inequalities generated by institutions. As Mill says: 'The most marked cases of injustice are wrongful aggression and wrongful exercise of power over someone.' In this regard the aim of justice is to give protection against arbitrary power. The most obvious way of assuring this is to entrust coercive power to a legitimate authority – the state – and to prohibit its use by individuals. Historically this involved a long and difficult process in the course of which systems of 'public' justice sought to control and eventually to eliminate private retaliation. Next, of course, the state itself may abuse its powers. Hence it is part of the theory of justice to define the limits within which state power may be rightly exercised. In the free societies the most important principles that have emerged are the division of powers, designed to avoid over-concentration, and the principle that the powers of the state are derived from the people acting through law and that the law itself is subject to limitations. These limitations may be embodied in the constitution in the form of fundamental rights, or they may be 'extra-legal' as is the case in Britain, where the theoretically unlimited legislative powers of Parliament are in practice limited by the freedom of the press and of association and assembly and the habit of responsible government under the party system. These limitations are not purely formal. They rest on the assumption of fundamental rights, and the problem of their validity leads back to the more general problem of the basis of moral rights and duties.

One of the instruments which society uses to curb arbitrary power is the criminal law. In following its historical development we can discern certain lines of advance in the conception of justice. (a) Early law fails to assure equality of protection. There are grades of rightlessness which deprive certain groups, such as slaves, serfs, aliens, of the full protection of the law, and there may be but poor protection for the mass of the people as against great nobles or high officials. (b) Punishments may be unequal and vary with gradations of rank. (c) In authoritarian states the methods of criminal justice are apt to be arbitrary and oppressive. It is only very slowly that rational procedure by evidence and argument replaces trial by ordeal, combat, or compurgation. Finally, the conception of punishment is humanized, greater stress being laid on the prevention of crime and the rehabilitation of the criminal than on retribution. The advance in all these directions is by no means in a straight line and there are periods of retrogression, yet on the theoretical side, at any rate, it is unmistakable.

If then we are to retain the term 'general' justice we should use it to indicate not the whole of righteousness, as Aristotle did, but as concerned mainly with the control of power relations and more particularly the exclusion of arbitrary power. We must next consider the two other forms of justice included in what Aristotle called 'particular' justice, namely corrective or rectificatory, and distributive, justice. The aim of corrective justice is to restore a disturbed equilibrium in the form of compensation for injuries arising out of breaches of faith or otherwise. It thus corresponds, as we have seen, to what in English law is covered by the law of contract and tort. But the moral issues raised by the latter are more complex than those Aristotle had to deal with. As he did not distinguish between civil injuries and crime, his account throws no light on the problem how the line is to be drawn between wrongs that give occasion for damages only and those that call for punishment, or on the distinction between liability for culpable injuries and liability for injuries without fault. The principle to be followed in rectificatory justice is, according to Aristotle, arithmetical equality; the parties are treated as equal and the judge aims at a mean between gain and loss. But the notion of 'equivalence' between injury and the corresponding remedy or of 'reciprocity' in contractual relations is very obscure, and its application to modern conditions raises legal and moral issues which are still in dispute.

The principle of distributive justice, according to Aristotle, is not arithmetical but proportionate equality. This notion seems to me to be of great importance, though the theory as a whole calls for revision in various directions. In the first place, while Aristotle used the principle of distributive justice to regulate the allocation of honours, office, and the like among a small body of free citizens, in modern times the principle has to be applied to the vastly more complicated problems of equitable distribution of the means of well-being, physical and mental, in highly differentiated, large-scale societies. This widening of meaning involves a re-examination of the significance of equality not only in the distribution of political power but also of wealth and income. It follows further that problems such as those dealing with the payment for services are not to be dealt with as matters only of commutative justice in the sense of equivalence of exchange between individuals, but of distributive justice conceived as a social or cooperative provision of the conditions of well-being, defined by communal standards.

In the second place, Aristotle took the principle of distributive justice to be proportion to merit. But he points out that what merit is, is differently interpreted in different societies: the standards adopted in democracies differ from those followed in oligarchic or aristocratic societies. For merit we should substitute 'relevant resemblances and differences', and what is relevant or not depends upon the particular right which is under consideration. For example, in the case of economic rights differences in needs are relevant, including the conditions necessary for the performance of specific functions and the more general conditions of well-being; in the case of educational rights differences in capacity or interest are relevant; in the case of electoral rights the principle of 'one man, one vote' is adopted in the interest of securing participation by all and in the absence of any agreed method of estimating differences of political capacity. In general, the criteria of relevance adopted by a society vary with the moral outlook prevalent in it and are thus a good index of the level of moral development attained by it.

In our own society the difficulty of deciding what differences and resemblances are relevant is perhaps greatest in dealing with 'economic rights'. There is general agreement that gross inequalities are unjust, and the right to minimum conditions of well-being is now widely recognized. But there is no agreement as to the distribution of property or the reward of service as above the minimum. Differences in needs, ability, productivity, or effort have all been put forward as relevant. But, apart from difficulties of measurement, none of these is free from objection on ethical grounds. It is arguable, however, that as judged by any of these criteria the wide differences in wealth now accepted are disproportionate and that there is, therefore, a strong case for reducing inequalities, even if there is no agreement as to what would constitute proportionate equality. In this, as in other contexts, it is easier to recognize injustice than to define justice.

The three forms of justice concerned with the control of power, the distribution of the means to well-being, and the provision of compensation for injuries are interrelated though distinguishable, and they are all linked by the formal principle of justice which enjoins the exclusion of arbitrary discrimination.

CHAPTER III

Rights and Duties

RIGHTS and duties are key concepts in jurisprudence and ethics. They have a long and complicated history. Here I am concerned to discuss them in relation to the ethical theory outlined in previous chapters.

A right may be defined as a claim that is or can be justly made by or on behalf of an individual or group to some condition or power. The moral justification of the claim is that the condition or power is an element of well-being or a means to it. Distinct rights and duties are based on distinct elements of well-being. But these are inter-related and not always harmoniously. In any given situation the claims which they justify may come into conflict. Problems of adjustment then arise which, from the ethical point of view, may involve a comparative evaluation of the goods involved and an inquiry into the conditions in which they may be reconciled or harmonized. The words 'on behalf of' in the definition are introduced to cover cases in which the subjects of the rights have not the capacity to make a claim, as in the case of infants or the mentally ill or animals. In such cases the claim may be made by others for them. In any case the validity of the right does not depend on the fact that a claim is made. A true right is a claim which a person is entitled to make or which he or others for him might or even ought to make.

All this applies to moral rights. Legal rights are claims enforceable at law. They may be defined as 'legally guaranteed powers to realize an interest'.[1] Whether or not they can be morally justified depends on the moral value of the interests involved and their relations to each other.

1. Cf. C. K. Allen, *Legal Duties*, p. 183. Professor Buckland says that 'the most accepted definition seems to be "an interest or an expectation guaranteed by the law".' (*Some Reflections in Jurisprudence*, p. 92.)

In general, a right implies an obligation, but it is not so clear that a duty or obligation always confers a right. There are duties of 'imperfect obligation', such as those of helping the needy or going to the aid of those in distress, in which the mode and manner in which the duty is to be fulfilled is left to the choice of the agent and which accordingly do not confer any specified rights on particular people. Again there is a duty to refrain from suicide, but this does not confer a definite correlative right on anyone. The argument has been generalized with reference to legal duties enforced by the criminal law. The state forbids the sale of certain drugs or of alcoholic liquors or compels children to be educated or vaccinated. In these and similar cases no doubt the duties are intended to serve the general interest, but it can hardly be maintained, so it is argued, that each single individual has a determinate right in these respects.[1] How much weight to attach to these arguments, I am not quite clear. There seems no real difficulty in the notion of a right to education or to such conditions of health as lie within the power of the state to assure.

Rights and duties rest on the same ethical foundation. A person's rights consist of his claims to the conditions of well-being; his duties of what he is expected to contribute to well-being. This, however, does not mean that those who are incapable of performing their duties have no rights. They still have a right to the conditions of such good as they are capable of and which society is able to secure for them. The following points call for some further discussion.

(a) Rights imply obligations or duties. Thus a right to property vested in A implies an obligation imposed on B, C, D, etc. not to interfere with A's use of the property. Every right is a claim from someone. The claim may be towards forbearance, or acquiescence, or to some active support. At the very least it thus implies freedom from obstruction. This accounts for the historical association

1. Cf. Allen, op. cit., p. 189.

between the notion of right and the notion of freedom. It has led some thinkers to describe a right as a 'secured or protected liberty' and conversely to consider liberty as a body of rights or liberties.

Writers on jurisprudence have introduced several distinctions: rights in the strict sense, privileges, liberties, immunities, powers, etc.[1] The importance of these distinctions may easily be exaggerated. Thus liberties are rights in so far as they are protected. I can say 'I am at liberty' to get up at six in the morning; but this is really of importance only in so far as it implies a duty on the part of others not to interfere with my doing so. Powers are sometimes distinguished from rights in that there need be no duty on the part of anyone else corresponding to them. For example, my right to make a will corresponds to no duty to anyone else. But here again my right implies that no one can interfere with the way I choose to alienate my property. The stress is on the effect my action will have. So privilege is an exceptional right, a right possessed by a few, and immunity is presumably exemption from a liability. Thus a judge is immune from having to pay damages for defamation because of anything he has said in the course of a trial.[2]

(b) Rights and duties define social relations. Thus there are no 'natural rights' in the sense of pre-social rights, or rights of man as in a state of 'nature'. But there are natural rights in the sense of 'rationally justifiable rights' and there is 'natural law' in the sense of law as it ought to be, 'ideal law'. On this view there are moral rights and duties wherever there is human intercourse, though there may be no durable societies and no states; that is, politically organized societies. There are *recognized* rights wherever there are societies with a regular structure, though there may be no differentiated machinery for promulgation and enforcement. There are *legal* rights in societies that have a developed judiciary and organs of enforcement. The legal rights may or may not be in

1. Cf. especially Hohfeld.

2. Cf. Buckland, op. cit., ch. x.

harmony with recognized moral rights, or with moral rights not widely recognized but demonstrably justifiable as conditions or constituents of well-being. The validity of a right does not depend, on this view, on its recognition. Green thought otherwise. But his dictum that there is no right but thinking makes it so, must, as Hobhouse points out, be set aside as inconsistent with his own better teaching.[1]

(c) We must resist the tendency to regard rights as self-subsistent or absolute or to allow particular rights, for example property or contract, to dominate all others. Owing to the complexity of social relations rights founded on one set of relations may conflict with rights founded on other relations. A particular right formulates a *prima facie* claim and a *prima facie* duty. But taken by itself it may not be binding. To determine what is finally right involves a balancing of different claims. This balancing is effected by reference to a form or way of life accepted in a given society, and in given conditions some rights may be considered as more fundamental than others. Thus, in certain phases of historical development, religious duties were considered paramount, overriding all others. In other phases, the rights of private property may be given a prominence to which other rights are subordinate. The real difficulty lies here. From the ethical point of view, all we can say is that particular rights are subject to modification in a given situation by the claims arising out of other rights or of the body of rights as a whole. The distinction between legal and moral rights will be discussed later. At this point it is sufficient to say that legal rights and duties, in so far as they conform to ethical requirements, define those conditions of well-being which both require and permit of enforcement by the machinery of the law. This formulates an ideal. To this ideal actual legal systems approximate in varying degrees.

1. Cf. T. H. Green, *Principles of Political Obligation*, para. 31: 'Without recognition, or *claim to recognition*, there can be no rights,' and L. T. Hobhouse, *Elements of Social Justice*, p. 40.

(d) In the period since the French Revolution the system of rights and duties has undergone a complex development involving radical changes in outlook and organization. Firstly, inequalities or rights based on differences of sex, wealth, religion, and colour have been greatly reduced. Secondly, the notion of rights has been extended from the political to the social and economic sphere. Thirdly, the ancient idea of human rights has been, so to say, socialized. There has been a movement away from the conception of rights as inhering in individuals and limiting the law to a conception of rights as defining social relations and of law as based on rights so defined. Finally, there is a growing consensus of opinion about the principal rights and duties essential for full membership of a democratic community. They include the following:

1. Security of individuals or groups under the law.
2. Minimum conditions necessary for physical and mental development, including the right to personal property and to the best available education.
3. The right and the duty to work and to choice of employment.
4. Political membership of the community; that is, participation in the framing and working of political institutions.
5. Freedom of association and of contract.
6. Freedom of expression, of conscience and religion, of assembly in public meeting. More broadly freedom from interference in the sphere of self-development.

These rights are in many cases explicitly recognized in constitutions. It is worth mentioning that the Soviet Constitution, 1936, Ch. 10, includes freedom of speech, of the press, of assembly, of uniting in public organizations and societies; freedom of conscience; the right to work, to rest, and to leisure (by limiting hours and by assuring holidays), to maintenance in old age, sickness, or disability (provided by non-contributory insurance), to personal property and inheritance; the right of collective farm households to have their own holdings; the right to education; the right to personal freedom (such as the inviolability of the person and of the home) and to privacy of correspondence.[1]

We have now to inquire how far and in what ways these rights are in conformity with the formal requirements of justice. The fundamental aim is to assure that like cases should be treated in like manner, or, negatively, to exclude arbitrariness, to assure that in so far as different classes of persons receive different treatment such differences should not be due to personal favour or disfavour on the part of the law-makers but to some relevant difference in the grounds on which the right is based. The principles may be set out thus:

1. In allocating rights everyone concerned is entitled to be considered, or, negatively, no one concerned should be ignored or have his claims merely overridden (Equality of Consideration).
2. In allocating rights like cases should be treated in like manner. A difference of treatment requires justification in terms of relevant and sufficient differences between the claimants (Exclusion of Arbitrariness).
3. If differences are justified on the ground of relevant differences in the grounds of the claims, the allocation should be proportionate to the differences. Where the differences cannot be estimated with precision, it is generally held that it is right to assure a minimum for all and perhaps to see to it that differential awards do not endanger the minimum (Principle of Proportionate Equality).
4. Since no single right is absolute, claims based on any one right may be subject to qualifications in accordance with claims based on other rights or the requirements of the total order or way of life (Principle of the Common Good).

1. See Denisov and Kirichenko, *Soviet State Law*, 1960.

The principle of equality of consideration is based on the fact that all men are capable of enjoying and suffering, of happiness and misery, of morality and membership of a society. I take it that this is partly what is meant by saying that all rational beings should be treated as ends and not merely as means, or that every human being has value as such. The notion of ends as applied to persons is obscure, for ends are, as objects of desire, things that do not yet exist. What Kant meant is better expressed by him by saying that we ought to aim at 'the advancement of humanity' – that is, the fuller development of what exists potentially in man; in other words, that there is something in every man, his capacity for attaining objects of value, including morality, which is worthy of respect and which it is our duty to promote. The respect for persons as such is thus based on the recognition that each person has potentialities for good. In his later writings, Kant lays down the rule: promote perfection in yourself and happiness in others. In other words, the injunction to treat manhood as an end has two meanings, according as it is manhood in ourselves or manhood in others that we are considering. The ground for this distinction is the belief that moral perfection is self-sustained and inward and cannot be promoted by others; while it cannot be our duty to further our own happiness, since in any case we are naturally inclined to do so. Both these points can be disputed. Kant gives no ground for believing that it is not our duty to promote the capacities for good in others, so far as this can be done without affecting the inward character of virtue, or for denying that there are duties of self-control in the interest of our own happiness.

The second principle, namely, that like cases should be treated in like manner, needs no further elucidation at this point. It is an axiom of all rational ethics and is implicit in the notion of a norm or law of action as such.

The principle of proportionate equality is needed in order to deal with differences between individuals or in their circumstances. As Aristotle explained: injustice arises when equals are treated unequally, but also when unequals are treated equally. He was clearly right in pointing out that actual societies differ in what they consider relevant grounds of apportionment. This brings home the difficulties of distributive justice, but it does not follow, as some conclude, that the divergence of views cannot be overcome. The divergence affects some rights more than others, as we shall see. But even in the most disputed rights, such as those relating to property, fuller knowledge of the psychological and sociological facts may do a good deal to bridge the gap between the opposed ethical views.

What I have called the Principle of the Common Good requires further definition. The term 'common good' is highly ambiguous. We may speak of a good as common to a community in a distributive sense, meaning that each member possesses it or ought to possess it. We may, for example, say that mental and physical health is part of the common good, implying that each member is entitled to the conditions of mental and bodily health, so far as these can be secured by communal effort. The community as a unit cannot be healthy, but it can maintain the standards of hygiene and nutrition which might make it possible for each and every member to be healthy. But the term 'common' may be used in a collective sense. The common good then stands for a way or form of life characteristic of the community as a whole. The term is then applied to the relations between the members considered as a pattern or form. Thus we may say that one type of family life is better than another, meaning that the relations between the members considered as constituting a way of life are better in the one case than in the other. This seems to imply that we can attribute goodness or badness to the relations between the individuals and not merely to the individuals entering into them. But strictly it is the individuals-in-certain-relations that we have in mind and not the relations apart from the members.

When we consider the things or rather modes of activity we call good, we soon see that they can only be possessed by individuals. It is only individuals that can be well or ill, happy or miserable, it is only individuals who can appreciate beauty or truth or enjoy the give and take of the affections. A community may, however, be good as a whole, if it encourages and maintains an order or form of life in which these goods or values can be attained by its members, and if it seeks to distribute the means needed to attain them fairly; that is, in accordance with the principles of distributive justice.

If this analysis is on the right lines, then it would follow that *ideally* there can be no conflict between the good of the community and the good of the individuals composing it. For the good of the individual is what he ought to aim at, and this cannot be determined without reference to the way or form of life which is the good of the community. I say 'ideally', for the argument only holds on the assumption that the common good is rightly interpreted both by those who speak for the community and by the individuals who constitute it. But this assumption is rarely, if ever, realized in practice and consequently conflicts in fact arise quite frequently. It is important therefore to sort out the different ways in which this happens.

In the first place those who act for the community may have a false conception of the common good, and thus embark on a policy which is not likely to promote the good of its members. They may, for example, engage in an aggressive war, in pursuit of glory or power, in which case the sacrifices they demand from the members are not morally justifiable. On the other hand, there may be cases when war is justifiable. But then it must be shown to be necessary to ward off greater evil or to promote the good of mankind as a whole. In the former case the end set is a false or illusory end, its pursuit contributes neither to the good of the community nor to that of its component members. In the latter cases, the individual may be required to sacrifice even his life, but then it is for the sake of a greater good, which in the last resort is the good of individual human beings either of the present or of future generations.

In the second place, conflicts arise when there is a failure of justice; as for example, when a dominant section within the community imposes its conception of the common good upon the whole community and thus confuses or identifies a sectional good with the good of the entire community. Thus a community may be wealthy as a whole while the majority of its members are poor. In such a case the problem from the ethical point of view is how far the mode of distribution which prevails is justified; as, for example, it might be by the effect it produces on the total available for distribution. If, on the other hand, it can be shown that an approximation to equality is not economically injurious, then the wealth of the community taken as a whole cannot be regarded as ethically right if it leaves the majority of its members in a state of poverty.

A third type of conflict between the good of the community and the good of individuals is illustrated by the argument that in the past great achievements in the arts, in knowledge, and in invention have been made possible by the subjection of the many and the elevation of a leisured aristocracy upon their shoulders. Whether this is true as a matter of history I will not inquire. But, if so, it does not follow that the inequality was a necessary condition without which civilization could not have advanced. Since Engels it has been taken as axiomatic, for example, that without slavery there would have been no civilization. But as far as I know there is no real evidence for this view. That everything that happened had necessarily to happen is just a metaphysical dogma. In any case it does not follow that inequality is necessary now in the interests of art or the advancement of knowledge. We know very little about the conditions which favoured advances in the arts and sciences at certain periods and not at others. The burden of proof lies with those who maintain that the higher values of civilization cannot now be attained without a privileged social class. Ideally the common good should be such that all concerned in it are not only enabled but stimulated and assisted to make the best of themselves. In this connexion too there is no inevitable discrepancy between the good of individuals and the good of the community.

A fourth and more serious difficulty from the theoretical point of view arises when there is conflict between the various ideals within the same order of life or between some of the ideals and the entire order. Thus, for example, in certain circumstances religious values may seem so important as to reduce the rest to insignificance, or the threat to the entire social order so serious as to justify the sacrifice of such values as the freedom of thought and its expression. In such cases, given good faith on both sides, the conflict may be genuine in the sense that it may be rooted in a real difference of opinion regarding either the constituents entering into the total way of life or their order of importance. In the extreme case the moral innovator may advocate a radical change in the whole order of life. A tragic clash may then become unavoidable.

Taking these arguments into consideration, it would seem that apart from the clashes that may arise between component ideals within the entire order or way of life, or between the accepted order and the revolutionary moral innovator, the conflicts that occur are rarely analysable in terms of a divergence between the good of the individual and the good of the community. More commonly conflicts reflect a failure of social justice: either because the community has set itself false or illusory ends, which, in the last resort, will conduce neither to the good of the individuals nor of the community, or because a dominant section identifies its own interests with the interest of the community and parades its good as *the* good of the community. The matter may be summed up in the words of Hobhouse:

Where an organized society has a 'good' opposed to the summed-up gain and loss of its component members, it is either that some of those alleged members are treated merely as instruments external to the body they share or that the good is a false one, cheating even those who partake of it.[1]

If we can now return to the two senses of the term 'common good', it will be seen that if 'common' is used distributively the principle of the common good can be taken as asserting that, in so far as they can be secured by collective action, the conditions necessary for the good life ought to be made available to each and every member of the community. This requirement, however, is already covered by what I have called the principles of equality of consideration, the exclusion of arbitrariness, and proportionate equality. If 'common' is used in a collective sense the principle of the common good points to an order or form of life in which the different values are graded and balanced and the conditions necessary for the maintenance of the entire order defined. It is in the light of this form or pattern of life that public policy as a whole should be judged or determined. The principle of the common good, in this collective sense, is, therefore, of great importance in dealing with conflicts of rights or in defining the limits of particular rights.

1. *Metaphysical Theory of the State*, p. 131.

CHAPTER IV

The Right to Personal Security

WE have now to consider the main rights and duties regarded as essential for full membership of a democratic community and to examine the bearing of the principle of equality on each of them. It will be seen that, while in some cases equality is in Aristotle's terminology 'arithmetical', in others it is 'proportionate' equality, that is, adjusted to relevant differences.

I deal first with the right to personal security. Article 3 of the Declaration of Human Rights states that everyone has the right to life, liberty, and the security of person. This seems to me vague. The notion of liberty is too wide to be considered as a right among others. Liberty in general is a sum of guaranteed 'liberties' or rights. To define it as freedom from wrongful interference with others does not help, since what is wrongful can only be determined by asking whether the act violates specific rights. The term security is also ambiguous. It may be used in the wide sense as meaning protection which an individual may claim in asserting all or any of his rights. But it may mean, and here I am using it in the restricted sense, protection against violence, coercion, or intimidation. The law provides for security in this sense by prohibiting murder, wounding or inflicting bodily harm, intimidation or molestation, cruelty to or neglect of children, rape or indecent assault.

It will be seen that in regard to the rights of personal security arithmetical equality applies. Everyone is equally entitled to the protection of the law and no difference in capacity or desert is relevant. It is slowly recognized that, to assure equal protection for all, the legal system itself must satisfy certain standards. Thus it must guarantee the individual against arbitrary arrest, or detention, assure him the right of public trial by an impartial tribunal and to be judged by a law in effect at the time the alleged offence was committed. Further, it is important that the accused be provided with adequate legal representation and facilities for the preparation of the defence and be allowed the possibility of appeal in serious cases. The independence of the judiciary has rightly been considered of great importance in this context. Independence does not mean that the judge is entitled to act in an arbitrary manner. His duty is to interpret the law and the fundamental assumptions on which it rests. The danger must be avoided of using the judges as political instruments. Under the Nazi régime, for example, none but the politically pliable judges could either attain or retain their office. They were expected to administer the law in accordance 'with the healthy instincts of the people'; that is, with what the Leader wanted, irrespective of statute or precedent. Formally the judge was, according to Nazi jurisprudence, independent, but in fact he could be dismissed or compulsorily retired if he did not satisfy the régime. His duty was to interpret the ideas of the people 'in the light of fundamental principles laid down by the leader'.[1] Similar conditions prevailed in Italy under Mussolini. Professor Buckland quotes a conversation which the late Professor Kantorowicz had with an Italian judge. In the early days of the Fascist régime, he said, the matter was simple. In any litigation the judge had only to ascertain which of the parties was fascist. Later when everyone was a fascist it was not so easy, and you had even to go into the merits of the case.[2] In such circumstances, it is doubtful whether there is a *Rechtsstaat* at all.[3]

In defining the right to life and security of person formidable difficulties arise. There is, firstly, the question

1. Cf. Kollreuter, *Deutsches Verfassungsrecht*, p. 177.

2. *Some Reflections on Jurisprudence*, p. 35.

3. For the way in which different legal systems deal with the appointment, removal, or reappointment of judges, see *The Rule of Law in a Free Society*, pp. 258 ff.

whether or in what circumstances the state has a right to deprive the individual of his right to life or to subject him to force. This I propose to deal with under corrective justice or theories of punishment. There is, secondly, the question whether the killing of seriously deformed babies ('monsters') or the terminating of a pregnancy when the mother's physical and mental health is endangered by its continuance is morally justified and whether laws relating to such acts call for modification.

Among preliterate peoples and in early civilization, the killing of infants was in many cases allowed or tolerated, and generally the child, if not suffered to live, had to be killed in its earliest infancy. The restriction to the weak and deformed, as Hobhouse shows, marks the decay of the practice.[1] Christianity changed radically the attitude to infanticide prevalent in the Pagan empire. The Church Fathers strongly condemned the practice of exposing new-born infants and they brought infanticide under the rule condemning murder. Furthermore, in their view, the crime was the more heinous because the infant, by being deprived of the opportunity of baptism, was doomed to eternal damnation. It seems from a legend cited by Lecky that killing a newly born child was a worse sin than killing a baptized adult.[2] According to Westermarck and the authorities cited by him, infanticide was, until the end of the eighteenth or the beginning of the nineteenth century, a capital crime everywhere in Europe, except in Russia. In the course of this century there have been great changes. In most European countries, whether infanticide is considered as murder or not the death penalty is rarely inflicted. In England, a way of avoiding a sentence for murder was opened up by the Infanticide Act of 1922 as amended in 1938. This provides that in cases where a woman causes the death of her child under the age of twelve months while the balance of her mind was dis-

1. *Morals in Evolution*, p. 340.

2. Cf. Westermarck, *Origin of Moral Ideas*, I, p. 412, and Lecky, *History of European Morals*, I, pp. 23–4.

turbed by reason of her not having fully recovered from the effect of her giving birth to the child or by reason of the effect of lactation consequent upon the birth of the child, she should be guilty of infanticide and might be dealt with and punished as if she had been guilty of manslaughter. The jury may return a verdict of manslaughter on a trial for murder. In Scotland the charge of murder would not be preferred; the woman would be charged with culpable homicide. The statistical evidence shows that in fact women so charged since 1922 have been leniently treated. About two thirds of those convicted were bound over with or without supervision.[1] There is no reason to think that the change in the law has led to any increase in this form of crime. In 1955 thirteen women were charged with statutory infanticide and all were convicted, but most were discharged without punishment or put on probation; only two were sent to prison, one for a year and the other for three years.[2]

In addition to the Infanticide Act there is now another way of avoiding a sentence for murder. By the Homicide Act of 1947 it is possible for the jury to return a verdict for manslaughter by reason of diminished responsibility. Since this Act was passed there have been three or four occasions in which the defendant had put an end to the sufferings of his child who was hopelessly defective and in pain or of the spouse who was suffering dreadfully in a long-drawn-out and fatal illness. The jury took a lenient view and the defendant was sentenced to one or two years imprisonment. Professor Glanville Williams points out that, as the Act is worded, a great strain is put on the conscience of the jury who have to find an 'abnormality of mind arising from inherent causes'; that is, an abnormality due to inherited causes. This cannot cover cases of deep mental stress caused in other ways and makes the section in the Act inapplicable to the mercy-

1. *Royal Commission on Capital Punishment*, pp. 57–9.

2. Glanville Williams, *The Sanctity of Life and the Criminal Law*, p. 37.

killing cases. He recommends that the Act should be amended to allow the jury to give the judge discretion in all cases where the circumstances are such as substantially to diminish the culpability of the accused.[1] Behind all these perplexities, there is, I think, an underlying difficulty arising from a lack of clarity regarding the place of moral assessment in juridical punishment. Whatever view we take about retribution, the gradations of punishment as administered by the state cannot be based on any estimate of the degree of moral guilt. This is, in difficult cases, such as those we are now considering, beyond the power of judge or jury. It does not follow that the state of mind of the offender is irrelevant. It is important from two points of view: as throwing light on the best way of dealing with the offender and in estimating the probable deterrent effect on others of the way he is dealt with. Thus in some cases probation may be appropriate as likely to help enable the unfortunate mother to deal with her difficulties. In others psychological treatment may be necessary. As to deterrence, severity is even less likely to be effective in these cases than in other crimes. There is no reason, for example, for believing that leniency is likely to precipitate a rush of parents to destroy their badly deformed infants. I suggest, accordingly, that it should be open to the judge, on the jury's recommendation, to take into consideration the state of mind of the offender, not with a view of estimating guilt, but of doing the best possible for the offender, while at the same time bearing in mind the effect her treatment is likely to have on others.

We may next consider whether the right to life extends to the unborn child and whether its protection should come under the law. Most legal systems have laws prohibiting abortion, but these often lack enforcement and there is widespread demand for their abolition or reform. There are many who think that the termination of pregnancy should be the mother's own responsibility, while

1. *The Times*, Nov. 1962.

others would legalize abortion under specified conditions and subject to impartial judgement.

The issues raised are very complicated. There is first the moral question: in what circumstances, if any, is the termination of pregnancy morally justifiable? Second, what part is to be played by the criminal law in these matters? Should women who procure their own abortion and qualified surgeons who perform it for them be subject to legal penalties? It should be remembered that, if the termination of pregnancy be considered morally wrong, it does not follow that it ought to be legally punishable. Both these questions raise a third, namely, at what point is the embryo to be regarded as a human being, endowed with moral and legal rights? Does human personality begin at the moment of fertilization, or when the embryo is viable, that is, capable of being born alive, or at birth. From the point of view of the criminal law it is of the greatest importance to determine at what point legal protection of the embryo should begin. There is a good deal of evidence to show that very few illegal abortions take place after the twenty-eighth week; in fact very few occur after the first few months. It is arguable that if the protection of the criminal law is to be extended to the prenatal period it should commence at the time of viability (now generally taken to be the twenty-eighth week of pregnancy) and not go beyond.

From the ethical point of view the general principle appealed to is the value of human personality, it being assumed that the viable child must be considered a human being. Whether the values of personality are to be ascribed also to the foetus which is not yet viable is a matter of dispute; and some would hold that up to the time of viability a woman should have the right to decide whether she shall continue a pregnancy or not. There may well be grounds which might justify termination: (a) when continuance would seriously endanger the life or health of the mother. In such a situation there is a conflict of values, and in extreme cases a choice may have to be made between destroying the foetus and saving the life of the mother, or allowing the mother to die in the hope of saving the foetus. (b) Termination may be thought justified when the pregnancy is the result of illegal acts; for example, of rape, or seduction of a girl below the age of consent. In such circumstances continuance of the pregnancy may wreck the mental balance of the mother and hold out no happiness for the unwanted child. (c) There is possibly a third group of cases, namely, when the mother knows herself to be the carrier of a grave hereditary disease, mental or physical, or when the child is likely to suffer from a disease contracted by the mother during pregnancy. In all these cases, even if it be conceded that abortion is itself an evil, it may well be a lesser evil than the misery to the mother or to the child that would result from the continuance of the pregnancy. The mother and her medical advisers have to choose, and in making their choice the principle of the sanctity of the human life will not carry them very far: the problem is one of grading evils.

On the legal side, many countries allow therapeutic abortion; that is, operations performed by medical practitioners to terminate a pregnancy likely to endanger a woman's life or seriously to affect her health.[1] In England the present law of abortion rests upon the Offences Against the Person Act, 1861, which lays down a maximum penalty of imprisonment for life, even when the abortion is attempted before the foetus is viable. In practice, however, the law is not applied to the consenting mother, who is rarely prosecuted: and the Court recognizes a defence on the ground that the operation performed was necessary to save the life of the mother. Whether danger to the health of the mother, mental or physical, would constitute an equally valid defence is not quite clear, though it seems likely that when serious injury to health is feared the Court will not look too nar-

1. Cf. Herman Mannheim, *Criminal Justice and Social Reconstruction,* ch. III, for a full summary.

rowly into the question whether there is a danger to life.[1]

It is widely recognized that the law against abortion is ineffective. Instead of eliminating abortion it tends to drive women to unqualified persons operating often under dangerous conditions and without proper safeguards. Estimates of the number of illegal operations in England and Wales vary widely, some giving the figure 100,000 others as not less than a quarter of a million every year.[2] Equally high or higher figures are given for other countries. The small number of convictions shows that the law is not or cannot be enforced, and this suggests that it is out of touch with widely prevalent attitudes or opinions.

From the ethical point of view popular opinion is not a sufficient guide. We have seen that in considering the moral principles involved there may be cases when termination of pregnancy within the time limits referred to may be justified, though it must be confessed that the decision involves balancing of good and evil of great difficulty. Whether the conduct in question should be brought under the criminal law is another matter. I am inclined to agree with those who argue that the evil consequences of treating all cases of abortion as crimes are greater than the evils of keeping them out of the sphere of law, and that a termination of pregnancy by qualified practitioners should therefore cease to be a criminal offence.

1. Cf. Glanville Williams, *The Sanctity of Life and the Criminal Law*, p. 154.

2. ibid., p. 192.

CHAPTER V

Economic Rights

IN its application to the second group of rights, now sometimes called economic and social rights, the principle of equality presents difficulties. Approximations to the principle are to be found in most democratic societies in the laws fixing minimum wage rates, in the provisions made by the social services, including free elementary education, insurance schemes against unemployment, sickness, and old age.[1]

1. The following articles in the *Declaration of Human Rights* are of interest in this context:

Article 22

Everyone, as a member of society, has the right to social security and is entitled to the realization, through national effort and international cooperation and in accordance with the organization and resources of each State, of the economic, social, and cultural rights indispensable for his dignity and the free development of his personality.

Article 25

1. Everyone has the right to a standard of living adequate for the health and well-being of himself and of his family, including food, clothing, housing, and medical care and necessary social services, and the right to security in the event of unemployment, sickness, disability, widowhood, old age, or other lack of livelihood in circumstances beyond his control.

2. Motherhood and childhood are entitled to special care and assistance. All children, whether born in or out of wedlock, shall enjoy the same protection.

Attention may also be drawn to Article 17:

1. Everyone has the right to own property alone as well as in association with others.

2. No one shall be arbitrarily deprived of his property.

It will be seen that these articles make no attempt to define the nature and limits of property rights. With it may be compared the articles in the Soviet Constitution of 1936 (Articles 6 & 7) which assign property in the 'means of production' to the State, but give the individual property rights to income from work, savings, dwelling house, and other personal requisites.

These measures may be regarded as satisfying the principle of equality in seeking to assure the minimum conditions of physical and mental development for all. But they leave open the question of what is to happen above the minimum, and, if the principle of proportionate equality is to be used, what the basis of apportionment is to be.

We come up here against the old and complicated question of the ethical basis of the rights of property. Broadly, there seem to have been three distinguishable, though not mutually exclusive, types of theory. There are, firstly, natural right theories. These regard property as a fundamental right independent of particular institutions, though they may leave open the question what institutions are likely to be most in harmony with the requirements of natural law. Secondly, there are theories which base property on modes of origin or acquisition, e.g. first occupation, labour; or on an analysis of the factors which contribute to the value of the products of labour. Thirdly, there are the theories according to which property rights, like other rights, are to be tested by their contribution to public good or well-being. For my present purpose I can deal with these theories briefly.

It is worth noting that neither in Stoic nor Patristic doctrine is private property a natural right. 'By nature all things are held in common', is Stoic doctrine; the Fathers tell us: 'Before the Fall' there was 'no mine and thine distinct'. Private property became necessary and is therefore justified because man's greed and avarice have to be kept in check. By convention, therefore, laws are instituted to define the conditions and limitations of ownership. In medieval theory, as formulated by Saint Thomas, it seems that private property is not part of the natural law, but is not contrary to it and is added to it by human reason.[1] In modern scholastic writings, if I have

1. Cf. *Summa Theologica*, Part II, 2, Qu. 66; Cf. A. J. Carlyle, 'The Theory of Property in Mediaeval Theology', in *Property: its Duties and Rights*, ed. Charles Gore, 1915, p. 128.

followed them aright, a distinction is drawn, following Saint Thomas, between the general or primary right of man to the goods of the earth, and a sort of 'secondary natural right' based on reasoning about the practical conditions in which the primary right has to be exercised. The forms of ownership as defined by law do not belong to natural law and are subject to criticism in the light of natural law. Property arrangements ought to be, Pope Pius XII is quoted as saying,

> . . . an element of the social order, a necessary presupposition for men's initiatives, a stimulus to work for the securing of both the temporal and the transcendent ends of life, for securing, therefore, the dignity and liberty of man created in the image of God, who, from the beginning, has given to man dominion over material things.[1]

It will be seen that from the general right to use material goods, whether this is called 'natural' or not, very little can be deduced about the forms of ownership. In other words, natural law theories have in practice to appeal to the more general theories which judge property rights not by *a priori* principles, but by their observable effects on social well-being.[2]

The vagueness of natural right theories becomes apparent when we consider the way in which they have been used by lawyers. Blackstone, for example, includes property among absolute rights. But, it seems, that this only applies to 'possession', i.e. 'for the time only that the act of possession lasts'. Continuance and with it the right of inheritance and bequest is 'no natural but merely a civil right'.[3] It is thus not at all clear what rights are to be

1. Cf. Calvez and Perrin, *The Church and Social Justice*, p. 206.
2. 'Examine the writers on the laws of nature and you will always find that, whatever principles they set out with, they are sure to terminate here at last, and to assign as the ultimate reason for every rule which they establish the convenience and necessity of mankind.' Hume, *Enquiry*, Sect. III, part II, p. 189.
3. *Commentaries*, II. ii. Locke, on the other hand, thought that a father can dispose of his possessions as he likes. *Second Treatise*, 65.

considered 'natural', i.e. independent of social enactment. In other words, from the general right of possession no principle can be derived as to the scope and limits of the right of property.

The attempt to base the right of property on natural law appears in another form in Locke. A man, he argued, has by nature a right in his own person, in his own labour, and in that with which he 'mixes his labour'. The vagueness and ambiguity of the conception of nature are here once more apparent. Locke recognizes that on his view a person is only entitled to such products of his labour as he can use and that everything beyond this is 'more than his share and belongs to others'. In the case of land, in particular, appropriation can only confer a right 'when there is enough and as good left, and more than the yet unprovided could use' (para. 33). But instead of using his theory as a basis for criticizing existing inequalities, he accepts and justifies them. 'It is plain,' he says, 'that the consent of men have agreed to a disproportionate and unequal possession of the earth – I mean out of the bounds of society and compact, for in governments the laws regulate it, they having by consent found out and agreed how a man may rightfully, and without injury, possess more than he himself can make use of, by receiving gold and silver.'[1] The conception of nature thus provides no principles for regulating inequalities.

In socialist theory, Locke's principle that a person has a right to the fruits of his labour reappears in the form: 'the labourer has a right to the *whole* produce of his labour'. What is perhaps more distinctive of socialist thought is that a distinction is drawn between property in the means of production and property in the fruits of labour. It is clear that, if the instruments of production are appropriated by a few, the rest are deprived of the freedom to apply their labour. Combining these two points a conclusion is drawn which is the very opposite of Locke's individualism, namely that property in the

1. *Second Treatise on Civil Government*, v.

means of production must be held in common, that all must be given access to apply their labour, and that the assignment or apportionment of the results should be a matter of collective regulation. The principle adopted in making this assignment is not arithmetical but proportionate equality. Under socialism the basis of distribution is the quantity and quality of the labour expended; under communism distribution is according to needs. The problem before the socialist is how to reconcile central control with individual freedom – a problem rendered the more acute if political and economic control are concentrated in the same hands.[1]

To these problems we must return when we have considered other theories of the ethical basis of property. Of these the most important are those of the Utilitarians and the Idealists. The former justify private property as a condition of general happiness, the latter as a condition of self-dependence and self-fulfilment. The difficulty about both these theories is that they tended to conclude too readily that the particular form of private enterprise and of the distribution of capital and income that prevailed in their day were more likely than other arrangements to promote these ends. The Utilitarian philosophers and economists were only able to support this conclusion by making psychological and sociological assumptions of doubtful validity in their own time and certainly not

1. Cf. Marx, *Critique of the Gotha Programme*, Lenin, *State and Revolution*. Stalin sums up the position in the following way: 'Equality signifies that (*a*) after the capitalists have been overthrown and expropriated all the workers are equally liberated from exploitation; (*b*) after the means of production have been made the property of all society, private property in them has been abrogated for all equally; (*c*) that all are equally obligated to work according to their capacities, and have an equal right to remuneration according to their labour (socialist society); and (*d*) that all are equally obligated to work according to their capacities and all the workers have an equal right to remuneration therefore according to their needs (communist society).' 'Questions of Leninism', cited in *Soviet Legal Philosophy*, Babbs and Hazard, p. 388.

applicable to all stages of development. Thus they assumed that the individual's love of his own pleasure is the supreme motive in human conduct, that people can be relied upon to know their own interest best and to take the best means needed to attain them, and that individuals acting separately are more clear-sighted than when acting as a group. In the later developments of Utilitarian theories these assumptions are either abandoned or greatly modified. Yet, on the whole, economists in the classical tradition continue to maintain that the system of private enterprise, despite the inequalities inherent in it, is more likely than other arrangements to provide the necessary incentives to effort, to promote production, and best to satisfy consumer's demands. The attitude of the later writers to equality is particularly instructive. They all think equality in itself to be desirable.[1] They all wish the conditions of well-being to be more widely diffused among the masses of the people. On the whole, however, they still maintain that inequality has to be tolerated as a necessary evil, on the ground that equalization would tend to discourage effort, decrease saving, and, by lessening efficiency, diminish the total available for distribution, and so would not benefit those for whose benefit it is advocated.

It will be seen that these conclusions turn not so much on questions of ethical principle as on questions of fact. Thus it may well be that inequality of distribution was an important factor in the earlier stages of capitalism, but is no longer so in a stage of high technological development and large-scale organization. Indeed, at such a stage egalitarian redistribution may not only be compatible with, but a condition of, increased productivity. The problem of incentives completely changes its character as industry moves from the type which prevailed when the factory owner formed and managed his own business

1. Sidgwick, *Principles of Political Economy*, p. 521; Marshall, *Principles*, pp. 46 ff.; Cannan, *Theories of Production and Distribution*, concluding chapter; Pigou, *Economics of Welfare*, p. 83.

to that which exists under Joint Stock institutions in which ownership of capital and management are almost completely dissociated. If these arguments be accepted, it follows that the Utilitarian position calls for drastic revision, if it is to be applied to present conditions.

On the philosophical side, the most important changes in Utilitarian theory that have been made in recent times are that most Utilitarians now reject the theory of psychological hedonism, agree that happiness is not to be identified with pleasure, and that there are other intrinsic goods than happiness. Among intrinsic goods are generally included moral qualities and the exercise of the creative faculties, cognitive and aesthetic. These modifications of Utilitarianism have their importance for theories of the ethical basis of property. For, if accepted, it would follow that in estimating the consequences of different types of property we have to consider not only their bearing on happiness, but also on qualities of character and personality. In this way Utilitarian defenders of private property can adopt as their own the doctrine of the Idealist philosophers that private property is necessary for the development of individual character.[1]

I believe that it is now generally recognized that private property in some things can be thus justified. It does not follow that the theory provides justification for the capitalist system *en bloc* in the form in which it existed at the time when the Idealist philosophers were putting it forward. They made no attempt to show that the distribution of property in capitalist societies was in any way proportionate to capacity for personal development or the striving for such development. With some exceptions they failed to note that, if private property was really an essential condition of freedom for the individual, then all had a claim to it, and that no system could be just which did not secure for the many such elementary conditions of freedom as security of employment and the

1. Cf. Hastings Rashdall, 'The Philosophical Theory of Property', *Property: Its Duties and Rights*, ch. 11, ed. Charles Gore, 1915.

power to choose a career. Again, if private property is defended on the ground that it encourages initiative and a sense of personal responsibility, then it would follow that an industrial system stands condemned, if it tolerates irresponsible power in the few, while depriving the many of any effective share in controlling the basic conditions of their lives. The root of the difficulty, I think, is that in most of the discussions the notion of private property is used too vaguely. It is necessary to distinguish at least three forms of private property: (i) property in durable and non-durable consumers' goods; (ii) property in the means of production worked by their owners; (iii) property in the means of production not worked or directly managed by their owners, especially the accumulation of masses of property of this kind in the hands of a relatively narrow class. While the first two forms of property can be justified as necessary conditions of a free and purposeful life, the third cannot. For this type of property gives power not only over things, but through things over persons. It is open to the charge made by socialists again and again that any form of property which gives man power over man is not an instrument of freedom but of servitude.

So far I have been dealing with ethical theories of property formulated in the latter part of the nineteenth and the early decades of the twentieth century. I have now to consider what bearing these theories have on the situation today. The following points immediately suggest themselves for our consideration:

Firstly, experience of communist societies has shown that the problem of power is not resolved by transferring the ownership of property in the means of production to the state. For this adds political power to economic power, rendering the individual more helpless than in capitalist systems, in which power and responsibility are more widely diffused.

Secondly, in western societies property for power is of less importance than it was when political power was directly linked with property and freedom of association was limited or non-existent. Nowadays the direct power of employers over workers is kept in check by trade unions, and wage-earners have learnt to use the political machine to remodel the economic system.

Thirdly, the new industrial revolution has led to the emergence of economic structures which have broadly similar characteristics irrespective of the type of political system – a concentration of control, unified direction, a vast increase in clerical labour and the number of administrators and technicians, aggregations of large masses of people in giant, impersonal concerns, with everywhere much the same patterns of relationships and behaviour. In all these structures, whatever the political type, there arise problems inherent in large-scale organization – how to avoid bureaucratization and administrative tyranny, how to reconcile control at the centre with local vigour and independence, how to maintain effective contact between the central and local agencies, and so forth. These are problems which both democratic and totalitarian systems have to face, though they are aggravated in the latter by the fusion of economic and political power.

Fourthly, western experience has shown that the function of managing, directing, including the ensuring of saving for future development, can be performed by professional administrators who are not owners. Management has been largely dissociated from ownership in large-scale organizations. It does not follow that this involves a radical change in the relations between the class structure and the property system, since in most cases the administrators and technicians may well belong to the same social strata and share the same outlook as the property owners. If the dangers of the managerial personnel hardening into a caste are to be avoided, it is necessary that the field of recruitment should be widened to include the working classes.

Fifthly, the capitalist states have not in fact followed the line of development predicted by Marx. They have shown powers of adaptation and reconstruction not foreseen by him. To this development numerous factors have contributed: (a) the relations between the classes have been affected by political factors, and these, together with the rise of the standard of living, have tended to reduce the antagonism between the classes; (b) in many countries nationalized sectors have arisen within the capitalist economy, a situation again not foreseen by Marx. In Britain, as in France, for example, between forty and fifty per cent of all fixed capital investment is done by public authorities including the nationalized industries, as well as the central and local government; (c) planning was formerly considered distinctive of socialism, but nowadays it is undertaken in varying degrees by capitalist governments. The prediction that planning must necessarily lead to serfdom has not so far been fulfilled. In western societies the power of the state has been held in check by associations which retain a measure of independence. In communist societies there are trends indicating an increasing demand for decentralization and a wider diffusion of responsibility.

Bearing these considerations in mind we will now return to the problem of the general principles of an equitable industrial order. We have seen that the ethical basis of property is that some control over material things is a condition of well-being and development. This justifies property in personalia, i.e. non-durable and durable, consumable or enjoyable goods necessary for physical and mental health, and, more generally, in all those things that a person needs to guide his own life and work out his purposes in his own way. It is clear that this does not exclude all forms of private property, but only those which give to some power over others. Next, if individuals have a right to the conditions of well-being, then it is the duty of the community to provide these conditions so far as this lies within its power. It follows as a corollary (1) that the final directing power over the economic system must be in communal hands, (2) that corresponding to the right of the individual to the conditions of well-being there is a correlative duty, i.e. the duty of work, to play one's part in the task of providing the means of well-being (this does not mean that the community has no duty to those who cannot work), and (3) that the system must be so organized that no individuals can, through the possession of property, have power over the lives of others.

These considerations themselves yield no principles of distributive justice. To arrive at them we must go back to the principle of equality. As we have seen, the right for everyone to the minimum conditions of life is now widely recognized, though in different forms. There remains the question of the distribution of property or income above the minimum. 'Arithmetic' equality has few defenders. If the principle of proportionate equality is appealed to the question is, proportionate to what? What differences are ethically relevant?

Among the criteria which have been widely discussed are needs, ability, productivity, effort. Apart from difficulties in measurement none of these is free from objection on ethical grounds. It is not obvious, for example, why a person highly endowed by nature should be treated better than others. Distribution according to product does not seem to be possible, since the value assignable to individuals is not assessable. It is clear that the major part of the value of a product depends upon the available raw material, differences of site and climate, level of technical development, the kind and amount of available skill, administrative security, and other social factors such as those influencing the level of demand. Distribution according to effort was persuasively defended in the last generation by, among others, Lowes Dickinson, at any rate for people doing the same kind of work. On this basis it follows that a person who finds his task difficult and irksome should have higher remuneration than those who perform it with ease and pleasure. The notion of desert or merit is particularly perplexing in this context. If merit means intrinsic worth it might be argued, as we have seen above, that between it and external reward there is no necessary connexion, and certainly no assignable proportion. Even if distribution according to merit could be defended in principle, its administration would require an amount of wisdom and humanity hardly likely to be generally available. Merit may be used in another sense to refer to actions which would not be performed without extrinsic reward. But this has nothing to do with any necessary relation between intrinsic worth and external conditions. It is based on the need, on occasion, of providing an additional stimulus to effort.

I should like to suggest a different approach. Firstly, it is fitting that individuals should have the means to well-being and this, not as a reward, but as a necessary condition. Secondly, there are two sorts of conditions, functional and more general. The functional conditions include the tools or equipment needed for one's work. The more general conditions go beyond one's work to the broader requirements of physical and mental health, the opportunity to exercise one's faculties and to pursue worthwhile objects. Both these kinds of conditions differ for different persons and, if so, may justify differential treatment. It is easy to see that they may point in different directions. Those who pursue occupations which are irksome or least worth pursuing for their own sake may be entitled to claim special facilities in compensation. Finally, since distribution depends on production, an equitable scale would have to take into consideration the bearing of the principle adopted on the total available for distribution. Thus an additional ground for differentiation may be found in the necessity to provide an incentive to effort with a view to encourage greater production.

The practical difficulties remain, of course. There is no reliable method of estimating the differentials that follow from the application of the above principles. We cannot know in advance of experience what conditions are needed, say, by an artist, a philosopher, a bishop, a lawyer, a coalminer, a road-sweeper, to enable them to make the most of their capacities for good, and at the same time to induce them to put out their best efforts in the performance of their specific functions. Since it is desirable to leave individuals the right to choose and vary their occupations, we have to rely in the end on the forces of supply and demand. The problem is therefore whether a scale so based can be operated in a manner to satisfy the demands of equity.

To bring about a state of affairs in which a scale based on equity would tend to coincide with the results of supply and demand, the following conditions would seem to be necessary, though they may not be sufficient. Firstly, there must be a narrowing of the range of differentials to avoid great disparities in earned income. This, together with the erosion of property-derived incomes, would tend to reduce differences in the standard of living, and so make possible a greater approximation to equality in educational opportunity and in the choice of occupations. Formal equality of access to education will not meet the requirement here contemplated, since gross differences in social and home backgrounds tend to make it more difficult for the less fortunate to develop whatever powers they have in the early stages of education, and to avail themselves of the opportunities for higher education formally open to them at later stages. Secondly, a system of education is required likely to maintain a high level of intelligence and taste and so generate and sustain a demand for interest in the 'higher' kinds of work. Thirdly, it is desirable that there should be a change in the prestige-value of occupations other than that which properly attaches to positions of responsibility and the exercise of authority in the different spheres of activity. Fourthly, given freedom of association, ways must be found to prevent powerful industrial or professional organizations from obtaining special differentials for their members not justified by the above principles. Granted conditions of equal opportunity there would be a stronger tendency than now for people to choose their work in accordance with their interest and capacity, and this is not only likely to conduce to greater well-being, but may be an important factor also in enhancing productivity. On the other hand, less agreeable work would have to be given sufficient differential advantages to overcome the resistance to engage in it. In general, then, differentials have to be justified by showing that they are required either in the interest of efficiency, or as necessary conditions of well-being, and, in any case, they ought not to be of a magnitude likely to endanger the minimum to which all are entitled.

I agree with G. D. H. Cole that at present the demand for higher income for jobs which have a higher social status is affected by the presence of large unearned incomes, which set standards of consumption to which the occupants of superior posts in industry and other occupations naturally aspire. If unearned income were to disappear, or to be greatly reduced, it would become possible to narrow differences of earned income to a very substantial extent without any adverse effects on them as incentives. The highest income could be reduced to no more than is at present earned by a highly qualified professional man working as a salaried employee in some branch of public service.[1]

In highly industrialized societies these requirements cannot be satisfied by reverting to the methods of individualist production – the peasant proprietor, the one-man business. The only course available is to vest the ultimate control of the industrial mechanism in the community, and to safeguard the freedom of individuals by giving them the right to participate in the exercise of this control, particularly in those decisions which concern them most directly in their working life. Two questions arise on which opinion is now sharply divided: (1) can ultimate control by the community be assured without complete or extensive social ownership of the means of production? (2) what form is the right of individual participation in

1. *The Case for Industrial Partnership*, p. 98.

the control of the industrial set-up to take, or in other words is 'democracy in industry' possible?

It is interesting to note that L. T. Hobhouse, writing in the twenties as a social liberal or, better, as a liberal socialist, was in favour of a mixed economy on lines which have much in common with those now advocated by democratic socialists in most western countries. He refused to accept nationalization as a universal panacea, but he looked forward to an extension of public ownership and management in a variety of forms, while allowing a certain scope to individual enterprise both in industry and the professions. The final ownership of capital had to be dealt with by controlling inheritance, and he thought that the graduation of death duties should be supplemented by adopting some such proposal as that of Rignano, imposing extra taxation at each passage of property by inheritance. The effect would be that inherited wealth would be a diminishing asset and the balance would go to the community. In general, he thought that wealth should be linked with function. The state had the duty of exercising ultimate control over the direction of industry without necessarily, or in all cases, assuming managerial responsibility. Unearned wealth would accrue to the community; the general conditions of work and remuneration would be laid down by the law and adjusted in detail by appropriate boards, who would gradually build up a set of principles analogous to the ways in which principles of case law have been reached; the actual management would be in the hands of joint boards of consumers and producers, municipalities, co-operative associations, or private enterprise, according to the requirements of particular industries.[1]

Since the twenties, western governments have increasingly accepted responsibility for maintaining full employment, and have been led to policies involving more and more planning and control. Thus they have sought in various ways to influence the rate of growth, the location

1. Cf. *Elements of Social Justice*, 1922, ch. x.

of industries, the degree of monopoly, and the distribution of incomes, and to deal with the problems arising out of the relation of full employment to the balance of payments. Furthermore, many of them have experimented with varying forms of semi-socialism by nationalizing certain industries or entrusting them to public or semi-public corporations. It is perhaps fair to say that the general tendency has been to lay more emphasis on planning and general control than on public ownership. On the economic efficiency of these kinds of semi-socialism opinions differ widely. From the point of view of social justice efficiency has to be judged by two fundamental requirements: there must be a reduction of inequalities not only in income but in property, and this has to be achieved without introducing new inequalities based on hierarchies of power.

Short of a revolutionary expropriation which in western societies is unlikely to succeed, or to do so only at the cost of generating new tyrannies, the best method of attacking inequalities of property is through the restriction of inheritance. This can be achieved as we have seen by the methods suggested by Rignano or by the modified scheme put forward by Hugh Dalton.[1] This provides that when an estate is inherited there should be, besides estate duty in its present form, a second duty against which the inheritor is given an annuity, roughly equal to the income that would have been yielded by the sum taken under the duty, and to terminate at his death. By reducing inequalities in property ownership, measures such as these would also indirectly reduce inequalities in income and so, in some degree, hinder the further accumulation of property. If the assets thus accruing to the community took the form not of money payments, but of shares or bonds or other forms of property, such as landed estates, private businesses, etc., they would provide a new route to socialism. As G. D. H. Cole argued,[2] the state

1. *Inequalities of Incomes in Modern Communities.*
2. Cf. *Is this Socialism?*, Fabian Pamphlet, 1954, p. 20.

would become a part-proprietor of enterprises which might remain in private hands but controlled by directors especially appointed, who would help shape policy in the public interest and in harmony with the wider schemes defined by the government planning agencies. The long run effect would be 'to establish socialized production over a wide field without setting up giant organizations in forms of enterprise better suited to relatively small and, within limits, competitive operation.'

The organization of industry which would thus emerge would be one permitting considerable diversity and elasticity of method. While some forms of enterprise would be directly managed by the state or by public corporations established by it, others would be carried on by municipal or regional bodies, cooperative societies, non-profitmaking institutes, or by enterprises whose funds would be derived partly from investment by public bodies and which would therefore be subject to public direction. In addition, there might well be various small-scale activities carried on by self-employed persons without substantial use of employed labour, for example, some professional services, shopkeeping, and perhaps farming by smallholders. In general, the greater the diversity and the decentralization of power, the greater the opportunity for the energy and initiative of individuals.

We may deal next with the idea of democracy in industry. This has a long history in socialist thought. Before the world wars it was expressed most clearly in theories of revolutionary syndicalism and in this country in the various forms of guild socialism. In our own day the difficulties inherent in the idea have been brought home to us by the experience of communist countries, where the ultimate control of industry is concentrated in the party leadership and there are no free or independent trade unions. In this connexion the Yugoslav experiment is of great interest. It is based on the principle of full scale workers' management. Industry is publicly owned. The various enterprises are run by Workers' Councils of 15 to

120 members elected by all the workers. The day-to-day management is in the hands of boards of three to eleven members elected by the Council. It is widely believed that the system has achieved a measure of decentralization. It appears, however, that the Communist Party is over-represented in the Councils and that major decisions reflect Party policy rather than the views of the workers.

In western societies socialists generally assume that, whatever the ultimate ideal may be, a mixed economy is likely to survive for a considerable time to come. They differ, however, in their attitude to the problem of workers' participation in management and, in particular, in their views as to the part to be played by the trade unions. In Germany, for example, stress is laid on direct participation by workers in management. This right is guaranteed by the *Betriebsverfassungsgesetz* 1952 (Works Constitution Law). According to this, all firms have to establish a Works Council which has the right to express views on the business affairs of the concern, as well as co-management rights in decisions on wage payments, conditions of work, and dismissals. In Joint Stock companies the workers are not represented in the Board of Directors (*Vorstand*) but they occupy one-third of the seats in the *Aufsichtsrat* or Board responsible for overall policy.

In the Coal and Steel industries there is a greater degree of workers' control. *Mitbestimmungsrecht* or Co-determination guarantees them fifty per cent representation on the *Aufsichtsrat* (nominated by the workers in the enterprise and the trade unions) and the right to nominate a Works Director on the *Vorstand* (Board of Directors) nominated directly by the Union. It has to be added that every labour agreement is a contract in law and cannot be broken without recourse to the courts. The contract system does not permit illegal strikes and a union cannot order a strike until its contract has expired.

On the working of this system opinions differ. According to some observers it has given the German worker a higher sense of security and better conditions of work than are enjoyed by workers in Britain. Others think that the Works Councils do nothing more than can be achieved by shop stewards or local secretaries in their day-to-day negotiations with the management. At the higher levels of management representation on the Boards has admittedly given the workers greater power than they formerly enjoyed, but their general influence on management is said not to be as great as that exercised by British or American unions through collective bargaining from outside the managerial structure.[1]

In France and more clearly in Britain there is nowadays little enthusiasm for the idea of a direct share by workers in management. It is felt that joint management gives rise to conflicts of loyalties and that, though a good deal can be achieved by joint consultation at different levels, nothing should be done to interfere with the independence of the trade unions and their traditional methods of action, or decrease their militancy in pressing working-class claims. On the other hand, the problem of the function or status of trade unions in a completely or dominantly socialized economy seems so far to have received little attention.

An interesting contribution to these problems has recently been made by Mendès-France in his book *La République moderne*. He begins by assuming that a mixed economy is likely to survive for some time. He envisages a system in which the government of the country is carried on by (a) a legislative assembly or parliament responsible for initiating and formulating legislation, elected geographically as at present; (b) a second chamber to be called the Economic and Social Council, an extension of the existing Economic Council, but unlike it, composed of representatives of the various social, economic, and regional groups and responsible primarily for planning and controlling the industrial system. His scheme differs from that propounded by the Guild Socialists in the twenties in that, unlike them, it is not based on any radical

1. Cf. Crossland, *The Conservative Enemy*, p. 221.

or sharp distinction between economic or political functions. It is the business of the Economic and Social Council to formulate a plan and to submit it for the approval of the Legislative Assembly. On the other hand, all legislation proposed by the latter body has to be submitted to the Economic and Social Council, which decides whether the matters under discussion call for its intervention or not. In case of a deadlock, machinery is provided for joint consultation and decision.

As far as the public sector is concerned it is the duty of the Economic and Social Council to assure that the various enterprises do not go each their own way, but are coordinated to meet the overall requirements of the plan. The private sectors, too, have to submit any considerable extensions that may be contemplated for approval. The relative part played by the public and private sectors is not fixed by appealing to any inflexible rule of nationalization, but is to be determined according to the prevailing conditions, the tasks which have to be undertaken, and the degree of cooperation which the public powers can appeal to. Whatever is done in the private sector must not be incompatible with the general plan. And, in those areas in which private enterprise shows itself to be too timid or to lack initiative (e.g. in moving industries to depressed areas), it is the duty of the state to step in and itself undertake the necessary action.

Mendès-France lays great stress on the importance of instructing the general public in economic and social matters, so as to enable them to take an active part in the shaping of policy. Without widespread education, democratization of the economic system cannot be obtained. So long as the privilege of knowledge is reserved to a minority, so long as information remains tendentious or dominated by group interests, democracy is impossible or illusory. Mendès-France does not discuss in this book the problem of the principles of payment for services, but he insists on the importance of abolishing hereditary privileges. 'The non-inheritance of social advantages alone can provide an answer to the problem of class conflicts.' There have to be '*élites*' but these must not be allowed to harden into castes. This is not an easy matter. He quotes a speech by Khrushchev in which he deplored the fact that in the U.S.S.R. sixty to seventy per cent of the students in the universities and other schools of education were the sons of functionaries and intellectuals. Perhaps the most important point in his discussion is the stress he lays on decentralization of power, involving as it does a complete reversal of the main trends in French history. Not only is there to be a second chamber to scrutinize and control the administrative acts of the government, but there are also to be regional, social, and economic councils constituted on the same model as the main Economic and Social Council and allowed considerable independent power. Decentralization is further strengthened by the role assigned to Trade Unions. Unlike the position of the latter in totalitarian societies, they are to retain their independence, but are expected to play their part in the democratization of the economy in various ways. Thus they must try to secure a more adequate representation of workers in the various economic commissions concerned with the definition and execution of the plan. In existing commissions only one-tenth represent labour, the rest being divided between the functionaries and the employers. Secondly, they must retain the right of criticizing and opposing the plan by any methods traditionally employed by them. Finally, they must contribute positively to the general plan by doing all they can to ensure its success and by taking an active interest not only in the formulation but the execution of the schemes adopted.

The idea of an economic assembly supplementing the general legislature, once ardently supported by the Guild Socialists, has now almost completely disappeared from public discussion in Britain. How much agreement there is on other matters, it is difficult to say. The following points need to be emphasized. British democratic socialists would agree with Mendès-France in the stress he lays on decentralization of power and in leaving open the question of the relative part to be assigned in the economy to public and private sectors. The ultimate aim is to reduce inequalities in property and income not justified by the principles of distributive justice. To achieve this aim it is necessary (a) to bring about a redistribution of wealth by the control of inheritance and by other methods of taxation; (b) to allow no more than relatively modest differences of income and only such as can be shown to be required either in the interest of efficiency or as necessary conditions of well-being. These differentials would not be fixed once and for all, but would be subject to changes in the occupational structure and the values put on different kinds of work. It is hardly likely that a scientific method of evaluation will ever be discovered which will enable experts to lay down objectively the values to be assigned, say, to a director of a physics laboratory, a medical general practitioner, a parish clergyman, an unskilled labourer, or a routine operator of an automatic machine. The range of differentials can only be determined empirically and by consent. But it is essential that claims to income shall be judged in terms of a common standard applied and defined by collective agreements reached by bodies representing management, workers, and consumers. Further, it is of the greatest importance to leave scope for free choice by encouraging diversity of structure and a measure of competition both within the public and the private sectors. To achieve popular control power has to be divided. Hence it is desirable that the unions should not be state organs but shall retain a measure of independence and bargaining strength. As to management, workers should be able to feel that they have a real share in deciding under whose orders their daily work is to be done. This can be assured by giving them the right to elect their supervisors from among those who have the necessary technical or educational qualifications. The structure and functions of the higher management in both the public and private sectors must vary with the requirements of particular industries. Whatever the structure, facilities should be provided for joint consultation of management and workers, especially when innovations involving changes in working conditions are involved. The general principles regulating wages, hours, conditions affecting health, and the status of the workers should be defined by collective agreement, given legal force, and adapted by special tribunals to the particular needs of each trade. The method is to reach agreement between employers and workers under the guidance of an impartial adjudicator, and in this context it makes no difference whether the employers are private individuals or state or municipal officials. The problems involved and the methods of solving them are the same.[1]

In reviewing the whole question of democracy in industry it is necessary to be clear on the point that democracy in this context means government by all concerned, consumers as well as producers. To make such government effective, it is important to distinguish the general control of the industrial system from the managerial function concerned with the actual direction of particular concerns and from the control of the day-to-day conditions under which the worker is to live. The final controlling power must be in the hands of the government, but in exercising this control legal compulsion should be employed only in marginal cases, and the legislation itself should be based on collective agreements between the employing body and the workers under the guidance of independent adjudicators. The managerial structure must vary with the requirements of the different industries. The problem of security of tenure for the worker, the right of dismissal, and the general status of workers cannot be left to individual concerns, but should be dealt

1. For a valuable discussion of the problems relating to security of tenure, dismissals, and redundancies see G. D. H. Cole, *The Case for Industrial Partnership*, ch. VII.

with by Trade Courts, consisting of representatives of employers and workers and independent adjudicators, and capable of reviewing the conditions prevailing in different industries.

CHAPTER VI

The Right to Education

THE right to education is part of the right to the conditions of mental and physical development. Two questions call for discussion here: How far and within what limits should this right be enforced? And, how is the right affected by the principle of equality?

In dealing with the first question we may begin with the Individualist approach. This can be seen at its best in the discussion by J. S. Mill. In general, Mill thought, governments should not interfere with individuals for their good. Education, however, was an exception. There are things of the mind the want of which is felt least where the need is greatest. These cannot be left to the demands of the market. 'The uncultivated cannot be judges of cultivation. Those who most need to be wiser and better usually desire it least, and, if they desired it, would be incapable of finding their way to it by their own lights.' In principle, therefore, it is right that governments should make provision for education. As far as elementary education is concerned he would go further. Failure by parents, whether from indifference or avarice or jealousy, to provide instruction is a failure of duty towards the children and to the rest of the community who are liable to suffer from the consequence of ignorance. Hence parents should be legally obliged to see to it that their children should receive instruction. It follows that it is the duty of the government to make instruction accessible either gratuitously or at trifling expense.

T. H. Green does not carry the matter much further. He brings compulsory education under his principle that the sphere of the state acting through law is the removal of obstacles or the 'hindering of hindrances' to the development of personality. Ignorance is such a hindrance and its removal by law is therefore justified. He adds that compulsory education will not be felt as a burden except by those who have no spontaneity to be deadened. This is hardly in keeping with Green's general teaching. It could be used to justify all kinds of interference from above on the ground that the individuals concerned have no spontaneous need of what, in the opinion of the would-be reformer, may nevertheless be good for them, and that once accepted the law will not be felt as imposing a constraint.[1]

Green's attempt to bring the law relating to education under the principle that the function of the law is to remove obstacles to free development is spelled out in some detail by Ernest Barker. He distinguishes three kinds of obstacles, and shows how the law has dealt with them. There is, first, the obstacle that there may not be schools for all. This was met in 1870 by the establishment, in addition to the voluntary schools, of a general system of schools maintained by state funds. Second, there is the obstacle that parents may not send their children to school. This was met in 1880 by the law making education up to a certain age compulsory. Third, there is the obstacle that parents may not have the means to pay. This had been partly met in 1870 by allowing the School Boards to remit fees and was carried further in 1891 by making the remission of fees general. In Barker's view, the law removes obstacles by providing the external conditions which make development possible, but must leave the inner life to self-directed growth.[2]

These views, resting as they do on a profound belief in the value of freedom, are worthy of respect. Yet it seems odd to consider education as removing an obstacle, or providing the 'external' conditions for development. The case for compulsion is rather that education is a positive condition of development and the main instrument for the achievement of the ends of social life, and that experience has shown that great advances in general education

1. *Principles of Political Obligation*, paras. 208–9.
2. *Social and Political Theory*, Book III, sec. 7.

can only be made by state action. The duty of the state is to ensure that all its future citizens are given the opportunity of acquiring that degree of education which will enable them to make an intelligent decision as to their own capacities or potentialities and provide the basis for the knowledge and discipline needed for active participation in the work and collective decisions of the community. Two corollaries follow from this principle. First, education of the general or preliminary type should be raised to the level and prolonged to the point at which capacity for intelligent choice of a future career may be said to be attained. This, it is generally agreed, cannot be placed earlier than at sixteen and in all probability should be eighteen years of age. The second corollary is that education in its preliminary stage should avoid premature specialization and should aim rather at developing the art of acquiring knowledge and the cultivation of a sense of values.

It is at this point that Mill's warnings of the dangers of monopoly must be remembered. 'A government which can mould the opinions and sentiments of the people from their youth upwards can do with them whatever it pleases.' Mill himself would meet this danger by permitting non-state schools even for the elementary stages of education, subject to certain minimal requirements and thus allowing a certain freedom of choice to parents. 'Government may require that instruction be given in certain things, but it must not prescribe how or from whom they shall obtain it.' To this it may be added that even in state schools a good deal can be done by encouraging freedom of initiative among teachers and by avoiding excessive centralization. In this as in other areas of life freedom has to be gained and regained in each generation, and in its defence independent educational associations have an important part of the play. In the case of higher education the important thing is to assure diversity and to prevent financial control by the state or others from being used as instruments for controlling thought.

The most difficult problem is that concerning the teaching of religion in schools. The problem has been dealt with in different ways according to the form taken by the struggle between the spiritual and temporal powers. In countries so diverse in respect of religious development as the United States and France religious teaching is entirely excluded from state schools. In England an uneasy compromise solution has been adopted providing for 'undenominational' teaching in state schools and 'denominational' teaching in voluntary schools. In totalitarian countries the educational system is dominated by a system of beliefs which has many characteristics of a religion and is more exclusive and intolerant than most religions.

It is odd that the problem of religious teaching has been discussed mainly with reference to the primary schools, in which by all accounts it is not very effective, and entirely ignored in the case of the secondary schools and the universities, where it might be taught at a deeper level and with greater hope of success. But, on the whole, it seems reasonable that in countries in which opinions on religion differ widely the state should not intervene to weight the scale. Religious instruction should therefore be voluntary and is perhaps best left to the churches. This, however, does not mean that the study of religion should be excluded from schools and universities. For religion is part of man's effort to come to terms with the world and part therefore of the history of culture. If for the moment we confine ourselves to western culture it is obvious that no intelligible conception of it can be formed without some knowledge of the Judao-Christian tradition and the impact of Greek thought on it. The study of these developments should begin in the later years of school life and be continued and deepened at the university level and be open to all students whatever their specialism. Provision should also be made for the comparative study of religions other than those in the Judao-Christian sphere and, in particular, of the conceptions they form of man's place in the universe and their bearing on the ordering of human relations. How these matters are to be taught and whether by philosophers, historians, sociologists, or theologians is a difficult question. But I have no doubt at all that in the present state of our knowledge it is perfectly possible to present a scholarly and balanced account of the interpretations offered by the religions of the order of nature and the purposes of life and of the way in which these interpretations are related, on the one hand, to science and philosophy and, on the other, to ethics. No scheme of education can be regarded as satisfactory which makes no provision for the study of these interrelations. How it is to be adapted to the different stages of education and in particular to the specialized disciplines pursued in the universities is a question which requires careful investigation. But in one form or another it is essential to any system of education which aims at being more than technical and careerist, and which seeks to provide students with the equipment they need to form a clearer conception of the nature of civilization and the possibilities open to it.

Education and Equality

As a minimum the principle of equality requires open access to primary and secondary education. Above the minimum account has to be taken of differences in ability and interest, though these are not necessarily to be determined exclusively by competitive tests at specific ages. On the other hand, differences of sex, social class, or wealth must be considered irrelevant. In theory these requirements are met to a considerable extent by free primary and secondary education and by providing access to higher education to those who give proof of capacity or show promise. It is also widely agreed that further development along these lines should aim at raising the educational minimum and increasing the opportunities of access to the higher levels.

In fact, gross inequalities remain. Thus to begin with, as between the state schools and the independent schools, there are very great differences in the size of classes. To give one example. In 1953 more than half the total number of pupils were in schools which had more than 30 for each teacher; for almost a quarter the number exceeded 35, and for 231,000 it was over 40. Even in secondary modern schools, out of 38,000 classes 17,900 had between 30 and 40, and nearly 2,600 more than 40; and in grammar schools, out of 18,700 classes more than 7,500 had more than 30.[1] In 1961, classes in the preparatory schools ranged from about 10 to 20; while in the primary schools in England and Wales 73 per cent of children were being taught in classes over 30, 49 per cent in classes over 35, and 19 per cent in classes over 40.[2] Next, for local and historical reasons the facilities for higher types of education are very unevenly spread over the country, so that it is much harder to obtain entry to a 'grammar' or 'technical' school in some places than in others. Finally, it is obvious that education is bound in practice to be shaped by the economic and social structure and particularly by the opportunities which are open to pupils and students when their period of formal education is over. From this point of view the significant factors are the length of the period devoted to education and the age at which the young are expected to begin their earning lives. The persistent inequalities can be seen clearly by comparing full-time attendance at schools in the different age groups. In 1953 the attendance was as follows:

Ages	
16	1 in 6
17	1 in 10
18	1 in 18
19	1 in 20
20	1 in 25

1. G. D. H. Cole, *The Post-War Condition of Britain*, p. 343.
2. *Statistics of Education*, 1961, part 1, tables 5 and 11.

The difference between 1 in 6 and 1 in 18 shows the relative sizes of the groups that begin their earning lives at 16 and 18 thus stopping short of the University or College level. The recruits to higher learning at 20 or more are 1 in 25, a mere 4 per cent.

Some light on the extent to which working-class parents avail themselves of the opportunities for a full course of secondary education is shown by a Report on Early Leaving. The authors took a 10 per cent sample of all those admitted in England to maintained grammar schools in 1946. They show that 43·7 per cent were children of skilled manual workers, 15·3 per cent of semi-skilled, and 5·8 per cent of unskilled manual workers. The Census of 1951 gives the proportion of men aged 20–64 as 43·6 per cent skilled, 15·6 per cent semi-skilled, and 12 per cent unskilled. The children of the unskilled parents are thus under-represented among the entrants. The reasons are probably to be found in the unwillingness of the parents to accept places for their children, or the children's relatively poor performance in the tests. The latter, again, may be due to a lower average of intelligence, or to lack of parental encouragement and facilities to study at home. One important point that emerges from the Report is that in fact one in six in the maintained grammar schools leave before the age of sixteen and that it is the children of manual workers who leave early. The attitude of parents towards continued education, which is one of the main causes of early leaving, is slowly changing according to recent investigations.[1]

In the universities the proportion of students coming from working-class homes is in the neighbourhood of 25 per cent. According to the Inquiry Committee of the Vice-Chancellors 1955–6, 26 per cent of men admitted to English Universities were sons of manual workers. At Oxford

1. Cf. A. M. Carr-Saunders, D. Caradoc Jones, and C. A. Moser, *A Survey of Social Conditions in England*, ch. 6.

the number was 13 per cent; at Cambridge 9 per cent; for London the percentage is 21 and for other English Universities 31. The Report further shows that among men who had attended maintained Grammar Schools 36 per cent were sons of manual workers, 30 per cent of these being skilled, 5 per cent semi-skilled, and just over 1 per cent unskilled. Since about 72 per cent of males aged 20–64 are manual workers, the under-representation of the sons of manual workers is very marked and cannot possibly correspond to the distribution of ability in the population as a whole.

The class character of education is most marked in the survival and growth of the Public Schools. Their history and the character they assumed in the nineteenth century have often been described and need no further discussion here. 'The "middling orders of society" ', says Trevelyan 'found in the reformed Public School the door of entrance for their sons into "the governing class". The old landed gentry, the professional men, and the new industrialists were educated together, forming an enlarged and modernized aristocracy, sufficiently numerous to meet the various needs of government and of leadership in Victoria's England and Victoria's Empire.'[1] The classes thus welded together were by the same process divided and continue to be divided from the rest of the nation brought up under a different system. In recent decades the public schools have shown great vitality and resilience. There is no doubt about their efficiency, but there is increasing resentment against the part played by wealth in their mode of recruitment and their tendency to perpetuate and even sharpen existing class divisions. They still hold a key position in the selection of those who fill positions of influence over a very wide field, and this is the more striking as between them the independent schools take charge of only about 7 per cent of boys in secondary schools, and less than 1 per cent if twenty of the more prominent

1. *English Social History*, p. 520.

among those represented at the Headmasters' Conference are considered.[1]

In dealing with the problems raised by these considerations, we may first of all agree with Mill that it is not desirable that the whole of education should be in the hands of the state. Hence the Public Schools and other privately organized schools have a right to exist and parents have a right to choose among them. There ought to be room for initiative and experiment in education subject to certain minimal requirements.

The case against the Public Schools and the Preparatory schools connected with them is that by their mode of recruitment they sustain and even sharpen class divisions. This was recognized by the Fleming Committee, who agreed that the independent schools should not be confined exclusively to the children of those able to pay full fees. They recommended accordingly that these schools should offer 25 per cent of their places to non-fee-paying pupils from maintained schools, the proportion to be increased stage by stage 'with a view to the progressive application of the principle that schools should be equally accessible to all pupils and that no child otherwise qualified should be excluded solely owing to lack of means.'[2] The proposal has not been implemented and it is very doubtful whether, if it had been, it would have had any appreciable effect on the class structure. It is now being discussed again, but the objection remains that, unless it is attempted on a larger scale than originally contemplated and accompanied by a radical reconstruction of the governing bodies, it would simply have the effect of lifting a few boys of quality out of their class, but leave the class system intact or perhaps even invigorated.

In so far as class relations can be affected by changes in the educational system, the interests of equality can be better served by concentrating effort on the primary and

1. Carr-Saunders, Jones, and Moser, op. cit.

2. *The Public Schools and the Educational System*, H.M.S.O., 1944, reprinted 1959.

secondary schools. Among the reforms most likely to be effective in the direction of equality are raising the school leaving age to eighteen, reducing the size of classes, attracting men and women of high ability to the teaching profession, and, in general, raising the level of education in the state system. Given these changes many parents will be less inclined to send their children to the 'independent' schools, so that in time the maintained and the independent schools will not be so sharply segregated along class lines as they are now. The proper function of the various types of independent schools will then be seen in clearer light.

It will have become obvious that the problems of educational equality cannot profitably be considered in isolation from the problem of economic and social equality. So long as society is divided between those whose children are expected to begin their earning life at fifteen and those who are not expected to do so, there are bound to be enormous differences in the attitude of both parents and children to higher education and, therefore, in their readiness to avail themselves of the opportunities which formally are open to them. Equality of educational opportunity must include equality in the early stages of upbringing and therefore of the home environment. There can be no such equality in a social order which tolerates wide differences in the standard of living, differences which cannot be reduced without radical changes in the distribution of property and income. Given these changes and given a more open system of education there will gradually come about a change in the prestige value attached to different occupations. It would then become possible for persons of ability, energy, or initiative to attain distinction within a wider range of activities and without a change of social status. Success will no longer be judged by standards of consumption made possible by large unearned incomes, and the social ladder will no longer operate in such a way as to draw the highly talented away from what are now called the 'lower ranks' of society. For a genuine egalitarianism it is important that ability and distinction of character shall not be concentrated at the top, but shall have an opportunity to express themselves in widely diversified ways in all spheres of social life.

CHAPTER VII

Political Rights

'EVERYONE has the right to take part in the government of his country.'[1]

In the democratic societies of the West this right is implemented in the sense that there is an accepted procedure to enable all adult citizens to elect a parliament. In countries where the government is of the cabinet type the representative assembly thus elected forms or helps to form a 'government', able to command the confidence of the majority of the representatives. In countries where the government is of the presidential type the electorate chooses both the representative body and the government. In the United States the electorate elects simultaneously but separately the Parliament or Congress and the Head of the Executive or President who in turn appoints his cabinet. Constitutional procedure varies greatly, but what a modern electorate in fact does is to choose one out of a number of competing parties, which submit to the votes of the electorate candidates for election to Parliament. The parties are voluntary associations, and the right to form them rests on the more general right of association, the right of public meetings, and the freedom of opinion.

What then is the justification of representative government? Broadly, three types of theory may be distinguished; those appealing to 'natural' rights, those associated with the Idealist philosophers, and those based on Utilitarian ethical theories.

The natural-right theories of government start by assuming that 'No one has by right the command over others'. 'Every man,' says Locke, 'has an equal right to his natural freedom, without being subjected to the will or authority of any other man.' From this it follows that

1. *Universal Declaration of Human Rights*, Article 21.1.

every man has the right to refuse obedience to laws to which he 'has not consented personally or through his representatives'. The justification of representative government is then that it is government by the consent of the governed.

The Idealist philosophers start from the principle that a moral imperative must be self-imposed, that moral obligation consists in the adoption by the self of its own law. The problem of political obligation thus presents itself in the form of what has been called the 'paradox of self-government'; that is, the problem how, in obeying the commands of a government, a person may still be obeying himself. The paradox is resolved not by insisting on the consent of every individual to governmental orders, but by distinguishing between the 'actual' will of a person at the level of explicit consciousness and a deeper or 'real' will, in which 'we will our own nature as a rational being'. This will is the 'general' will as distinguished from the 'will of all'.[1] The general will, it is then maintained, is embodied in the state, and in obeying its injunctions the individual is obeying his own will and is therefore 'self-governed'. If a theory of this type is to be used in defence of representative government as developed in democratic societies, it will have to be shown that in such societies there grows up through action of mind upon mind a common conviction of what is right or just, that this generates an effective common will, and that it is this will which is embodied or expressed in legislation.[2]

By contrast with these theories, Utilitarians defend representative government on empirical grounds as a

1. This doctrine is generally traced back to Rousseau's distinction between the *volonté générale* and the *volonté de tous*. According to Barker, however, the idea of the will of *omnes ut universi*, as distinct from the will of *omnes ut singuli*, had already been current in the School of Natural Law. Cf. his Introduction to the *Social Contract: Essays by Locke, Hume, and Rousseau*, p. XL.

2. Cf. Bosanquet, *The Philosophical Theory of the State*, ch. V, and E. Barker, *Principles of Social and Political Theory*, Book V, sec. 3.

device more likely than other forms of government to promote the general good. Their views have been stated in many forms, not necessarily in harmony with each other. Perhaps the clearest is to be found in Sidgwick's *Elements of Politics*. He argues, firstly, that legislation is an art which cannot safely be entrusted to lawyers or other experts. What is needed is a body of persons who combine general ability with a varied experience of social life. Strictly speaking, the members of such a body should have not only the kind of knowledge of social conditions which only experience can give, but also the ability to utilize such knowledge as is available of the general tendencies of social development and the effects of different social causes. The sociological equipment involved is hardly to be expected from all the members. Hence it is important in constructing a representative assembly to aim at an adequate selection of persons who, in addition to their general knowledge, have some special experience in some department of social life, and thus in the aggregate possess the special knowledge that is most indispensable.

A second argument for entrusting the main part of legislation to a representative assembly is the necessity of ensuring not only that legislators should have insight of the way in which the law affects the lives of individuals, but that they should have a keen *concern* for the interests of those whom they represent. Popular elections for a limited time are more likely to attain this object than other methods of appointing a legislative assembly. A third reason in favour of an assembly so elected is that, even if it is not necessarily the wisest that could be achieved by other methods, it is more likely to be acceptable to the governed and consequently to cause less friction and discontent. A fourth argument is sometimes given prominence not only by Utilitarians such as J. S. Mill, but also by such writers as T. H. Green and, more recently, Ernest Barker. This lays stress on the educative effect of representative institutions. Active participation is supposed to further intellectual and moral development by eliciting the energies of individuals and affording them the opportunity of rising above their partial interests and enabling them to look at particular issues in the light of general principles. Of the value of this type of argument Sidgwick had his doubts. He was not convinced that taking part in general elections, or even continuing vigilance in observing the consequences of their decisions, could give the mass of electors the kind of intellectual training required for making well-grounded social judgements. Participation in local government was, he thought, perhaps more likely to achieve some of these alleged results. Mill, it may be remarked, had in mind not so much the experience gained during elections, as the stimulus provided by sharing in the activities of other public bodies and more particularly voluntary associations, such as trade unions.

On the whole, then, the Utilitarian defence of legislatures appointed by popular election is not based on any appeal to absolute principles of constitutional equity, or even on generalizations with regard to human nature claiming to be universally valid. All that is contended is that, in societies of a certain level of intellectual and moral development, the well-being of the members is more likely to be promoted by a legislature which they are allowed to elect than by one over which they have no methods might be preferable. They would then have to control. Circumstances are conceivable in which other be judged on their merits in the light of their capacity to promote the general well-being.

The theories which account for political obligation in terms of the consent of the governed, whether in the form of a contract or of acceptance by a real or general will, are highly ambiguous and confusing. It is never very clear whether laws are taken to be justified by the fact that they are willed or accepted by those subject to them or by the value or justice of what is enacted. Locke, for example, bases authority on contractual consent, but behind the contract are the laws of nature and of reason and, ultimately, the standard is the 'good of the community' or the 'public good'.[1] How is this to be determined? The answer is the decision of the majority which 'determines, as having by the law of nature and reason, the power of the whole'.[2] Now, the rule of majority is, no doubt, tolerable in homogeneous populations and allegiance to it justifiable in general. But this is not to say that what the majority enacts is always right or necessarily consonant with the 'law of nature and reason'.

There is an even deeper ambiguity in the theory of a general will. Ever since it was formulated by Rousseau it has tended to waver between two different conceptions which it does not succeed in bringing into an intelligible relation to each other. On the one hand, the general will is identified with an ideal good, that in which human purposes would be unified and harmonized. In this sense it is not what is actually willed by any one or by all, but is something which is taken to be logically implied in human endeavour as that which, if attained, would make it complete and systematic. On the other hand, the general will is conceived as something determinate, an 'effective community of will'. Now, actual institutions, including the state, no doubt, embody human striving, though not always at the level of deliberate willing or conscious purpose. But what reason is there for believing that a given state represents 'mind at its best', or the 'rational will', and by what criteria are we to be guided in deciding whether particular states or institutions conform to these lofty requirements?

But there is an even deeper difficulty. Nothing is gained by assuming that what *ought* to be willed really *is* willed by someone, whether this be his own real will or the will of a common 'self'. For this leaves open the question what this real or general will wills, and how this is to be ascertained. Rousseau's attempt to solve this puzzle wavered between the will of all and the will of the wise legislator.

1. XIV, 163–196. 2. VIII, 96.

Bosanquet's metaphysical construction gets us no nearer a solution. The general will cannot speak for itself. Whether we ought to conform to the laws or imperatives purporting to emanate from it must depend on our judgement whether in so doing we are acting justly. The medieval theologians raised the question whether what God commands is good because he commands it, or whether he commands it because it is good. The problem remains the same, if for God we write universal self. We still have to ask with regard to any particular state whether its laws are just. If the state is the 'operative criticism of institutions', the really important question remains by what principles this criticism is to be guided. The notion of obligation as based on the acceptance of a command rather than on the justice or value of what is commanded thus breaks down. Neither moral nor legal validity depends on consent.

An attempt to reinstate the theory of a general will as the basis of political obligation has recently been made by Blanshard among others.[1] In essentials Blanshard defends Bosanquet's theory while discarding its metaphysical implications. There is nothing here of the conception of society as a continuous self-identical being – a social universal. But he accepts and reinterprets Bosanquet's distinction between an 'actual' and a 'rational' will. The latter is 'an ideal to which a man commits himself by implication every day of his life and whose claims he cannot repudiate without turning his back upon himself'. As to this I can only say that this confuses logical implication with actual acceptance. It is not even obvious that the logical implications of the will of any individual would necessarily be rational in the sense of being acceptable in the light of reflection and criticism based on wider and deeper insight than he is capable of. Next, Blanshard argues that this rational will is general because 'the end or object of a rational will is the same in everyone'. This is asserted as a statement of fact, namely, that there

1. Brand Blanshard, *Reason and Goodness*, 1961, ch. XIV.

is agreement about ultimate ends, existing differences being mainly about means. All this is very doubtful, as can be seen by the disagreements that exist now, say, about distributive justice, divorce, legal punishment, euthanasia. We have here again the confusion between 'logical implication' and actual agreement. Nothing is gained by saying that what would be willed by everyone in a society of individuals, all of whom were rational, is actually willed by implication by individuals in actually existing societies. We have to distinguish between (a) a joint act of willing; that is, a decision reached by a number of individuals after discussion and the give-and-take of argument; (b) an object which a number of individuals will, severally or jointly, and (c) a rational good; that is, something that ought to be willed by all jointly or severally. Here again it is confusing to identify the rational good with a general will. Finally, Blanshard accepts Bosanquet's view that the general will is embodied in the state. Since *de facto* there is no general will, this cannot be true. The most that you can say is that the state ought to provide the means of realizing a rational good, and that this includes provision for cooperative thinking and willing. Bosanquet, like Rousseau, tried to distinguish between the will of all and the general will. But the confusion remains. Bosanquet says the general will is not to be found in public opinion, that it is revealed in action quite as much as in discussion, that it *is* a *de facto* tendency only in so far as this tendency reveals active ideas with regard to connexions of persons or groups of persons, that it is only in part self-conscious.[1] All this is very confusing. It blurs the distinctions between willing, what is willed, and what ought to be willed.

The whole problem of political obligation has been unnecessarily complicated by the metaphysical theories of the state. Why should I obey the law? I agree with Buckland's pedestrian approach. The reasons are the same

1. 'The Reality of the General Will' in *Aspects of the Social Problem.*

as should guide us in any other matter of conduct. The fact that an act is forbidden or commanded by the law is morally important. How important depends on the choice that has to be made. I recognize that there must be laws and that to disregard them may lead to anarchy. I have to ask myself whether disobedience of this particular law which I take to be unjust may not lead to general disobedience, including disobedience of laws which are just, and whether the law may not have other functions than the provision of justice.[1] But a point may be reached at which the evil of the commanded act may be so great as to outweigh these considerations and there may then be a moral right to disobey. I do not see how this problem is illuminated by a vague conception of a general will. The point has been well stated by MacIver.[2] We obey the law not necessarily because we think that the law is right, but because we think it is right to obey the law.

We must, in short, distinguish between the will *for* the state and the will *of* the state. In states in which the spirit of citizenship is widely diffused there is a readiness to accept the decisions of government, even though particular decisions may not be considered right. But this will to maintain the state does not determine policy or make the laws 'continuously and directly', as Rousseau thought. The will to accept governmental policy is not identical with the will that makes the policy. The doctrine that government ought to be by the consent of the governed cannot mean that for every enactment the consent of every individual, however perverse or wilful, is required; otherwise the obedience of every minority would rest on compulsion. The community is not a voluntary association which men can enter and leave as they choose. But, being in a community, they come to recognize that organization is a necessity of social life and that its ordinances may have to be imposed on the reluctant. There may be a desire for an ordered common life, but this does not

1. See Buckland, *Some Reflections on Jurisprudence*, pp. 28–9.
2. *The Modern State*, p. 154.

imply that particular ordinances are recognized as just by everyone or that their ethical validity depends on such acceptance.

It is interesting to note that Durkheim, who believed in the reality of a collective mind, did not think of the state as a collective mind. The latter is diffused throughout society and is never comprehended in its entirety by the state. The state thinks and decides for society, but it is not true to say that society thinks or decides through or with the aid of the state.[1]

But this is not to say that consent is not important. The root of the matter is that coercion is *pro tanto* evil, but nevertheless necessary in order to avoid other evils, or to promote conditions of well-being which cannot be attained without a certain uniformity of regulation. The first step in this direction is to prevent abuse of power by individuals over other individuals. This means taking the power of coercion out of the hands of individuals and entrusting it to a common authority capable of ensuring the universal observance of common rules and the settlement of disputes without the use of force by the individuals involved. A second step is to reduce whatever coercion has to be employed by the common authority to a minimum. This implies that we can find ways of distinguishing between those classes of morally good or evil acts which should be brought under legal sanctions, and those which ought to be left to moral choice. It implies further that, whatever the laws may be, it is better that they should be acceptable to as many as possible who are subject to them than be imposed upon them by force or the threat of force. A prime condition of such acceptability is a share in the making of the law and a widespread realization that there are ways of changing the law without resort to violence.

The principles of representative government as understood in democratic societies follow from these considerations. Adult citizens are given the opportunity of sharing in law-making by the right to join political parties, to

1. *Leçons de sociologie*, pp. 62 ff.

help in the formation of policy and in choosing candidates for the legislative assembly. Decision by majority is inherent in government by discussion. To insist on unanimity would enable the few to coerce the rest or to delay decision indefinitely. On the other hand, the majority has no divine right to impose its will on the minority. Majority rule is thus a convenience, and to be acceptable has to satisfy a number of important conditions. Firstly, the minority must be made to feel that they have been properly heard and only then overruled. When there is a feeling that contrary opinions have not been elicited or not had a fair hearing the majority should not seek to exert all the power it possesses formally. Secondly, it is important to avoid decisions by bare majority. One difficulty that arises in this connexion in certain conditions is that the parliamentary majority of one side may be clear, though in every constituency the other side commands a large minority. This, as has frequently been pointed out, may create the impression of a general trend of public opinion which overcomes the reluctance to use bare majority power. Various devices have been suggested to overcome this difficulty, but none seem to be quite satisfactory.[1] Perhaps this is not a question of machinery, but of inculcating an attitude of tolerance and respect for contrary opinions. Thirdly, the minority must be able to feel that, though in a minority today, it may be in the majority tomorrow, and, especially, that a change in government may be brought about by constitutional methods and without resort to violence. Herein lies the justification of an organized 'opposition', which on the one hand has enough in common with the party in power to contribute effectively to discussion, but which on the other is sufficiently different in outlook to hold out the possibility of an 'alternative government'.[2] Finally, none

1. Hobhouse, *Elements of Social Justice*, p. 190.

2. 'The test of a free country is to examine the status of the body that corresponds to His Majesty's opposition.' Sir Ivor Jennings, *The Law and the Constitution*, 4th ed., p. 60.

of these conditions can be fulfilled in a society divided by deep-seated national or class differences or without a certain measure of equality in the economic and social sphere. Equality in political power is thus closely interconnected with equality in economic power and educational opportunity.

Equality in political rights is seen first of all in the slow but still far from universal recognition that certain differences between individuals are irrelevant as grounds for discrimination. Examples are differences of sex, religion, property, race, or colour. On the other hand, the problem whether there are any differences that *are* relevant, for example, differences in intelligence, interest in and knowledge of public affairs – is still sometimes raised. As far as the right to elect representatives is concerned, democracies have adopted the principle of 'arithmetical' equality – 'one man, one vote' – and have excluded weighted voting because of the lack of an agreed method of estimating differences in political capacity. The equalization of electoral constituencies is another example of arithmetical equality. Where constituencies are unequal, the principle of 'one man one vote' in the assembly would conflict with the principle of 'one man, one vote' in the electorate, since in the smaller constituencies each voter would have a proportionally greater share in the making of the government. It must be confessed that no device has yet been discovered which can ensure that each will counts, still less that each counts equally. This difficulty can be seen in the complex problems raised by the movement for proportional representation. This is defended on the ground that it would secure the individual voter or party a fair share in the composition of the legislature. As against this, appeal is made to the need for a strong executive which, it is claimed, cannot be assured unless the party in power has an adequate majority.

Turning from the allotment of the right to elect to eligibility, the principle of equality applies in the sense that candidates are not formally required to possess a definite income or show evidence of educational attainments. It is interesting to note that Sidgwick, writing in the nineties, felt it necessary to refute the argument that only those whose income is above the average are likely to have had the time and the means to acquire the degree of culture that legislators ought to possess. He makes the point that the knowledge acquired in schools and colleges is not necessarily of the kind that is really useful for purposes of practical politics, while the requisite insight may well be within the reach of able people in all classes of society, despite the disadvantage of a short education and a life spent in manual labour.[1]

In fact, of course, differences in wealth and education count. Throughout the nineteenth century the accepted view was that parliamentarianism had worked successfully because the personnel of parliaments and cabinets was still predominantly upper class and the function of the lower orders was limited to giving the system a popular *imprimatur* by helping to choose which of two aristocratic parties would hold office.[2] It was not until 1906 that a substantial body of lower-middle-class representatives entered the House of Commons. Since the Second World War the personnel of the House is more like a cross-section of the population, but the professional classes still constitute the largest element in both parties.[3]

It is clear that political and economic equality are deeply interrelated. The gravamen of the socialist criticism of bourgeois democracy has always been that equality in political rights is of little importance, so long as there remain gross inequalities in economic power. The criticism was put in its sharpest form by Lenin. Political democracy, he argued, can be defined as a system by which the working class chose, at given intervals, which member of the governing class was to rule over them. As applied to

1. *Elements of Politics*, ch. xv.
2. Ensor, *England 1870–1914*, p. 387.
3. Cf. G. Campion, *Parliament: A Survey*, ch. I; and G. D. H. Cole, *Studies in Class Structure*, ch. v.

the nineteenth century this definition was apt enough. Writing in 1865 Bagehot quotes the *Saturday Review* as saying that 'at the door of the House of Commons there was a differential duty of at least £2,000 a year'. But the twentieth century presents a different picture. In the 1906 elections nearly all of the fifty-three Labour M.P.s had been manual workers, and a large proportion of the huge liberal contingent consisted of men with small means, and in the Cabinet itself sat Lloyd George, the orphan son of an elementary school teacher brought up by his uncle who was a village shoemaker.[1] It is true that there is still a lag between the democratization of the electorate and the democratization of the House of Commons. Nevertheless, Lenin's description of British representative government as a process by which rival portions of the ruling class compete for the wage-earners' vote has become increasingly inapplicable. The wage-earning classes have learnt to exercise power directly and are using it increasingly to reshape the economic system in their interests.[2]

Political power is thus being used increasingly to bring about a closer approximation to economic equality. This, however, is not to assert the primacy of the political factors over the economic. Owing to the great complexity of social facts and the difficulty of isolating cause factors, causal relationships in the social sciences cannot be stated in the form of uniform sequences or connexions between specific events, but rather in the form of changes of pattern within a series of inter-linked events. As far as the movement towards equality is concerned, we can say that historically the immense increase in the industrial power of the wage-earners was brought about not so much by the extension of the franchise as by the growth of voluntary associations and, especially, the trade unions. On the other hand, the trade unions would hardly have become so powerful without acquiring a measure of political power either by forming a political party them-

1. Ensor, op. cit., p. 388.
2. Cf. Strachey, *Contemporary Capitalism*, p. 160.

selves, or by forcing other parties to make concessions to the wage-earners in return for their votes. Thus what has happened in the movement towards greater equality is that there has been a shift in the balance of political and economic power or, in other words, a change in the pattern of relationships between representative institutions and the economic associations of employers and workers. Political power has ceased to be linked exclusively with property in the means of production; the direct power of employers over the workers has come to be balanced by the power of the trade unions, and the wage-earners have learnt to use political power to re-fashion the economic structure. The problem of political equality is thus inextricably linked with the problem of the balance of power between the governmental structure on the one hand and the economic associations on the other.

CHAPTER VIII

Association and Contract

1

THE right to associate is the right to unite for a common purpose not forbidden by the law. In the Universal Declaration of Human Rights (Art. 20) it is formulated thus:

> 1. Everyone has the right to freedom of peaceful assembly and association.
> 2. No one may be compelled to belong to an association.

In all countries this right is limited in various ways. The problem is on what principles? Associations are intermediary between the state and the mass of individuals. Historically the freedom of the individual has sometimes involved his emancipation from the absolute control of associations, e.g. the patriarchal family, the Church. On the other hand, in certain circumstances associations may be important agencies of freedom in resisting a tyrannical state, e.g. the Churches in Communist or Fascist countries. The problem is how to limit the power of associations over their own members and over the public at large without interfering with their right to pursue legitimate common purposes or to fulfil important social functions.

The right of association has not always been recognized. In Revolutionary and Napoleonic France all combinations were prohibited by law as inimical to the state. In the comparable period in England the Combination Law of 1800 aimed at the suppression of strikes and trade unions. The right of the workers and of employers to combine was conceded by the Acts of 1824–5. Thereafter the history of the law of combinations is complicated. The Act of 1871 left the legal position of trade unions ill defined and, though the right to strike was recognized, they were vulnerable to common law charges of conspiracy or wrongfully inducing breaches of contract. The Taff

Vale decision of 1901 brought this to light by laying it down that a trade union could be sued in tort by calling out men in breach of contract. But the exposure of unions to action for damages was in effect to deprive the union of the strike weapon. The law of 1905 went to the other extreme and relieved the unions of liability for any tort whatever. Now, it seems, an aggrieved member has a remedy against wrongful expulsion where there is a clearly defined contract of membership (Bonsor Case, 1956). On the question of the 'closed shop', that is the question whether unions should be allowed by agreement with the employers to deprive an individual of his freedom to remain outside a union, or a particular union, opinion both of employers and trade unions is divided. The Courts, however, will not intervene, with the result that a union can in fact by non-admission or expulsion exclude an individual from a trade.

The problem of limiting the right of association is not, of course, confined to trade unions. Equally great or greater difficulties arise in connexion with the huge industrial corporations of the modern world. By a concentration of capital resources they are able to control the direction and tempo of production, influence standards of consumption, shape price policy and conditions of employment. How to control these powers is a standing problem of democratic societies. As far as monopolies and restrictive practices are concerned, the tendency of the law in Britain was not to interfere. But recently opinion has hardened to the extent of recognizing that these have to be regulated in the public interest, though there is still a reluctance to condemn them outright. Instead, provision is made by the Restrictive Practices Court and the Monopolies Commission for registration, inquiry, and possible control to prevent abuse. It is to be noted that the majority of the Court are not lawyers but 'persons appearing to the Lord Chancellor to be qualified ... by virtue of knowledge of, or experience in industry or public affairs'. How this works out in practice is still uncertain. Much depends on how widely the Court construes the 'gateways'; that is, the plea that the agreement in question is not against the public interest.[1]

From the ethical point of view, it is important to distinguish between the right of individuals to associate for a common purpose and the rights and duties of the associations once formed. For it is clear that, as a result of association, new entities come into being with functions which may differ from the sum of the functions which individuals severally can aim at and powers far greater than the sum of the powers individuals can exercise. The question of their rights and duties is therefore to be settled by considering not only how they came into being, or the terms on which they were constructed, but what in fact they can do to their members and the public at large. Legally, the tendency has been to regard the relations between the members as purely contractual. But this has proved unsatisfactory, as can be seen from the history of the law relating to trade unions. The status of non-incorporated bodies remains ill-defined. Attempts have been made to clarify their position by such notions as 'demi-personality'. But it is not clear what this implies and to what groups it may be ascribed.[2]

Dicey, in reviewing the way in which the problem was handled by the Utilitarians, was of the opinion that the difficulty had not been resolved. 'How,' he asked, 'can the right of combined action be curtailed without depriving individual liberty of half its value; how can it be left unrestricted without destroying either the liberty of individual citizens or the power of the government?' There is, he thought, no theoretical solution and the problem has to be solved in practice by what must necessarily be a rough compromise. The need to balance rights is, however, not peculiar to this case, and, once it is realized that no single right is absolute, we can see that there

1. Cf. Sir David Cairns in *Law and Opinion in England in the Twentieth Century*, ed. M. Ginsberg, p. 190.

2. Cf. G. W. Paton, *Textbook of Jurisprudence*, pp. 277–81.

is no inconsistency of principle. The right of association when applied to given circumstances has to be defined in relation to other rights in such terms as to make for the maximum of liberty and equality. The emancipation of the trade unions was in the main made necessary by the need to place the workmen on terms of equality with the employer, especially as tacit combinations of employers could never, in fact, be prevented by law. Nowadays it is clear that combinations of both employers and workers may act oppressively towards others and to their own members. The problem is to prevent inequalities of power from being abused and so to generalize freedom.

In totalitarian countries the knot is cut by allowing formal freedom of association, but turning the large associations, such as the trade unions, into what are virtually state organs. This must be rejected by democratic societies as depriving the individual of his freedom and society of an important source of diversity. A diametrically opposite solution was found by the Guild Socialists in the doctrine of plural sovereignty. This would give sovereignty in its own domain to each association. The weakness of the doctrine was that it was based on an unworkable distinction between economic and political functions, and a failure to realize that the actual power exercised by different guilds would vary considerably and would call for control by institutions which would bring back the state under another name.

There remains a third possibility which may be called social, as distinguished from political, pluralism. Social pluralists would admit that, while legal sovereignty cannot in the nature of the case be plural, adjustments of conflicts arising out of the power of associations cannot always be resolved by legal methods. The state must retain ultimate power of control, but need not always resort to legal compulsion. It may well leave a good deal of autonomy to associations, but provide machinery for the adjustment of conflicts by negotiation between the parties aided by impartial or independent adjudicators. The agreements so reached may or may not be given legal force. In this respect the western democracies differ greatly. In Britain the tendency has been to leave matters to collective agreements and to resort to legislative compulsion only in those marginal cases where the conflict of forces is too stubborn to be handled by argument and persuasion.[1]

2

Contracts become important with the growth of private property, exchange of goods, and free enterprise. In earlier stages exchanges are of the nature of instantaneous transactions completed then and there. As commerce develops it becomes necessary to rely on promises for the future by either one party or both, and there arises the notion of contracts as binding in morals and law. At first, however, their scope is limited. Every man has his place fixed in the social world, individuals can hardly enter into obligations on their own account, and there are, in any case, few opportunities for entering into voluntary relations. As the barriers of status are broken down the sphere of voluntary agreement expands and there is greater mobility both of men and goods. Societies based on free enterprise have increasingly to rely on a law of contract with sanctions assuring performance or compensation for breach. In general, contracts are held to be legally valid (i) if they are entered into by persons capable of knowing what they are agreeing to, and (ii) without coercion or intimidation or wilful or negligent misrepresentation of material facts on either side, and (iii) provided that the effects intended involve no violation of law, damage to third parties, or injury to the community.

On the ethical justification of the validity of contracts opinions differ. According to some the ground is that a contract is the expression of a concurrence of will and the

1. Full a full discussion see the essay on Labour Law by Prof. Kahn-Freund in *Law and Opinion in England in the Twentieth Century*, ed. M. Ginsberg.

'will is inherently worthy of respect'. The utilitarian explanation is that agreements satisfying the above requirements are likely to promote the interests of the parties agreeing without injuring others, on the assumption that sane adults can on the whole be trusted to provide for their own interests, if secured from interference. A third view appeals to the principle which enjoins the avoidance of injury to others. The moral basis of the law of contract is on this view not that the promisor has agreed to be bound, but that he has by his promise created a reasonable expectation that it will be kept and that it is right that the recipient should not be disappointed or suffer from its breach.[1]

Freedom of contract creates difficulties of its own and in fact contracts are not left wholly unregulated. The need for regulation was early recognized within the liberal camp. J. S. Mill pointed out that in the case of children 'freedom of contract is but another name for freedom of coercion'.[2] But the argument may be generalized. Firstly, the right of contract is no more absolute than any other right; and when it comes into conflict with other rights, e.g. the right of workers to minimum conditions of a good life, its claims may have to be balanced in the interest of greater freedom on the whole. Again, it was part of the individualist doctrine of contracts that they were only valid when entered into freely and not under duress. But this implies substantial equality between the parties, and it could be reasonably argued that there was no such equality of bargaining power between a factory owner and unorganized adult workers. In this way legislation governing safety in factories or limiting hours of work for juveniles and women was justified on the ground that, if it interfered with the freedom of the owners, it protected the freedom of the weaker party, and that such protection could not safely be left to voluntary agreement.

1. Cf. M. R. Cohen, *Law and the Social Order*, 92; and Sidgwick, *Elements of Politics*, VI. 2. 2. *Principles of Political Economy*, V, XI.

Whether recent legislation concerning contracts constitutes an 'interference' with freedom cannot be discussed in general terms, but must be decided on the merits in each case. I am not competent to undertake this task. There has been a good deal of talk about a reversal of the trend from status to contract which Sir Henry Maine took to be characteristic of progressive societies 'hitherto'. But I doubt whether this way of putting the matter is really helpful. The definition of status is not very clear. Perhaps the best is that suggested by C. K. Allen[1]:

> A fact or condition of membership of a group of which the powers are determined extrinsically by law, affecting not merely one particular relationship ... but generally, though in varying degrees, a member's claims and powers.

It is not easy to see how recent legislation concerning contract[2] can be considered as a return to 'status'. May it not be viewed rather as an attempt to protect the weaker party or to equalize bargaining power? To take but one example, the regulations fixing minimum wage rates on the recommendation of tripartite councils by a process akin to collective bargaining can hardly be regarded as interfering with the freedom of contract; they make for greater freedom by equalizing bargaining power[3] and providing the opportunity for an independent or judicial review of the issues involved. The results of negotiated agreements cannot fairly be described as a return to status in the sense above defined.

In Soviet jurisprudence contracts were at first dismissed as instruments of bourgeois society. Later, however, they came to be used as instruments of administrative decen-

1. *Legal Duties*, pp. 28 ff.; and G. W. Paton, *Text-Book of Jurisprudence*, p. 256.

2. As reviewed by Mr Sales in *Modern Law Review*, vol. 16, p. 318, and discussed by Professor Gower in *Law and Opinion in England in the Twentieth Century*, pp. 161–2.

3. It must be admitted, however, that in practice, though not in law, such agreements bind others who were not parties to the negotiations.

tralization and of making local enterprises accountable to the authorities at the centre. They are thus used as an administrative part of planning between different state bodies. There are, for example, penalties for an unjustified delay in the conclusion of a local contract.[1]

A form of contract of special importance is that of marriage. It should be noted that it differs from other contracts in important ways. Firstly, its terms and consequences cannot be modified by the agreement of the parties, however clearly stated before entry into the union. Secondly, it cannot be dissolved by the mere agreement of the parties and, indeed, such agreement may be regarded as 'collusive' and be a bar to divorce. Thirdly, it invests the parties with certain rights and imposes on them certain duties, not only towards one another but towards members of the community generally. In particular, the interests of the children have to be safeguarded and they are not parties to the contract.[2].

Family law is a subject of great interest to social philosophy. Here I propose to confine attention to the problem of divorce, on which religious and ethical opinion is still sharply divided. Contemporary legal systems reflect this difference of opinion. Most of them base the law of divorce on the principle of 'faults' or matrimonial offences. In other words, the dissolution of marriage is regarded as a relief which one party may claim on the ground of the other party's delinquency and, in a measure, as a punishment of that delinquency. In some modern codes, however, a different principle is emerging: the principle that the ground upon which a divorce may be granted should be that the marriage had irretrievably broken down.

The list of 'faults' varies greatly in different countries, but generally includes adultery, cruelty, desertion. It is to be noted that insanity is often admitted as a ground of divorce, though, of course, it cannot be brought under the

1. For a short account see Friedmann, *Law in a Changing Society*, pp. 110–12, and the references there given.

2. Cf. E. Jenks, *The Book of English Law*, p. 274.

principle of 'faults'. The 'breakdown principle' may be implemented in various ways, be made subject to various safeguards, or be combined with the 'faults' principle. A few examples may be cited to illustrate these points.

Thus the West German Marriage Act of 1946 allows the parties to sue for divorce if there has been irretrievable disruption for three years. If one party is mainly responsible for the disruption, the other may object to the divorce. The court may, however, disregard the objection if, after considering the behaviour of the spouses, it decides that the continuance of the marriage cannot be justified. The court may further refuse the application for divorce, if this is thought to conflict with the interests of one or several minor children of the union.

The Swedish Marriage Law of 1920 has perhaps gone furthest in the direction of accepting the 'breakdown' principle. According to the account given by Professor Friedmann,[1] this law makes the following provisions: a joint application for separation on the grounds of lasting and profound disruption is accepted by the court without examination; separation may be obtained unilaterally when the court finds that there has been 'profound and lasting disruption'; divorce can be obtained one year after a judicial separation decree, provided the parties have in fact lived apart; divorce can also be obtained without foregoing judicial separation on certain 'breakdown' grounds, e.g. separation for three years or insanity for more than three years without the hope of recovery.

In sixteen American states divorce may be granted after separation for periods varying from two to ten years, though in some the court has a discretion to withhold a decree and in others a divorce will not be granted if the separation was due to the applicant's conduct. In Czechoslovakia, Hungary, Poland, and Russia the court has complete discretion to grant a divorce, if satisfied that the marriage does not provide normal conditions for a joint life and the upbringing of children. The interests of the

1. *Law in a Changing Society*, ch. 7.

children have to be considered and the conduct of the applicant may bar him or her from obtaining a decree unless the other spouse consents. In Greece and Switzerland either spouse may ask for a divorce when married life has become intolerable, but the spouse who is chiefly at fault will not be granted a divorce on this ground.[1] In England attempts to make separation for seven years a ground of divorce have so far not been successful.

In matters so controversial and so subject to religious and social cross-currents, the various trends of opinion are difficult to evaluate. I can best sum up the situation as I see it in the following way:

(i) There is wide agreement against divorce by mere consent. The very few legal codes that accept it as a ground make it subject to restrictions to ensure that the consent was not lightly arrived at and had been freely given.

(ii) There is stronger support for granting divorce after a separation by agreement or under a court order which had lasted for a number of years, or after separation lasting for seven years or more.

(iii) The gap between those legal systems which base divorce on 'faults' and those that admit 'breakdown' as a ground is in practice narrowed by elastic interpretations of such grounds as 'mental cruelty', 'contingent desertion', or '*injures graves*' in French Law, and by the acceptance of 'hotel evidence' of adultery. There is abundant evidence that divorce may in fact be obtained by concealed mutual agreement despite the formal insistence on 'faults'.

(iv) The main objection to the principle of 'breakdown' is that it sets the court a task of great difficulty, the task of deciding whether the disruption is beyond hope of repair. As against this it might be argued that there is a similar difficulty in determining guilt or innocence in applying the principle of matrimonial offences. Furthermore, it must be pointed out that, from the ethical point of view,

1. See appendix III, *Report of the Royal Commission on Marriage and Divorce*, 1956.

it is very doubtful whether the commission of an offence should be regarded as sufficient ground for a divorce in the absence of further objective evidence that the marriage had broken down completely.

On the whole, it seems to me that the whole notion of 'guilt' is of dubious applicability in this context and that the doctrine of matrimonial offence should be abandoned. In its place the general ground for divorce should be evidence that the marriage had broken down and that there was no probability of reconciliation and further cohabitation. Where there are children it will, no doubt, be difficult for the court to decide whether their interests will be best served by the maintenance of the marriage or by its dissolution. But this is a difficulty that arises equally if the principle adopted is based on 'fault' or matrimonial offence.[1]

1. For further discussion see O. R. McGregor, *Divorce in England,* 1957, and W. Friedmann, *Law in a Changing Society*, 1959, and the references there cited.

CHAPTER IX

Rights in the Sphere of Thought and Belief

EVERYONE has the right to freedom of thought, conscience, and religion; this right includes freedom to change his religion or belief, and freedom, either alone or in community with others and in public or private, to manifest his religion or belief in teaching, practice, and observance.

Everyone has the right to freedom of opinion and expression; this right includes freedom to hold opinion without interference, and to seek, receive, and impart information through any media and regardless of frontiers.

(Articles 18 and 19 of the Universal Declaration of Human Rights).

With the history of the struggle for religious liberty and its effect upon the struggle for the freedom of thought and opinion generally we are not here concerned. Our problem is how these rights are to be justified. The main principles have been long laid down. As to religious beliefs Locke showed that what is of value in religion depends upon an 'inward persuasion of the mind' and this cannot be achieved by coercion.[1] 'Such is the nature of the understanding that it cannot be compelled to the belief of anything by outward force.' Locke pleaded further for liberty of thought within the churches themselves. There is much in the creeds which ordinary men do not understand. No one is authorized to pronounce them damned: 'It is too bold an intrenchment upon the prerogative of the Almighty: to their own master they stand or fall.' Intolerance is the real cause of immense evils that have been ascribed to different sources. 'It is not the diversity of opinion, which cannot be averted, but the refusal of toleration to those that are of different opinions, which

1. *Letter Concerning Toleration, 1689.*

might have been granted, that has produced all the bustles and wars, that have been in the Christian world, upon account of religion.'

The case for freedom of thought in general was put eloquently by Milton in his *Areopagitica: a Speech for the Liberty of Unlicensed Printing* (1664). Censorship, he argued, will lead to the 'discouragement of all learning and the stop of truth, not only by disexercising and blunting our abilities in what we know already, but by hindering and cropping the discovery that might be yet further made both in religious and civil wisdom.' Knowledge is advanced through openness to new ideas. If the waters of truth 'flow not in perpetual progression, they sicken into a muddy pool of conformity and tradition'. That strict control of opinion is useful in promoting morality is, he shows, not borne out by the example of countries where the censorship is severe, such as Italy and Spain. It is not the case that they are 'one scruple the better, the honester, the wiser, the chaster since all the inquisitorial rigour that hath been executed upon books.' Milton goes so far as to place liberty of thought above all liberties: 'Give me liberty to know, to utter, and to argue freely according to conscience, above all other liberties.'

In more modern terms the arguments may be summed up thus. The permanent interests of man as a progressive being, to use Mill's description of utility, depend upon or at least can be furthered by the advancement of knowledge and the use of it in adapting habits and institutions to new conditions. But knowledge flourishes best in an atmosphere of free discussion; and in order to direct social policy wisely it is necessary that there should be freedom to criticize existing institutions and to put forward unpopular opinions, no matter how offensive they may be to prevailing attitudes. From the point of view of individual development freedom is equally essential. The qualities most admirable in man – sincerity, integrity, impartiality, vigour in the search for truth and beauty – cannot be developed in an atmosphere of surveillance and constraint.

The conditions needed in the pursuit of truth cannot be assured without imbuing people with the readiness to listen to contrary opinions and a willingness to understand them. Repression can only lead to moral pauperization, to an atrophy of will and intellect alike. A distinction is sometimes drawn between freedom of thought and freedom of expression. But thought languishes if not expressed. The consideration of these enduring values of freedom in the sphere of thought and belief must outweigh any calculation of particular advantages which may from time to time be thought to demand its violation.

In the past, restrictions upon religious freedom have often been due to political considerations. The persecution of Christians in the early Empire was undertaken mainly in the interest of political stability – to discourage secret assemblies and movements likely to cause a breach of the peace.[1] Even Locke denied that toleration should be extended to those who uphold the doctrine of religious intolerance, to such as Roman Catholics, 'who deliver themselves up to the protection and service of another prince', and to atheists, on the ground that they could not be relied upon to respect covenants, promises, or oaths.

Nowadays we have no difficulty in recognizing that religious diversity is no threat to political cohesion and that, whatever be the philosophical relation of religion and morality, in practice, men may form moral judgements outside any religious faith and let these guide their actions as firmly as might believers whose morality is rooted in religion.

In western civilization the granting of religious freedom has been associated with the secularization of the state and the separation, not always complete, of spiritual and temporal powers. It has been plausibly argued that the dynamic quality of the western peoples was enhanced by the conflicts and rivalries between the secular and religious powers, and there are many who would agree with Lord Acton that political liberty owes much to the fric-

1. Cf. J. B. Bury, *History of the Freedom of Thought.*

tion thus generated. Our age has its own problems. The question may be raised whether the separation of religion and politics can be maintained in an age when political decisions turn upon issues involving the whole spiritual life of man. The problems raised are particularly acute in the Communist countries, since in a sense they have reverted to the fusion of spiritual and temporal powers by subjecting art and science to political control. Such a fusion of powers is surely as great a menace to freedom now as in former ages. In non-Communist and Communist societies alike the problems involved bristle with unresolved difficulties.

Christian opinion on these matters is very divided. There are those who take the view that the spheres of religion and politics are distinct and should be kept distinct. There are others who hold that under modern conditions the separation cannot be maintained, in view of the fact that political decisions, such as those relating to war or to economic conflicts within and between states, are not purely technical, but imply fundamental moral and religious assumptions. There is an intermediate position which appears to be widely held. This rests upon the distinction between the functions of the Church as an organized body and the duty of its members in their capacity as citizens. While the Church as such should, on this view, keep out of politics, it is the duty of individuals to decide on the issues that arise in the light of Christian principles. But at this point divergencies of view reappear. Some would take the view that the principles inculcated by Christianity are of necessity highly general and can afford no guidance on such concrete issues as, say, the forms of property best suited to modern conditions, or the methods which should be adopted to secure world peace. On questions such as these Churchmen are as likely to differ as other men. On the other hand, some would say that such a dichotomy is defeatist and call for a modern casuistry capable of dealing with problems of this sort. Similar difficulties arise for other religions.

However they may be resolved, freedom of thought and expression remains an essential requirement for Church and State alike.

On the question whether we should tolerate the intolerant, Renan's well-known remarks are still worth quoting:

> Liberty is the best weapon against the enemies of liberty ... Science can endure the virile rule of liberty; fanaticism and superstition cannot endure it.... The essential thing is not to silence a dangerous doctrine, to quench a discordant voice; the essential thing is to put the human intellect in a condition in which the mass may see the uselessness of these outbursts of anger. When such a spirit becomes the atmosphere of a society, the fanatic cannot find anything more to live on. He is himself vanquished by the prevailing gentleness.[1]

This is true for societies at a certain level of inner stability and outward security, and it is a sign of a highly developed society that it can afford to take risks. But in certain conditions, as we need hardly to be reminded, a fanatical and intolerant group may become dangerous to the survival or revival of freedom. Countervailing action may then become unavoidable.

It is important to insist that the case for freedom of thought and expression does not rest on any theory of the relativity of knowledge and belief. A person may be fully convinced of the truth of his beliefs, and at the same time recognize that he is not infallible and that in any case it would be wrong to impose his views on others by force. The ground for this refusal to use force is that error is best met by reason and that to suppress anything unheard is to abdicate the function of reason to coordinate all possible data. The refusal to constrain opinion may express not faltering but assured faith in the power of rational appeal.

In English law I take it there is no unrestricted freedom of expression. Dicey's summary of the situation still holds good:

1. *Conférences d'Angleterre*, Hibbert Lectures 1880, pp. 205–7 (cited: Ritchie, *Natural Rights*, p. 186).

Freedom of discussion in England is little else than the right to write or say anything which a jury consisting of twelve shopkeepers think it expedient should be said or written. Such 'liberty' may vary at different times from unrestricted license to severe restraint, and the experience of English history during the last two centuries shows that under the law of libel the amount of latitude conceded to the expression of opinion has in fact varied greatly according to the condition of popular sentiment.[1]

The theory underlying the law seems to have been clearly stated by Locke in his comments on the refusal by the Commons in 1695 to continue the Licensing Act:

> I know not why a man should not have the liberty to print whatever he would speak; and to be answerable for the one just as he would be for the other, if he transgresses the law in either. But gagging a man for fear he should talk heresy or sedition has no other ground than such as will make gyves necessary for fear a man should use violence if his hands were free.[2]

A person, in other words, may say or publish what he likes, but if he libels anyone or offends against the laws of treason, sedition, or blasphemy he may have an action raised against him. In practice, therefore, everything depends on the way the laws are interpreted and applied in particular cases. In regard to sedition, for example, there is the difficulty of drawing the line between criticism of governmental policy and threats to overturn the state by force. Lord Denning quotes the case of an Australian communist who had said that in a war with the Soviets the Australian communists would fight with the Soviets. The words were held to be seditious, though the High Court was evenly divided on the point. In Lord Denning's view the right way is to leave the decision to the jury who can be trusted to draw the line fairly between what is dan-

1. *Law of the Constitution*, 3rd ed., p. 231.
2. Lord King's *Life of Locke*, pp. 202–8 (cited: Ritchie, *Natural Rights*, p. 154).

gerous and what is not.[1] Similar difficulties are met with in dealing with utterances likely to incite ill will between different groups or classes. Recently proposals have been put forward to make incitement to racial hatred or prejudice a crime. Opponents of these proposals lay stress on difficulties of definition and interpretation, and they maintain that, in so far as violence is attributable to provocative utterances, the provokers are already liable to prosecution under the existing law.

Under blasphemy are included attacks on the Christian religion in a manner calculated to wound the feelings of its professors or to provoke a breach of the peace. Nowadays it is the manner rather than the matter that is said to be the gist of the offence. The object is not to prevent reasonable comment or criticism but to protect religious sentiments from insult and ridicule. The logic of this is not clear, as was pointed out by Sir J. F. Stephen. If the law were based on a desire to prevent the use of language which causes offence to believers, it would also have to punish such preaching as offends the feelings of unbelievers. In a careful historical survey he concluded that to say 'that the crime lies in the manner and not in the matter appears to me to be an attempt to evade and explain away a law which has no doubt ceased to be in harmony with the temper of the time.'[2] In any event, as the matter stands now it would be more straightforward to abolish the law against blasphemy as such and to deal with those using offensive language by applying the laws prohibiting acts liable to provoke a breach of public order.

The law against obscene publications raises similar problems. The Act of 1959 has the merit of giving authors and publishers the right to appear in court and to defend their publications against conviction and an order for forfeiture. They can do so if they can show that the 'publication of the article in question is justified as being

1. *Freedom Under the Law*, p. 45.
2. *History of the Criminal Law in England*, vol. 2, p. 475.

for the public good on the ground that it is in the interests of science, literature, art, and learning or of any other object of general concern.' The Act further provides that the book must be considered as a whole, that isolated passages deemed objectionable must be viewed in relation to their relevance to the author's main purpose, and that experts may be called to give their opinion on the literary or scientific merits of the work, though not on the question of obscenity. The Act of 1959 is an improvement on previous acts; but it remains open to the objection on the ground that the law ought only to deal with acts that permit of precise definition and specific proof and that 'obscenity' does not permit of such definition or proof. According to Section I (i) of the Act an article shall be deemed to be obscene 'if its effect is, if taken as a whole, such as to deprave and corrupt persons who are likely, having regard to all circumstances, to read, see, or hear the matter contained or embodied in it.' This is to define the obscure by the equally or the more obscure. We are not told how 'to deprave or corrupt' is to be defined or what kind of evidence is required to establish that the article in question will or will not tend to produce the effects alleged. If 'to corrupt' means to 'to incite to unchastity', what ground is there for believing that 'pure filth' is more likely to have this effect than the mass of sexually suggestive material that is now so readily available?

It is sometimes said that obscenity does not reside so much in the thing said as in the manner in which it is said.[1] But as in the case of blasphemy this interpretation is not borne out by an examination of the works that have been subjected to censorship. Thus the condemna-

1. See Lord Birkett's comments in *Does Pornography Matter*, ed. C. H. Rolph, ch. 1, and Dom Denys Rutledge, ibid., ch. 6, p. 90: 'Pornography matters to the State and other public authorities who have the duty of protecting the citizen from what he finds offensive . . . abstracting altogether from the question of whether what he finds offensive is morally wrong or not.'

tion not so long ago of such plays as *Waste*, or *Ghosts*, or *Young Woodley*, or such books as *The Well of Loneliness* was not based on indecency in the language used, but on the supposed social dangers of any public discussion of the ideas dealt with. In any case, the standards of decency vary greatly. The advocacy of birth control was regarded as indecent a generation ago; it is so no longer. As far as the stage is concerned, the official attitude tries to follow changes in public opinion, but, as Bernard Shaw pointed out, keeps always at a respectful distance; say, twenty years, behind it.[1] On the whole, I cannot but conclude that, since indecency and obscenity are vague and obscure notions, they are not matters which can be effectively handled by the blunt machinery of the law.

Writing in 1913 J. B. Bury concluded that, though the future of intellectual freedom was by no means assured, a setback was not probable, apart from a catastrophic sweeping away of European culture. He thought that, in consequence of the long conflict which was necessary to establish it, men had come consciously to realize the value of freedom and that this conviction was strong enough to resist any attempt to reintroduce restraints. Were he reviewing the situation today, he would have to qualify even his guarded conclusion. In many areas of the world, not confined to those under totalitarian rule, freedom of opinion is, despite formal safeguards, seriously restricted in practice. It is increasingly clear that this freedom, even more than other civil liberties, has to be won anew in each generation.

1. Cf. John Van Druten, 'Sex Censorship and the Theatre', *Sexual Reform Congress*, 1930, p. 318.

CHAPTER X

The Ethics of Punishment

THE previous chapters have dealt briefly with the principal rights and duties which constitute the substance of justice, and an attempt has been made to inquire in what sense the principle of equality applies to them. How far actual legal systems approximate to justice as thus defined is a question for comparative jurisprudence and quite beyond my competence. Theory and practice differ widely and often the spirit and purpose of the rights enumerated in constitutions are disregarded while homage is paid to the letter. The difficulty is greatest in respect of the rights of the individual to the conditions of physical and mental well-being. For these conditions must vary greatly with the different economic and social situations of the peoples of the world and can hardly be expressed in the form of general rules. Even political and social rights, such as the right of freedom of association, of speech and assembly may for large sections of the population remain more formal than real at certain levels of educational and economic development. The history of political and social theory in the free societies shows, I think, that the attempts that have been made to devise a formula to define the ends and limits of state action have proved inconclusive. The lesson has been learnt that liberty and control are not incompatible and that the limits are largely practical. They turn upon such questions as to what sorts of things can be achieved at different levels of development by the use of legal sanctions and cannot be achieved without them, what in given circumstances can best be done by individuals or voluntary combinations of individuals, and what things of importance would remain undone if the state did not do them. The problems involved are far from having been solved by western states, and are now being faced under varying conditions of strain and urgency by the newly emerging states.

The modern state protects the body of rights through the civil and criminal law. The distinction between the two, according to some authorities, is that the former deals with injuries to the individual and the latter with injuries to the community.[1] But this is misleading, since a violation of the rights of the individual is also an injury to the community. The difference is rather that the civil law aims at the redress of wrongs by ensuring restitution or compensation, while the object of the criminal law is the suppression of wrongdoing. From this distinction follows another. An individual suffering a civil injury need, if he so chooses, take no action, while where a crime has been committed the person injured cannot prevent proceedings being taken. The criminal cannot escape merely by making good the loss inflicted; if convicted, he is liable to be punished.

What, then, is punishment, and how far can it be ethically justified? For developed legal systems punishment may be defined as the authoritative infliction of pain or other deprivation on a person for (or because of) an offence which he has committed. Punishment thus inflicted is a deliberate act based on an impartial examination of the relevant facts by a competent authority which issues a verdict and has the means of enforcing it. Thus 'nature' does not punish, and the painful consequences, physical or moral, that follow 'naturally' from a wrong act do not constitute punishment. Legal and moral offences do not coincide completely, but in general serious crimes are acts which are condemned by the moral sense of the community and from which every man knows, or is presumed to know, he ought to refrain. Furthermore, the punishment is inflicted for an offence and this in advanced legal systems is taken as implying that the offence was committed 'with intent' and not involuntarily. Intent generally is taken to mean a specific intention to do a

1. Stephen, op. cit., Book V, ch. 1.

particular act prohibited by law. Sometimes, however, though this is disputed, the notion of intent has been extended to cover consequences not intended as such but likely to follow from the act. In other cases, again, lack of direct intention does not exempt from liability. In circumstances fraught with danger the law may lay down standards of care, and failure to satisfy them may make a person liable for negligence, though there was no intention or recklessness. To avoid conviction the accused may have to show that in fact he took the care that prudence requires.

All this applies to advanced legal systems. In early society the protection of the individual may not be concentrated in the hands of a differentiated authority, stress may be laid on the deed rather than on the intention, and the punishment may not be confined to the person who committed the offence, but may be inflicted vicariously on other persons or collectively on the group to which he belongs. The distinction between the intentional and the unintentional, the premeditated and unpremeditated, may not be clearly drawn. The development may be followed by comparing the way in which unintentional homicides are dealt with in the Hebrew Codes. Distinctions are drawn between accidental killing, killing in enmity, and 'lying in wait'. Cities of refuge are provided for accidental or unpremeditated killing, though even then the avenger may slay the killer outside the borders of the city of refuge.[1] There are similar hesitations in other codes of early law, and even in advanced legal systems the demarcation between intentional and unintentional offences is not always clearly drawn.[2]

Similarly, the principle that no one is punishable for acts committed by others has by no means been always accepted. Often the family or the kindred was made to suffer with the offender. Here again the transition to the

1. Cf. Exodus, xxi, 13; Deut., xix, 4–6; Numbers, xxxv, 15, 20–24.

2. Cf. Hobhouse, *Morals in Evolution*, p. 85.

notion of individual liability can be illustrated from the Old Testament. The declaration in *Ezekiel* that it was unjust that the children's teeth should be set on edge when the fathers had eaten sour grapes was a revolutionary advance on the earlier view that the sins of the fathers should be visited on the children. Similar developments have been cited from other early legal systems.[1]

Despite the survival of certain ambiguities in the notion of intent and occasional reversals to earlier views of collective liability, the general principle that no one shall be answerable for the crimes of others, and for his only to the extent that they are voluntary, is generally accepted. In other words, only responsible agents are liable to punishment. We have therefore to ask what is meant by responsibility.

It is useful to distinguish between being 'responsible *to*' and being 'responsible *for*'. Thus religious writers speak of responsibility as 'answerableness to God'. In ethical discussion it is often considered as answerableness to one's conscience. But this is metaphorical, implying a division of the self, one part of which is responsible to the other. In any case, to be accountable or answerable implies that there is a duty or obligation (legal or moral) to do something or to refrain from doing something, and that he on whom this duty falls has the capacity to be determined by the knowledge of this duty. In connexion with punishment responsibility relates to a past act or omission. A person is responsible for acts which he does or has done voluntarily (or which he could have avoided doing) with some understanding of the consequences of his actions and insight into the rightness or wrongness of what he is about to do. These three features, freedom, knowledge of consequences, and knowledge of the relevant moral or legal obligations, are susceptible of very different interpretations. It is not easy to define freedom

1. Cf. Sutherland's account of the laws of the Visigoths, *Origin and Growth of the Moral Instinct*, II, p. 168, and the numerous references in Hobhouse, op. cit., ch. III, 6.

or the measure of knowledge or insight required. The line of division between full responsibility, diminished responsibility, and lack of responsibility is, in fact, variously drawn, and on any view there remain many doubtful cases. A responsible person is accountable to someone. But even if there is no one to call him to account, he is still responsible in the sense that it is his duty to make reparation or in some way to restore the situation he has disturbed.

To be responsible *for* means either to have duties to others, for example, when a parent is said to be responsible for the well-being of his children or else to be accountable for the acts of others, for example, when a parent is said to be responsible for the debts of his children. To 'take on' responsibility means to take on duties to act without guidance from others. To train people in responsibility means to prepare them to take decisions without having to appeal to others. To act in a responsible manner is to take proper care in carrying out your duties and in estimating their relative importance, and to have a declarable reason for the decisions made. 'Responsible government' means that those who govern know they may be called to account for what they do and are ready and willing to do so. There are thus common elements in these different applications of the notion of responsibility, namely: (i) agency or authorship; (ii) an obligation to act or refrain and a knowledge of the obligation; and (iii) a capacity to be determined or influenced by such knowledge.

In this connexion it is usual to raise the metaphysical problem of free will *versus* determinism. I am inclined to agree with Sidgwick that this issue is not of decisive importance from the point of view of the regulation of conduct, except perhaps for those who accept a retributive theory of punishment.[1]

However this may be, I am proceeding on the assump-

1. Cf. Sidgwick, *Methods*, Book I, ch. v, and Rashdall, *Theory of Good and Evil*, II, book III, chs. 3 and 4.

tion that there is freedom in the sense of a capacity or power of acting with intent; that is, of forming a more or less impartial judgement of the alternative actions that are possible and of acting in accordance with that judgement. Common sense holds that there is such a capacity and, I think, this belief can be justified without entering into the difficult problem of the nature of the will or of uncaused causes. Consider first a cognitive judgement, where no decision to act is involved. In arriving at it I am, no doubt, influenced by my past experiences, beliefs, and prejudices. Nevertheless my judgement remains, while I am making it, to some extent at least, open, and modifiable by the evidence which I have or seek to find. I can to some extent check the flow of associations, resist the influence of strong desires and implanted prejudices. Furthermore, this power of weighing evidence, of making relatively impartial judgements, can be developed by practice and training or contracted by negligence and disuse. Knowing or judging in the light of evidence thus implies a measure of openness to alternatives. It is true that we speak of being constrained by the evidence. But this constraint or cogency of implication is something different from causal necessitation. A conclusion may follow from given premises, but this does not mean that the act apprehending the premises will in all cases be followed by another act of apprehending the conclusion. Validity and psychological constraint are different notions.

What has been said applies also to judgements about the consequence likely to follow upon action. This brings us to 'freedom of action'. This means, firstly, freedom from external compulsion. I am deprived of freedom if I am pushed or thrown. I also lose my freedom if I faint or am paralysed, and cannot do the things I might want or be required to do. Freedom means, secondly, the capacity of judging more or less impartially what consequences are likely to follow from my action and of being influenced (though not completely determined) by my judgement. This applies to actions which raise no moral issues. Moral freedom means the power or capacity of judging the relative value or worth, the rightness or wrongness of the alternative acts and their probable consequences and of acting accordingly. I agree with Sidgwick that the perception or judgement that an act is the right and reasonable act to be done is, or can be an adequate motive for doing it. Modern psychology in no way disproves this, so far as I can see. Freedom involves two elements, cognitive and affective. The agent must be capable of forming a judgement of right and wrong, and the judgement must have sufficient emotional or conative warmth and drive to enable him to act in accordance with it. Thus, when the affective and the cognitive elements are dissociated, there is a corresponding restriction of freedom in the sense here relevant. Broadly, freedom is subject to two kinds of limitations, limitations of scope or loss of affectivity. The former include (i) external conditions which may reduce the alternatives possible and so limit choice and (ii) limitations of knowledge. Thus a feeble-minded person may not be able to see the alternatives open to him and has so far a limited range of choice. On the limitations due to dissociation or loss of affectivity psychiatrists differ. It is not at all clear at what point the barriers between the conscious and the unconscious prevent people from knowing what they are doing, or deprive what knowledge they have of the power to induce or control action. The view that the teaching of psychoanalysis is incompatible with the belief in freedom and responsibility is based on a misunderstanding. I take it that the object of psychotherapy is to help the patient to regain control of his actions by bringing what was previously unconscious into consciousness and so to enable him to face realities, to form reasonably impartial judgements about himself and his surroundings and act on them; in other words, to become a responsible person.

On this view, then, freedom and responsibility are closely related. A person is responsible for what he does 'freely', that is, with some knowledge of what he is doing and insight into what is right and wrong, and who is emotionally capable of being influenced in his actions by such knowledge and insight. It follows that since there are degrees of freedom there are degrees of responsibility.

The legal idea of responsibility is usually expressed in terms of the doctrine of *mens rea*: no one can be convicted of a crime unless there was an intention to do an act which is unlawful. But, as we have seen, the notion of 'intent' covers not only intentions to do a specific act prohibited by law, but also cases of murder in which without aiming at causing death or grievous harm the accused does something which a reasonable man would normally realize to be likely to cause death or grievous bodily harm. There are also cases of 'strict liability' in which lack of intention is no defence, for example, selling adulterated food, even without knowing that it is adulterated, or selling liquor to an intoxicated person, though he is not known to be intoxicated. Here the aim of the law is to maintain high standards of care by making those who violate them do so at their peril.

A problem of peculiar difficulty is the legal responsibility of those suffering from mental disease or abnormality. The legal approach has been to concentrate almost entirely on the cognitive aspects of responsibility; that is, to establish whether the offender knew what he was doing and that what he was doing was wrong. But the climate of opinion is changing and it is slowly being recognized that in addition to knowledge there must also be the capacity or power to act in accordance with it. Thus some individuals may well be aware that what they are about to do is forbidden by the law, but the knowledge of this leaves them cold: they lack the emotional organization needed for control. Others may have too much conscience and, as in the case of the depressives, may be tortured by a sense of guilt but may nevertheless be indifferent to their ordinary duties and may even be driven to serious acts of aggression. Since the cognitive and conative capacities vary independently, and each capacity shows a very wide range of variation, we must expect that the degree of integration or power of self-regulation achieved will also vary widely. In short, we must expect to find an almost infinite range of degrees of responsibility. The problem from the practical point of view is whether it is possible to divide mentally abnormal offenders into a limited number of groups for the purpose of assessing criminal responsibility, and to what extent the law can and ought to take degrees of responsibility so assessed into account in fixing penalties or by way of mitigation of sentence and treatment after sentence.

We can now return to the problem of the ethical basis of punishment. The definition of punishment given above as consisting in pain or deprivation inflicted on a person for an offence or because of an offence might be taken at first sight as implying a retributive theory of punishment. But this is not necessarily so. For there might well be other reasons for punishing only those who have committed an offence, for example, the need to inculcate a sense of personal responsibility, or consideration for the rights of innocent persons. In any case, the definition of punishment, assuming it to represent accurately what punishment purports to achieve, is not in itself a justification of it. It may well be that considered as an end in itself it cannot be ethically defended, and that as a means better methods are now or may become available for maintaining the social order than in former ages.

Broadly there are three theories of the aims of punishment, the retributive, the deterrent, and the educative or reformative. Considered in the abstract they are often held to be complementary. Genuine reform, it is argued, can only be achieved if the offender is made to realize that his punishment was deserved, and such reform, in turn, is likely to be the most effective deterrent. In the actual conditions in which the criminal law operates, however, it is very doubtful whether any methods exist for combining punishment with reform, and it may even be argued that the concentration of criminals in overcrowded prisons, so far from dimishing crime, produces conditions making for more crime.

The retributive view is deeply rooted in the instinctive and emotional nature of man, but as a philosophical theory it is difficult to define with any precision. Those who defend it have this in common that they all insist that punishment should not be inflicted as a means to some other end but only 'because the individual on whom it is inflicted has committed a crime' (Kant). Both Green and Bosanquet assert emphatically that the demand for retribution must be clearly distinguished from the desire for revenge. It is rather a demand that the criminal should have his due, should be dealt with according to his deserts, should be punished justly.[1] But there are others who do not shrink from linking retribution directly with revenge. Thus Sir James Fitzjames Stephen writes: 'The criminal law regulates, sanctions, and provides a legitimate satisfaction for the passion of revenge; the criminal law stands to the passion of revenge in much the same relation as marriage to the sexual appetite.'[2] Elsewhere he adds that the criminal law proceeds upon the principle that it is morally right to hate criminals and it confirms and justifies the sentiment by inflicting upon criminals punishments which express it. ... It is highly desirable that criminals should be hated and that the punishments inflicted upon them should be so contrived as to give expression to that hatred. Accordingly he goes on to ask for increased use of physical pain by flogging and otherwise. This attitude is not quite dead. Thus Lord Goddard is quoted as saying in the Lords' debate on capital punishment: 'I do not see how it can be said to be non-Christian or other than praiseworthy that the country should be willing to avenge crime'.[3]

Other authorities speak not of revenge but of 'righteous indignation'. Thus Westermarck, in a very full discussion,

1. Green, *Principles of Political Obligation*, para, 183.
2. *General View of the Criminal Law of England*, p. 99.
3. 198 H. L. Debates, 5th Series, 743, 1956.

argues that, whatever theorists may say, the 'immediate aim of punishment has always been to give expression to the righteous indignation of the society which inflicts it.'[1] As to this, it must be said that, though the demand for punishment may be rooted in inborn resentment, it does not follow that we should allow our emotions or instincts to determine our deliberate policy. Hatred and anger are in their nature blind, while justice ought to be clear-sighted and administered without passion. As Sir Carleton Kemp Allen has argued: 'the borderline between indignant righteousness, impassioned retribution, and Pharasaical self-righteousness is thin and easily overstepped.'[2] It is interesting to note that Butler, who has given a profound analysis of resentment, nevertheless concludes that since it involves producing misery it ought never to be made use of except in order to produce some greater good.[3]

The term retributive is highly charged with emotion. There survive in it primitive, magical notions of 'undoing' what has been done, of wiping away sin or stain, of atonement, of expiation, and of appeasement of the injured party. But no doubt the clinging to retribution as the essence of punishment is due also to an obscure but deeply rooted belief that there is a necessary relation between guilt and punishment, a belief made articulate in the ethical theory that the proper basis of punishment, as of reward, is merit or desert.

Clearly great caution is required in analysing this complex notion. We may begin by citing a few representative accounts:

Juridical punishment can never be administered merely as a means for promoting another good, either with regard to the criminal himself or to civil society, but must in all cases be imposed because the individual on whom it is inflicted has committed a crime.... The principle is that of equality or

1. *Ethical Relativity*, p. 83.
2. *Aspects of Justice*, p. 25.
3. Butler's *Works*, ed. Gladstone, Vol. II, IX, 6.

talion which should be carried out in the spirit. Even if civil society were on the point of being dissolved with the consent of the members, as for example if a people dwelling on an island resolved to separate and scatter to all parts of the world, they would be bound first of all to execute the last murderer in their prisons, so that each may meet with that fate which his deeds deserve and the guilt of blood may not rest upon the people.[1]

The essence of punishment is not a threat, but to set a stamp of annulment on what has been done. Punishment is an act of repudiation which is at the same time a reflex stroke against the guilty person. Punishment is the negation of a bad will by the reaction of the social will for good.[2]

In discussing this matter the only important things are, first, that crime is to be annulled, not because it is the producing of an evil, but because it is an infringement of the right as right, and secondly, the question of what that positive existence is which crime possesses and which must be annulled; it is this existence which is the real evil which is to be removed, and the essential point is the question where it lies. ... If crime and its annulment are treated as if they were unqualified evils, it must of course seem quite unreasonable to will an evil merely because another evil is already there. ... In punishment the offender is honoured as a rational being, since the punishment is looked on as his right.[3] [McTaggart's gloss on this is that, according to Hegel, punishment is not 'vindictive'. It is pain inflicted on a man because he has rejected the moral law and in order that he may by the fact of his punishment be forced into recognizing as valid the law which he has rejected and so repent, and not merely be frightened out of doing it again. The assumption is that the pain as such will induce repentance. If this is achieved, punishment is inherently good. The criminal has a right to be punished in order that his crime may be annihilated and he himself rendered guiltless.[4]]

1. Kant, *Philosophy of Law*, transl. Hastie, p. 155.
2. Bosanquet, *Some Suggestions in Ethics*, ch. VII, 1919.
3. Hegel, *Philosophy of Right*, transl. T. M. Knox, pp. 69–70.
4. Cf. *Studies in Hegelian Cosmology*, ch. V.

> Punishment is punishment only when it is deserved. We pay the penalty because we owe it, and for no other reason; and if punishment is inflicted for any other reason whatever than because it is merited by wrong, it is a gross immorality, a crying injustice, an abominable crime, and not what it pretends to be. ... The destruction of guilt is a good in itself, whatever be the consequences and even if there be no consequences at all. And this not because a mere negation is good, but because the denial of wrong is the assertion of right and the assertion of right is an end in itself.[1]

> Retributive punishment, even in brutally vindictive forms, does at least treat its victims as persons and moral agents and has thus an ethical superiority to mere deterrence or to a merely medicinal treatment aiming at reformation.[2]

In commenting on these and similar statements, we may, I think, begin by dismissing all ideas of annulment, undoing, etc. as superstitious survivals. A deed once done cannot be undone nor can the punishment frustrate the endless consequences of that deed. It is true, as Bernard Shaw reminded us, that discharged prisoners like to believe that, having paid the price of the crime, they are entitled to begin again with a clean slate. But the bargain should never be made: society does not, and perhaps cannot, keep it. How can we be sure that the punishment has removed the guilt or that punishment as such can make a man feel guiltless? How, indeed, can we assess repentance? We are as bad judges of repentance as of guilt.

The connexion between guilt and punishment is sometimes put in another way. It is argued that every wrong brings its own retribution with it in the effects it has on the character of the agent. To this it may be replied that as a defence of punishment by courts of law it is an *ignoratio elenchi*. Evil following automatically is one thing, punishment deliberately inflicted another. If evil brings its own consequences with it, there is no case for helping the process by additional, deliberate action. If

1. Bradley, *Ethical Studies*, pp. 24–5.
2. Temple, *The Ethics of Penal Action*, 1934.

the argument is that it is right that the offender should realize that what he has done is wrong, and that such realization must involve pain or suffering, the answer is again that this is an inward process which can hardly be furthered by juridical punishment as usually administered. It is very questionable whether pain inflicted by another can be used to bring about repentance. As George Eliot put the matter: 'Men do not become penitent and learn to abhor themselves by having their back cut open with the lash; rather they learn to abhor the lash.'[1]

It has been argued, among others by McTaggart, that under certain conditions punishment may induce repentance, namely, when the culprit recognizes the punishing authority as one which embodies the moral law and has a right to enforce it. But this assumes the rightfulness of the retributive theory, the theory that punishment as such is the due consequence of the crime. Unless we can show that there is a due or fit punishment, legally ascertainable, the culprit's repentance rests on an illusion and will not survive exposure. In any case, McTaggart concludes that the function of inducing repentance is scarcely ever fulfilled successfully by the criminal law as at present administered, and that it is not more likely to succeed in performing it in the future. He was of the opinion that punishment in this sense was fast disappearing in jurisprudence, but that it retained some importance in education, in the sense that punishment can act as a moralizing agent when children can be convinced that the authority by which it is exercised acts rightly.[2] As far as the state is concerned the chief aim of punishment should be the prevention of crime. The task of 'purifying' the criminal is beyond its scope or capacity.

The defenders of the retributive view are shy of committing themselves to retribution in the sense of requiting an evil (the crime) by inflicting another evil (the suffering or pain). They have to convince themselves either

1. *Felix Holt*, ch. XLII.
2. Studies in Hegelian Cosmology, ch. V.

that there is something good in punishment as such, or that the combination of wrong-doing with the pain of punishment is as a whole a lesser evil than wrong-doing unpunished. The latter view is sometimes defended by Ideal Utilitarians or Intuitionists who are not definitely committed to a retributory theory of punishment. Thus G. E. Moore maintains that 'the infliction of pain on a person whose state of mind is bad may, if the pain be not intense, create a state of things that is better on the whole than if the evil state of mind had existed unpunished.' He adds that 'whether such a state of mind ever constitutes a positive good is another question.'[1] It is not clear, however, whether this is asserted as a direct and indubitable intuition, or whether behind it are not obscure notions of 'purging' or 'purifying' the offender's mind or, in psychoanalytic language, of satisfying his 'need of punishment'.

Similar difficulties apply, as I have argued above,[2] to Rashdall's view that 'wickedness humbled is better than wickedness successful and triumphant',[3] and to Ross's assumption that a combination of moral happiness is a greater good than either by itself, and wrong and pain inflicted as punishment a lesser evil than wrong-doing by itself. The argument can in any event have little bearing on human justice. It may be, as Kant thought, that the order of the world could not be regarded as moral if virtue were not linked with happiness and vice with suffering, though the two parts of this assertion do not carry equal conviction. In the phenomenal world, however, we are not in the position to review the merits of all the members of society and assure a proportionate distribution.

Despite all these arguments, the retributive theory still has some vitality. Thus the writers of the *Report on Capital Punishment* assert that 'retribution must always be an essential element in any form of punishment:

1. *Principia Ethica*, 214. 2. Ch. II.
3. *Theory of Good and Evil*, II, p. 294.

punishment presupposes an offence and the measure of the punishment must not be greater than the offence deserves.'[1] In a somewhat different form the point has been put vigorously by a recent writer. The distinctive feature of retribution, it is argued, is that it is directed exclusively to a specific act and not to the personality of the offender. The retribution should be: (a) 'act-adequate'; that is, proportionate to the degree of blame-worthiness of the crime; and (b) once the act has been 'retributed' the actor becomes free; he regains his dignity. A scale of punishments has to be established to fit each crime-type, and there must be no punishments in excess of the guilt reflected in each type of conduct on which it may be imposed. The standard should be based on the degree of blame-worthiness, presumably moral blame-worthiness.[2]

There are two points here and neither carries conviction. That punishment presupposes an offence is true, but this does not necessarily involve retribution. For, suppose that the main aim of punishment is the protection of rights. It might then be argued that, in order to secure this aim, it is necessary that individuals should be induced to believe that each will be held to be accountable for his actions. This would certainly be defeated if persons who had committed no offence were to be liable to punishment. Next, the argument that punishments should be made to fit the crime, so far from supporting, creates difficulties for the theory of retribution. For (a), as Green and Bosanquet saw clearly, the equivalence of offence and punishment is a meaningless superstition.[3] The state cannot estimate either pain or moral guilt, and the scale of gradations cannot be adapted to factors which cannot be known. Furthermore, (b) the crime as an inward state and the punishment inflicted by an external authority are not in *pari materia* and there can be no sort of proportion

1. Para. 53.
2. Helen Silving, in *Essays in Criminal Science*, 1961, ed. G. O. W. Mueller, ch. v.
3. Bosanquet, *Philosophical Theory of the State*, p. 228.

between them. The 'inner identity' of crime and penalty of which the Hegelians speak can only subsist when the pain experienced by the offender is that inherent in his realization that he has acted wrongly. But this, as we have seen, is an inward process and is not something within the power of the criminal law to bring about. From an educational point of view there may be something in making punishment fit the crime. Thus C. K. Allen was told by the headmaster of an Approved School that, when dealing with a certain boy who was an incorrigible thief, the only effective method which he had found was himself to arrange a series of 'thefts' of the boy's own pocket money. But this obviously has its limits. What penalty equals the crime of rape, brutal assault, or perjury? The retributive theory is sometimes defended on the ground that it rules out penalties more severe than can be justified by the gravity of the offence. But here again, if gravity means moral blame-worthiness, how is it to be assessed and how is the impact of the punishment to be determined? Professor Silving says the retribution should be 'act-adequate', but if this means 'guilt-adequate' it involves an impossible apportionment of penalty to moral blame-worthiness, and it is difficult to see how moral blame-worthiness can be ascertained, if attention is confined to the specific act and the personality of the offender ignored.

Some writers find an element of truth in the retributive theory in another way. If the natural desire for vengeance is not met and satisfied by the orderly procedure of the criminal law, men would revert to the more bloody private vengeance of lynch law, the feud, or vendetta. The problem of an enlightened morality is not to suppress the natural desire for vengeance, but to control it and minimize or eliminate its brutality.[1] This is appeasement rather than retribution. Historically the efforts to control private retaliation are important factors in the growth of public justice. But the popular demand for punishments may be very unenlightened and subject to waves of pas-

1. Cf. M. R. Cohen, *Yale Law Review*, 49, 1940.

sion, as the periodically recurring demands for flogging as a punishment for certain types of offence show. It cannot be right always to yield to popular clamour and the intensity of a demand is no criterion of its justice.

Finally, there is the denunciatory or vindicatory form of the retributive theory. According to this, the aim of punishment is to keep alive the sense of justice in the community by the formal repudiation of acts which violate the accepted code. This view, familiar to sociologists from the work of Durkheim, has been recently restated by Lord Denning. 'The ultimate justification of punishment,' he tells us, 'is not that it is a deterrent but that it is the emphatic denunciation of a crime.' But from the moral point of view a crime is not a crime merely because it is denounced or condemned: there must be a reason why it is condemned. Mere dislike or revulsion is no proper ground of punishment. There must be rights worth defending and, if punishment is to be justified, it must be shown to be necessary for the protection of these rights. The denunciation of offences cannot be the ultimate aim of punishment; it is important in so far as it serves the overriding aim of the protection of rights.

The reformative theory of punishment is no modern discovery. It was clearly formulated by Plato. 'No punishment inflicted by law is for the sake of harm, but in order to produce one of two results, either to make the sufferer better or to make him less bad than he would have been without it.'[1] In another passage this is combined with the deterrent or preventive view: 'Punishment is not retribution for the past, for what has been done cannot be undone; it is imposed for the sake of the future and to secure that both the person punished and those who see him punished may either learn to detest the crime utterly or at any rate to abate much of their old behaviour.'[2]

As usually stated the reformative theory is ambiguous. It is not clear whether what is meant is that we ought to

1. *Laws*, IX. 854.
2. *Laws*, XI. 934, and cf. *Protagoras*, 324, and *Gorgias*, 525.

reform our criminals *while* we punish them, or *instead* of punishing them, or that punishment as such is reformative. No one doubts nowadays that it is the duty of the state to do what can be done to enable criminals to resume normal life, to give them psychological treatment if necessary, to retrain them for suitable occupations, and so forth. The question is whether punishment as such is educative. The ambiguity is to some extent faced in some continental legal systems which adopt what is called the 'dual track' system (*Zweispurigkeit*) which distinguishes between the purely punitive reaction to crime and the protective and reformative 'measures' which the law may prescribe. The punitive part of the legal reaction is on this view retributive, backward-looking; while the reformative and protective measures look forward to the effects on the criminal and on others. The difficulties of this system are very clearly brought out by Professor Helen Silving in the essay cited above.

On the whole, it is clear that criminals have the right to be given such aid as is possible to enable them to live useful lives. But this is not to say that reformation is the main purpose of punishment. This could only be justified if it could be shown that punishment as such is reformative. But this, as we have seen, brings back the retributive theory, since it assumes that there is a morally just punishment legally determinable, or that it is right that the offender should be made to believe that there is such a just punishment, whether it is so or not.

It does not follow that the reformative approach is without importance. On the contrary, it has proved of value in several ways, not so much by what it contributed to the theory of punishment, as by directing attention away from punitive to non-punitive methods of dealing with crime. This can be seen in various ways. First, it has served to bring home the necessity of obtaining fuller knowledge than we have on the question to what extent criminals *can* be re-educated and by what methods. Second, it has stimulated inquiries into the psychological effects of the different types of punishment on those on whom they are imposed. In particular, it has drawn attention to the fact that in many cases imprisonment tends to hinder rather than to aid reform. In this way it may have contributed to changes in the law which make it possible for courts to avoid sending first offenders to prison or to ensure that young offenders should not be sent to the same institutions as adult criminals. Thirdly, the emphasis on reformation has inspired the demand for a radical review of prison régimes with the object of enabling them to provide the conditions needed for retraining or rehabilitation. Finally, the reformative or rather the educative aspect of punishment may be considered not only from the point of view of the particular offender but from that of the general public. The law may, by attaching penalties to actions to which current morality is indifferent or perhaps only mildly averse, induce the belief that they are morally wrong. Thus, for example, bribery of officials or at elections may for long be only mildly condemned or meet with no reproach until it is made legally punishable, when people come slowly to regard it as wrong in itself. In this way the law may serve as an instrument of moral education.

Our argument so far points to the conclusion that we must reject the theory of punishment as an end in itself. There remains punishment as a means, and so regarded, though clumsy and uncertain in its results, punishment is and must perhaps for long remain unavoidable. Society has the right and the duty to protect itself, and may do so not only by restraining the criminal but by deterring others through the threat of painful consequences of crime to the criminal. The greater the certainty of detection, conviction, and execution of the sentence, the greater the deterrent power of the punishment on potential offenders, including the offender himself. On this view, the punishment must be designed to do the least harm to the offender compatible with its efficiency as a deterrent.

Whether or to what extent punishments do in fact

deter is a question on which penologists differ widely. At the end of the nineteenth century Ferri argued on the basis of Italian experience that variations in penal policy had no influence on the rate of crime.[1] A similar conclusion based on a much broader survey was reached by Rusche and Kirchheimer in 1939.[2] The arguments are inconclusive because, quite apart from the difficulties of allowing for changes in police efficiency or in the methods of crime detection, no means are available for isolating the effects of changes in penal policy from other factors making for crime. There are similar difficulties in estimating the relative efficiency of imprisonment, probation, and fines. On the whole, it seems likely that for the minor crimes the threat of punishment does act as a deterrent. For the graver crimes and especially those associated with mental abnormality the effectiveness of punishment is more doubtful. It is certain that severity is ineffective and tends to defeat its own ends. Far more important is certainty of detection, conviction, and the carrying out of the sentence.

In this connexion the justification of corporal punishment for certain offences and of capital punishment for murder still gives rise to wide differences of opinion. In this country the Cadogan Committee set up to examine this question in 1938[3] came to the conclusion that as far as adults were concerned, there was no evidence to support the claim that corporal punishment is an exceptionally effective deterrent.[4] They added that it was highly probable that corporal punishment is apt to produce feelings of bitterness and resentment which make the offender more anti-social, more likely to commit other offences, and that at best it can exercise no positive reformative influence. Accordingly, they recommended the abolition of flogging for adults, except for those guilty of certain prison offences. They also recommended the abolition of

1. *Criminal Sociology*, pp. 220–25.
2. *Punishment and Social Structure*, ch. XII.
3. Cmnd. 5684.
4. Para. 59, p. 90.

corporal punishment for young offenders, on the ground both of its ineffectiveness in practice and the known harmful effects on those on whom it is inflicted. The recommendations were not implemented until the Criminal Justice Act of 1948. Since then there have been recurrent demands for the reintroduction of corporal punishment. The problem was reviewed again by the Advisory Council on the Treatment of Offenders in 1960. They supported the conclusion of the Cadogan Committee that corporal punishment had no special value as a deterrent and concluded that its reintroduction was unlikely to produce a decrease in the incidence of crime.[1]

The arguments about capital punishment so far as they are based on the deterrent view are of two kinds. The first, generally held by supporters of the death penalty, consist in showing that, on general grounds of what we know about human nature, the fear of losing one's own life is more likely than anything else to deter potential killers from taking the life of others. The second, more often appealed to by opponents of the death penalty, consist of various statistical arguments purporting to show that there is no evidence for the view that capital punishment is an essential or uniquely deterrent force. As an example of the first type of argument the emphatic statement by Sir James Fitzjames Stephen nearly a hundred years ago is often cited:

> No other punishment deters men from committing crimes as the punishment of death. This is one of those propositions which it is difficult to prove, simply because they are themselves more obvious than any proof can make them. ... In any secondary punishment, however terrible, there is hope; but death is death: its terrors cannot be described more forcibly.

The *Report of the Royal Commission on Capital Punishment* which cites this passage does not go so far as this. It asserts, nevertheless, that

1. Cmnd. 1213.

it is reasonable to suppose that the deterrent force of capital punishment operates not only by affecting the conscious thoughts of individuals tempted to commit murder, but also by building up in the community, over a long period of time, a deep feeling of abhorrence for the crime of murder. The fact that men are hung for murder is one great reason why murder is considered so dreadful a crime.[1]

The danger of relying on arguments of this sort can be seen from the fact that in the eighteenth century similar arguments were used to justify the death penality for sheep-stealing. Sir Lionel Fox quotes a judge as saying, in passing sentence of death: 'you are to be hanged not because you have stolen a sheep, but in order that others may not steal sheep.'[2] As is well known the dire (and often pompous) prognostications of the terrible consequences likely to follow the abolition of the death penalty for such offences as cattle-stealing, burglary, and stealing in dwelling houses were quickly falsified by subsequent history. Finally, if we are to rely on general arguments from human nature the following assertion by the late Archbishop Temple has at least as much claim to be heard as that of Sir James Fitzjames Stephen:

I believe that the example of the state taking life, even when it only does so in return for a life already taken, does more to lower the value of human life in the minds of its citizens than the deterrent influence of this penalty can do to protect the life of the citizen. In this way I believe that the main influence of the death penalty is rather to increase than diminish the number of murders.

The statistical evidence has been examined recently by the Royal Commission on Capital Punishment, 1947–53,[3] and in 1929–30 by a Select Committee. The latter felt able to give a quite definite opinion:

Our prolonged examination of the situation in foreign countries has increasingly confirmed us in the assurance that capital punishment may be abolished in this country without

1. Para. 59. 2. *The English Prison and Borstal System*, p. 11.
3. Cmnd. 9832.

endangering life and property, or impairing the security of society.

The Royal Commission *Report* is more cautious:

> The general conclusion which we reach after careful review of all the evidence we have been able to obtain as to the deterrent effect of capital punishment may be stated as follows: *Prima facie* the penalty of death is likely to have a stronger effect as a deterrent to normal human beings than any other form of punishment, and there is some evidence (though no convincing statistical evidence) that this is in fact so. But this effect does not operate universally or uniformly and there are many offenders on whom it is limited and may often be negligible. It is accordingly important to view this question in just perspective and not to base a penal policy in relation to murder on exaggerated estimates of the uniquely deterrent force of the death penalty.[1]

The Commission's caution is intelligible. As they explain, we can number the cases in which the threat of the penalty has failed, but we cannot number its successes, since we cannot know how many people have refrained from murder because of the fear of being hanged. The statistical evidence is full of pitfalls. No valid conclusions can be drawn by comparing countries differing in economic and social conditions, in the definition of murder, in the efficiency of the police and the skill of murderers. Nevertheless, scepticism can be overdone. There are countries with contiguous areas sufficiently similar in character to justify effective comparison. Some of these are particularly important because they contain areas or states, some of which have retained the death penalty, while others have abolished it or restored it after abolition. These cases provide conditions which approximate to those required for control groups. A good example from the United States is to be found in the states of South Dakota, North Dakota, and Nebraska, the evidence for which has been carefully reviewed by Professor Sellin. He concludes that the rise and fall of the murder rate re-

1. Para. 68.

mained much the same for those states, whether or not the death penalty was used, or whether executions were frequent or not, and that both penalty states and abolition states show rates which suggest that these rates are conditioned by other factors than the death penalty. The evidence from European countries lends no support to the view that the abeyance of capital punishment is likely to have an adverse effect on the number of murders. The general conclusion which the Royal Commission reaches on this point is that 'there is no clear evidence in any of the figures we have examined that the abolition of capital punishment has led to an increase in the homicide rate, or that its reintroduction has led to a fall.'[1] It may be added that Professor Sellin's investigations based on police reports in 265 American cities showed that the existence or non-existence of the death penalty 'deterrent' made no difference in the number of criminals prepared to use lethal weapons against the police. In his opinion 'the argument upon which the police rest their opposition to the abolition of capital punishment lacks any factual basis.' The Select Committee reviewing the evidence from other countries concluded that there was no proof that the abolition of capital punishment has led to an increase in the number of burglars arming themselves or in the carrying of lethal weapons.

In sum, I cannot but conclude that on the deterrent view of punishment no convincing case has been put forward for retaining the death penalty, and that the burden of proof lies heavily on those who resist its abolition.

It has been argued recently that, if retribution is not an acceptable aim of punishment, the legal concept of responsibility ceases to have any relevance and that it had better be allowed to wither away.[2] The logical basis of

1. Para. 68.

2. See Barbara Wootton, *Social Science and Social Pathology*, ch. 8; and 'Diminished Responsibility', *Law Quarterly Review*, 1960; and compare H. A. L. Hart, *Punishment and the Elimination of Responsibility*, Hobhouse Memorial Trust Lecture, No. 31, 1962.

this escapes me. For if by responsibility is meant the capacity of being influenced in one's conduct by a judgement of the consequences of actions (including the legal consequences) and the knowledge of right and wrong, then it is highly relevant both in considering deterrence or reform. For effective reform it is necessary to estimate the offender's sense of responsibility and to decide by what methods it can be strengthened. In the case of those suffering from an identifiable mental condition which can be treated psychiatrically, I take it that the object of the treatment is to break down the barriers between the conscious and the unconscious and to enable the patient to regain the power of conscious control; that is, of acting 'responsibly'. In other cases diagnosis of responsibility is needed to determine what other methods of education may be attempted, or, if none are available, whether repetition of the crime can be prevented by adding the infliction of a penalty to the foreseeable consequences of the conduct contemplated. From the deterrent point of view it is necessary to assume that people are capable of acting with intent; that is, with knowledge of the nature and consequences of what they are about to do. For, if they were not, it would not be possible to influence their behaviour by the threat of penal consequences.

There is a more important consideration. Since punishment is not an end in itself, it must be viewed in relation to the broad aims of the legal system. These, I take it, include the definition, maintenance, and adjustment of rights. The state tries to achieve these ends partly through the educational system and partly through the machinery of the law. In doing so it uses both penal and non-penal methods and it cannot succeed in either without appealing to intelligent will and respect for the rights of others. Such an appeal must aim at cultivating among citizens a sense of responsibility and the importance of acting responsibly, and this aim would certainly be defeated if the law failed to distinguish between intentional and non-intentional acts, or if persons who had committed no offence were liable to undergo punishment in the interests of deterrence. From the point of view of penal reform the important thing is to devise methods of encouraging a sense of responsibility increasingly independent of punishment or the threat of punishment.

If retributive views of punishment are rejected the question arises on what basis punishments are to be graded and on what ground extenuating circumstances ought to be taken into consideration in mitigation of sentence. I believe that Green's solution of this problem comes nearest to being acceptable. He insists that the law cannot possibly attempt to adjust the amount of punishment to the degree of moral culpability. The principle to be followed is that crime should be punished according to: (i) the importance of the right which it violates, and (ii) the degree of terror which needs to be associated with the crime in order to protect the right. As he explains, this does not mean that the punishment of crime serves no moral purpose. On the contrary, it does serve such a purpose in that it is founded on a sense of what is necessary for the protection of rights. Its justice thus depends on the justice of the system of rights which it is to maintain.

Similarly, Green argues that the admission of 'extenuating circumstances' as a ground for not inflicting the extremest penalty is not based on any estimate of the degree of moral guilt of the crime. It is true that this is the reason often given by judges for their decisions. But in this they are mistaken. The amount of punishment cannot be related to the moral guilt of the crime, for the latter is not ascertainable. The true ground is that a change in the circumstances may make it unnecessary to associate with the crime the degree of severity normally thought necessary to defend the right involved. Thus a woman who steals bread to feed her starving children cannot in normal circumstances be regarded as seriously endangering the rights of property and her sentence may therefore be lightened accordingly. On the other hand, in conditions where many people are on the edge of starvation stringent penalties will not only fail of their object, but will divert attention from the real problem which is to readjust property rights or to take other measures to save people from starvation.[1]

Green's views may be further clarified by reference to his discussion of drunkenness and of criminal negligence. As to drunkenness, he argues that, though the hurt caused may not have been intentional, the drunkenness itself may be and is perhaps preventable by the influence of adequate motives. 'The case of a crime committed by a drunkard is plainly distinguishable from that committed by a lunatic, for the association of penal terror with the latter would tend neither to prevent a lunatic from committing a crime nor people from becoming lunatics'.[2] In the case of criminal negligence, for example, that of an engine driver who neglects a signal and causes the death of many, the punishment is not to be based on any estimate of moral culpability, but on the importance of the right to be protected. In the case supposed, the right in question is the right to life of the passengers. This depends for its maintenance on the vigilance of drivers. Hence the punishment is justified which can be shown to be necessary in order to prevent the recurrence of a like failure in vigilance, without raising the question of the degree of moral guilt of the particular driver.[3]

The general conclusions that emerge from our discussion so far may be briefly stated. Whatever views we may have as to the intrinsic fitness of the sequence between penalty and wrong-doing, it is clear that retribution cannot be the concern of the law. As Bernard Shaw put it: 'Vengeance is mine, saith the Lord. This means it is not the Lord Chief Justice's.' The machinery of the law is plainly inadequate to the task of moral assessment. It cannot determine the degree of causality or culpability, nor the apportionment of penalty to guilt. As far as reform is concerned, the real question is whether punishment as

1. *Principles of Political Obligation*, para. 194.
2. Para. 199
3. Para. 198.

such is reformative. It is very doubtful whether prison life can ever provide the conditions needed for genuine moral improvement, or, in the case of the mentally affected, for effective psychiatric treatment; in other words, whether any methods exist for combining reform with punishment. In graver cases it may even be that punishment may not only fail to effect a cure but may bring about a state of affairs likely to prevent a cure. The difficulty is to decide which offenders should be handed over to non-penal agencies for treatment and at what point in the penal procedure the discrimination should be made and by whom. Progress in penal policy thus depends on advances in our knowledge of the causes of crime and of the relations of the various types of crime to mental abnormality.

The importance of 'individualization' is widely realized. The problem on which opinions differ is whether this should be done not only after conviction but also before. At best, punishment is a mechanical and dangerous means of protection. It can hardly be made equitable, and if used as a means of reform it requires a degree of wisdom and humanity rarely attainable. There will, it is hoped, be a shift from purely punitive to protective and remedial measures. Meanwhile, punishment is perhaps unavoidable. But we must look forward to a time when dangerous criminals will be segregated and for the rest society will concentrate on removing the conditions favouring crime and on the best means for securing a widely diffused sense of responsibility independent of punishment.

CHAPTER XI

Justice among States

1

IN approaching the problem of international justice we are met at the outset by the view, by no means confined to the cynical and disillusioned, that political relations between states and morality have nothing to do with one another, that the action of states cannot be judged by the same standards as those which apply to individuals.

In so far as assertions of this sort are intended as a warning against self-righteousness and as a protest against those who use the moral appeal to hide motives of power or domination, they may serve a useful purpose. Even so, it has to be remembered that charges of hypocrisy are easily made and may themselves be rooted in self-righteousness. Was the slogan of a 'war to make the world safe for democracy' merely a spiritual trap to catch the hesitant and to discourage the enemy? Is Russian diplomacy inspired by a desire to spread Communism, or is it merely carrying on, in a new world setting, the old Tsarist drive for expansion? Whatever the answer, it is clear that the moral appeal is thought necessary, and this implies a recognition that there is a deep-seated belief among men that moral obligations apply not only to individuals but also to nations or states. Philosophical reflection will show that this belief is justified. In principle there can be no difference between the morality of states and the morality of their citizens. In other words, statesmen acting on behalf of their state are not exempt from ordinary duties. We ought to expect them, for example, to keep their promises, to act in good faith, not to interfere with others to their injury, to be ready to make reparation for wrongs inflicted, or to come to the aid of other nations in distress. From the point of view of a rational ethic we must recognize that, if justice is no respecter of persons, neither is it a respecter of nations, that what is just for our own state must in like circumstances be equally just for other states.

Rational Utilitarians have seen this clearly. Thus Sidgwick rejects as immoral the view that a state is not subject to duties limiting the pursuit of its own interests. 'For a state, as for an individual, the ultimate end and standard of right conduct is the happiness of all who are affected by its actions.' Though it is true that the general happiness is more likely, in the Utilitarian view, to be promoted by attending to the interests which the agent knows best, namely his own, this does not mean that he is entitled to do so by means which are inconsistent with the general good. It is equally clear that, when there is a conflict, utilitarian justice requires that the interest of the part must give way to the interest of the whole. 'On this point of principle no compromise is possible, no appeal to experience relevant: the principle does not profess to describe what states and individuals have done but to prescribe what they ought to do.'[1]

A very different position was adopted by Idealist philosophers in the Hegelian tradition, notably by Bosanquet. Their views were widely discussed during the war of 1914–18, and in different forms they are still influential today. Hegelian exegesis is notoriously difficult; but it is clear that in Hegel's view states are autonomous or self-dependent beings. Their relations to others are governed by their own wills and there is no universal will with powers over them. International law rests on the principle that treaties are to be observed. But this principle can have no greater validity than the treaties themselves. 'This universal *proviso* of international law does not go beyond an ought-to-be, and what really happens is that international relations in accordance with treaty alternate with the severance of these relations.' Kant's idea for securing 'perpetual peace' by a League of Nations to adjust disputes is dismissed on the ground

1. *Elements of Politics*, ch. XVIII, 1.

that the agreement bringing it into being would ultimately depend on the will of particular sovereign states and would therefore remain 'infected with contingency'. In the last resort each state must be guided by its own conception of welfare, and if there is serious disagreement the matter can only be settled by war.[1]

Bosanquet's view is closely similar. There is no general will of mankind, no recognized scheme of values to guide the acts of states:

> A state cannot tell whether it is being less than just or merely just, or kind or generous. For it every act is under altering conditions and it is the sole judge in its own cause. A state may think that it is behaving with superhuman generosity, whilst its antagonist may think it is behaving like a bandit. There is no complete or detailed scheme and scale of conduct and sentiment to operate as a norm of feeling and judgement. ... As a supreme power a state has a responsibility for any choice, of which no precedent nor external recommendation can divest it.[2]

This does not mean that a state has no duties towards other states, but that these duties emanate from its own will and are subject to its own interpretation of them. Bosanquet also shares Hegel's scepticism about the value of leagues of states to prevent war. Such leagues, he says, are 'purely *de facto*'. They do not rest upon the spirit of a solid community and any powerful league tends to raise up a powerful counter-league against it, with grave risk of war.

On the fundamental point that in their relations to one another states have no common moral standards to guide them, Bosanquet realizes that he has rather overstated his case. He notes that in peacetime and over a great part of their conduct the course of states like that of

1. *Philosophy of Right,* transl. T. M. Knox, paras 330–37.
2. 'Patriotism in the Perfect State' in *The International Crisis in its Ethical and Psychological Aspects*, 1915, p. 138.

individuals 'may be considered as plainly marked'. But, he argues, at any moment problems may crop up which involve conflicting philosophies of history and decisions the effects of which on the world's future are incalculable. In such circumstances, each state will have only one certainty – the values of its own civilization – and will have to decide in the light of that 'form of the good life and that attitude to humanity with which it has so far identified itself'. Bosanquet does not inquire to what extent disputes between states in fact imply fundamental divergence in moral outlook, though he seems to think that the war of 1914 was a 'war of faiths'. It is worth noting that in alleged breaches of international law the parties impugned rarely deny the validity of the rules applicable to the case, but seek to prove that in fact no rule had been violated. Nevertheless, it is true that situations may arise in which statesmen have to make decisions about both internal and external affairs the effects of which are not calculable with any precision. Bosanquet gives the following example. Suppose the British Empire confronted by an opponent or an international tribunal with a proposed regulation which it judged fatal to sea power. In such conditions there is, he thinks, no recognized general moral order to guide decision, save the certainty of the value of the moral order of which it (the Empire) is the guardian, and, if this was seriously threatened, the consideration of this certainty 'would probably present itself as an overwhelming ground of action'.[1] We may test this argument in our day by considering the proposal that Britain should abandon its nuclear deterrent. Is it seriously suggested that, if such a proposal were made in the interests of general disarmament, Britain would be justified in refusing? Such issues are not, it is true, 'justiciable'. But there is a plain contradiction from the ethical point of view in allowing each state to act on the assumption that its own civilization is of higher value

1. 'The Function of the State in Promoting the Unity of Mankind', *Proceedings of the Aristotelian Society*, 1917, pp. 43–4.

than that of all others. It is a policy which cannot be universalized.

Perhaps the most objectionable feature in the theories following the Hegelian tradition is their readiness to accept war as a final arbiter and to concede not only that states tend in critical situations to act as though they were the sole judges in their own cause, but that they are right in doing so. They make no attempt to examine the nature of the differences in moral outlook that divide men, or to explore the possibility of widening the range of international law to include matters which at present states regard as falling solely within their domestic jurisdiction despite the fact that they are of vital concern to others beyond their territorial limits.

I conclude, then, that men acting in their political capacity are bound by the same principles as when they are acting in other capacities, though owing to a difference in the circumstances there must needs be a difference in the way the principles are applied. The axiom of justice holds for states as for individuals. What is just for our own state or nation must be equally just for other nations in similar circumstances.

2

The central core of the idea of justice is, as I have argued above, the exclusion of arbitrariness and, more particularly, of arbitrary power. Hence the enormous importance of the growth of legality, the emergence of the notion that persons are under the rule of law and not of men. This is equally important in the relations between states. From this important consequences follow. First, we must agree with Kant that states have a moral duty to work towards a rule of law, and that this involves the adoption of methods and institutions limiting the resort to war and tending eventually to its elimination. Second, experience shows that the rule of law cannot operate successfully either within or between states unless provision is made for changing the law without violence by the parties involved. As far as relations between states are concerned, it follows that the problems raised can only be resolved by the creation of an international tribunal commanding general confidence and with ample power to enforce its decisions. No such authority is within sight, but this does not alter the duty of all states to work towards its establishment, whatever be the difficulties in the way. As an important step there is much to be said for the proposal to set up a standing tribunal, capable of dealing impartially with grievances arising out of unequal treaties, or with other deeply felt grievances not resolvable on the basis of existing law, and of making recommendations, but without claiming the power of enforcement. It is arguable that such a tribunal might promote an awareness of the possibility and the urgent need of some middle course between leaving states to be judges in their own cause and expecting them to surrender the power of decision to a third party.[1]

The assertion that states ought to be just to one another is purely formal; it does not tell us what acts are just or unjust. As in the case of justice among individuals, substantive justice consists in a body of rights and duties, and these can only be ascertained by an examination of the needs and potentialities of states and an inquiry into the conditions in which they can be satisfied or fulfilled in an ordered society of states. Such an inquiry would involve comparative studies of great difficulty. My purpose here is to touch only on some of the fundamental points suggested by the analysis of the notion of justice in previous chapters.

Firstly, the rights of states must not be conceived as inherent in them in 'a state of nature', or independently of their social relations, but as defining the conditions in which they can best live together in a society of states. Secondly, rights imply correlative duties and, since states are only too ready to assert their rights, it is important

1. See J. Stone, *Aggression and World Order*, p. 176.

rather to lay stress on the correlative duties. Thirdly, as in the case of individual rights, no single right is absolute. Justice is concerned with the balancing of different rights, and in complex situations particular rights must be regarded as subject to adjustment or qualification by the claims arising out of other rights or of the body of rights as a whole. Finally, all rights and duties are subject to the principles of equality as I have defined them above. These principles do not assert that states are in fact equal: they obviously differ in size, population, wealth, power, and level of development. Nor do they assert that states ought to be treated in the same way. What they do assert is (a) that all states are equally entitled to consideration, that the claims of no state shall be ignored or overridden merely because it is too weak to make itself heard; (b) that like cases shall be treated in like manner; (c) that differences in treatment require justification in terms of relevant differences, and that the treatment shall be proportionate to the differences. As in the case of individuals, the criteria of relevance may vary with the rights and duties under consideration. Thus, as regards the right to security and territorial integrity and the right to independence, equality is 'arithmetical', all alike being equally entitled to them. On the other hand, political rights, for example, the right to a share in international law-making, may well be thought to involve an appeal to some form of proportionate equality. So also, if economic rights came to be recognized, differences in needs might be considered relevant.[1]

3

With these points in mind I propose to consider very briefly some of the generally recognized rights and duties of states.

1. Cf. A. D. McNair, 'Equality of States in International Law', *Michigan Law Review*, 1927; and J. L. Brierly, *The Law of Nations*, 6th ed., pp. 130–33.

Territorial integrity. The rights of states over the territories they occupy have a certain resemblance to ownership in private law, but their ethical basis has not received anything like the attention that philosophers have given to the rights of property. Usually the rights over territories are traced back to modes of origin or acquisition. These include occupation, continued possession, cession, and conquest. As to conquest, it is interesting to compare the views of an enlightened Utilitarian, like Sidgwick, writing towards the end of the nineteenth century, with those now coming to be widely accepted. Sidgwick was of the opinion that when conqueror and conquered are approximately equal in civilization, territorial expansion is not likely to benefit either party and is 'rightly disapproved of by the morality of civilized states'.[1] Where there is a marked difference in civilization, annexation by conquest can only be justified, if at all, when the war that led to it was made necessary by the obstinate violation of international law on the part of the conquered and continued occupation is likely to promote internal peace and improvements in industry and culture. As to expansion by colonization, Sidgwick was profoundly shocked by the barbarities which its history discloses, all the more painful because of the frequent evidence of benevolent intentions and even beneficent efforts on the part of the colonizing powers. He insists that the colonized should never be deprived of any rights of property without full compensation and that the cession of such rights should be voluntary, and, furthermore, that it is the duty of the ruling power to promote the education of the colonized to enable them to share in the life of civilized mankind. The ultimate end to be aimed at, he insists, is 'the aggregate happiness of all the human beings concerned, civilized and uncivilized, native or imported'.[2]

It is clear that Sidgwick's teaching was far in advance not only of the practice followed but also of the precepts

1. *Elements of Politics*, 1891, p. 310. 2. ibid., p. 323.

taught in his day. Throughout the nineteenth century acquisition by conquest was not only considered legally valid but was hardly condemned by public opinion. Witness among others the numerous incursions in Asia and Africa by Britain, France, and Russia which resulted in annexation or the imposition of a protectorate. The Covenant of the League of Nations marks an important change. It contains clauses declaring that acquisition of territory by conquest should not be recognized as valid by members of the League.[1] The principle was re-affirmed in 1932, but its concrete application in practice has not been consistent. Thus the Italian annexation of Ethiopia was recognized by Britain, and, though the U.S.A. and the Soviet Union refused recognition, the majority of the League states took the view that they were not bound by any obligation not to recognize.[2] The reaction of the various states to the German annexations in the Hitler period and to the incorporation of the Baltic republics into the Soviet Union shows the difficulty of dealing by law with territorial changes obtained by pressure or treaty violation, so long as war continues to be an instrument of national policy. The truth is, as Brierly tells us, 'that international law can no more refuse to recognize that a finally successful conquest does change the title to territory than municipal law can a change of régime brought about by a successful revolution.'[3]

The changes that have occurred recently in the attitude to colonies and dependencies are much more radical than Sidgwick could have anticipated; though, as usually happens in dealing with problems of social causation, it is difficult to estimate to what extent they can be attributed to moral factors. The changes are generally in accord with the principles enunciated under the Mandates system of the League of Nations and re-affirmed in

1. e.g., Art. 10.
2. I. Brownlie, *International Law and the Use of Force by States*, p. 414.
3. *The Law of Nations*, 6th ed., p. 172.

the Charter of the United Nations. Under these principles states undertake to promote the advancement of dependencies and colonies, and to assist them in the progressive development of free political institutions according to the particular circumstances of each territory and its peoples and the varying stages of advancement.[1] It is now clear that the aim is not only to improve the standards of colonial rule but to eliminate colonialism entirely. What has already been achieved is impressive. Between 1945 and 1962 forty-three formerly dependent areas have been admitted to United Nations membership. There is no doubt that the duty of states to facilitate the movement towards independence is now widely recognized.

The right of political independence. This is the right of a state to manage its own affairs without interference by other states. It has been described as involving, *inter alia*, 'the right of a state to establish, maintain, and change its own constitution or form of government and select its own rulers..., to negotiate and conclude treaties and alliances..., and to maintain diplomatic intercourse with other members of the international community'[2] The right can be best understood by reference to its correlative duties. These include not only the duty of states to refrain from direct attack on other states, but also from indirect interference with them, such as the encouragement of subversive activities or the permission or toleration of activities within a state likely to foment civil strife in another state.

The right of political independence is closely connected with the principle of national self-determination. This principle has never been very clearly defined and in international law, it seems, there are no recognized standards by which a group may be said to be entitled to

1. Art. 73.
2. Hershey, *Elements of Public International Law*, p. 147, cited in D. W. Bowett, *Self-Defence in International Law*, p. 43.

self-determination.[1] It was formulated with his usual moderation by J. S. Mill. 'It is,' he says, 'in general a necessary condition of free government that the boundaries of governments should coincide in the main with those of nationalities.' But he adds immediately that the principle is subject to various qualifications. There are areas in which nationalities are so intermixed that separate governments are not possible or desirable. How serious the difficulties are was shown clearly in the attempts made to apply the principle of self-determination in the treaties of 1919. Whether the western governments had it in their power to apply it more fairly or more consistently than they did is a question on which historians differ. It is clear, however, that under the banner of self-determination minorities were created and left to the mercy of states dominated by intense national feelings and anxious to assert their newly won power and authority. The minority treaties under the League of Nations lacked the power to remedy the evils thus arising. Attempts at international intervention were resented as limitations of national sovereignty and as a violation of the principle of majority rule. On the other hand, the minorities could not but feel that their grievances had not been met and that without a measure of autonomy they were not likely to be met.

Similar difficulties are now facing the states emerging in the British Commonwealth and elsewhere as a result of decolonization. These generally correspond to the administrative units created by the colonizing powers and are far from being homogeneous either in language or tradition. They are not self-determining groups, since as yet there are no selves, but self-making groups, or groups in search of a self. Whether they will succeed in generating sufficient community of will and feeling to enable them to weld the diverse elements of which they are composed into working units and how they will deal with the minorities within them no one can at present foretell.

1. Bowett, op. cit., p. 43.

A different type of difficulty may be illustrated from the Soviet attitude to the Jews. As is well known, the policy adopted during the early stages of the Revolution of encouraging Jewish cultural activities has been reversed. The theoretical justification for this reversal is that in Soviet theory the Jews are not a nation and, therefore, cannot rightly claim to have their own institutions. But this is a flimsy excuse. There is no ground for linking group rights exclusively with the elusive concept of nationality. Any section of a community with a sense of common interests ought to have rights based on such interests, providing they do not conflict with the equal rights of other groups. Various degrees of autonomy are in fact possible without endangering over-all loyalty; and provided there is a genuine respect for equal freedom, the administrative difficulties are far from being insoluble.

The present attitude to the claims of nationality is paradoxical. On the one hand, there is a widely held view that the principle of nationality has outlived its usefulness, that the independence not only of small states but of most large ones as well is illusory. On the other hand, the number of nations continues to rise. The League of Nations contained forty-two members out of a possible total of seventy. In 1962 the membership of the United Nations rose to one hundred and ten. The explanation of the paradox is partly that many areas of the world are now testing the national ideals cherished in Europe towards the end of the nineteenth century. They are in the stage in which nationalism plays a liberative role. So long as alien rule remains anywhere the peoples suffering from it will feel that their economic and cultural development will not be furthered without political independence. In these areas therefore nationalism is likely to continue as an active force. Whether it will follow the familiar sequence of liberation, unification, and aggression remains to be seen.

Despite the growing 'nationalization' of the world the need for larger units than the uni-national or even multinational state is not in dispute. But different types of organization may well be required for different purposes. Thus to secure peace a world organization is now necessary. For economic purposes, on the other hand, regional groups are needed and are coming into being. Cultural needs again may best be served by organizations of a different type. The problems of nationality would be completely transformed if matters of military security were taken out of the hands of sovereign states. There would then be less reason for states, large or small, to strive for economic self-sufficiency, and a greater readiness to recognize the claims of a wider society. In these conditions cultural diversity would not have the political significance it has at present, and the distinctive elements in national cultures would have a greater chance of survival. The problems of minorities will remain, but they would not loom so large if the major causes threatening the security of peoples were removed.

It follows that, from the ethical point of view, the right to political independence should not be interpreted as excluding interdependence. What it asserts is that no state has the right to claim superiority over another state or to reduce it to dependence. This does not exclude the common submission of all states to an international authority, or the acceptance by each state of limitations to its liberty imposed upon it by international law and policy. Independence, in other words, defines the relation of the members of the society of states to each other, as members of a legal and moral order which binds them all alike. The problem at bottom is how to define the relations between the independence and the interdependence of states; in other words, to determine what matters properly belong to domestic jurisdiction and what matters should be subject to international control or consultation. The solution of this problem is among the most important tasks confronting mankind. States are still unwilling to abandon any part of their sovereignty. The growing social and economic interdependence of the peoples of the world has not been accompanied by a parallel realization of the ethical implications of interdependence and their bearing on international law and policy.

Political rights. Among these must be included the right of states to participate in the shaping of international policy and especially the making of international law, its interpretation and enforcement. This of course formulates an ideal, since as yet there is no world legislature with adequate powers of enforcement. In our own day the most important organs of international organization are the United Nations and the agencies created by it or working in connexion with it. Their structure is therefore of importance in this context. Membership of the United Nations is open to all states which accept the obligations laid down in its Charter and, 'in the judgement of the organization, are able and willing to carry out these obligations'. In practice, however, no serious attempt is made to implement this latter requirement. In the Assembly each state has one vote. Differences in population, economic resources, or educational level are ignored. The Assembly takes its ordinary decisions by a majority vote, but if a question is considered 'important' a two-thirds majority of the members present and voting is required. It is clear that under voting arrangements of this sort decision by majority is only acceptable if the powers of the Assembly are strictly limited. The large nations are hardly likely to feel bound in matters they consider vital by a body in which their votes have no more weight than those of the smallest nation. If the Assembly is ever given greater powers to act on behalf of all the members the task of devising a system of 'weighting' on some agreed principle of proportionate equality will have to be faced.[1]

The difficulties reappear in sharper form in the case of

1. Cf. G. Clark and L. B. Sohn, *World Peace Through World Law*, 1960.

the Security Council, whose powers are far greater than those of any other organ of the United Nations. The Council consists of five permanent members – China, France, the U.S.S.R., the United Kingdom, and the United States – and six other members elected by the General Assembly for a term of two years, regard being paid to geographical distribution and the contribution of the members to the fulfilment of the purposes of the United Nations. The method of arriving at decisions gives the Great Powers a privileged position. Each of them has a veto on decisions. In existing conditions of mutual distrust the insistence on the right of veto is not surprising, but it is generally agreed that it has resulted in depriving the Council in the majority of cases of the ability to discharge its responsibilities under the Charter.

Finally, mention must be made in this context of the other principal organ of the United Nations, the International Court of Justice. This consists of fifteen judges elected by the Security Council and the General Assembly regardless of nationality from among persons with the highest judicial qualifications. It is understood that in making the election the representation of the main forms of civilization shall be assured. The basis of the Court's jurisdiction is voluntary. The Optional Clause by which states agree to submit their disputes to the jurisdiction of the Court has only been signed by about a third of the members of the United Nations and many of those who have signed have done so with reservations designed to exclude decisions on matters of 'domestic jurisdiction' and on condition of reciprocity on the part of the other states involved. These reservations have had the effect of weakening the influence of the Court, but, as Professor Brierly pointed out, they reflect the prevailing tensions and lack of mutual trust in the relations between states. It should be remembered, however, that, though the Court lacks powers of compulsory jurisdiction, it has made contributions of great importance to the development of international law through its decisions and advisory opinions.

The right to conclude treaties. Treaties have some analogy to private contracts. But there is an obvious difference between them. While contracts between individuals are invalid if made under duress, treaties imposed by a conqueror are as valid in law as those which are entered into freely. The ethical problem involved was discussed fully by Sidgwick from the point of view of individualist Utilitarianism. He saw clearly that it would not do to say that treaties made under coercion may be repudiated by the vanquished when they have the power to do so. For this would encourage the conqueror to crush his enemy completely and ruthlessly. On the other hand, it is clearly morally repugnant to condemn a nation for seeking release from a palpably unjust and oppressive treaty. In dealing with this difficulty, Sidgwick tried to distinguish between onerous conditions imposed by a victor who had just cause for war and cases in which the conqueror was in the wrong. But he recognizes the difficulties involved in distinguishing between just and unjust wars, and is compelled to conclude that, so long as war is recognized as a method for settling disputes between states, the problem cannot be satisfactorily resolved. He adds that the moral and jural difficulties encountered should serve to impress on the mind the essential barbarism of war – however ordered and regulated.[1] In this he clearly goes to the root of the matter.

Analogous difficulties arise in connexion with treaties which, owing to changes in circumstances, have become oppressive. They have usually been dealt with by appealing to the principle that treaties are made with the implied reservation that they will be binding only so long as circumstances remain the same (*rebus sic stantibus*). That this argument lends itself to abuse is obvious. Witness the appeal made to it by the Nazis every time they found a treaty inconvenient, though usually they put forward the additional argument that repudiation was made necessary on the ground that the treaty in question

1. *Elements of Politics*, pp. 278–82.

had become incompatible with the right and duty of self-preservation.[1]

It is clear that the problem of unequal and oppressive treaties cannot be resolved as long as international law is too weak to regulate *ab initio* the conditions in which valid contracts can be made, to deny the validity of treaties made under coercion, and to provide for the impartial revision of treaties when such revision has become necessary in the general interest. In English law 'freedom of contract' has been limited in various ways to protect the weaker party, or for other reasons of public policy. Until international law is in a position to impose similar limitations, we cannot expect it to deal adequately with the problems of a changing international order.[2]

4

The question as to the practical implementation of the rights and duties of states and of their relations to each other is very complicated. Its full treatment is beyond my competence. Here I can only offer some comments related to the points previously raised in my analysis.

I begin with the right of security against interference. This has been interpreted as carrying with it the right to arm in self-defence. In an era of nuclear armaments, it is now clear, self-defence involves intolerable risks. It has therefore to be examined in the context of the wider problem of world disarmament. The ideal solution would be to adopt a policy of complete national disarmament save only for such limited and lightly armed forces as are needed for internal security. The difficulties involved in giving effect to this ideal are only too obvious, but it must be remembered that so are the penalties for failure to do so.

Next, in regard to the right of territorial integrity we

1. Numerous examples will be found in Bristler, *Die Völkerrechtslehre des Nationalsozialismus*, 1938, pp. 154–6.

2. Cf. Brierly, *The Law of Nations*, ch. VII.

have to face the difficulty that in implementing it we have to start with the *status quo*, even though the *status quo* may be flagrantly unjust or felt by the peoples concerned to be so. On this, two points have to be made. On the one hand, the general principle stands that attempts to bring about territorial changes by force must be restrained. On the other hand, this principle is only acceptable on two conditions. First, that an international standing authority exists whose business it is to examine grievances before the point is reached at which peoples will be impelled to take the law into their own hands. Second, that this authority must be able to inspire a general and widespread belief not only in its ability to deal justly with claims, but to enforce its decisions irrespective of the strength of the parties in question.

Similar considerations are suggested by an examination of the right of political independence. For if a world authority existed capable of ensuring world peace, states would have less reason for insisting on political and economic autarky. Greater scope would then be given to international cooperation through governmental and non-governmental institutions, and there would be a greater willingness to widen the area of international law to include matters which states at present consider as falling solely within their domestic jurisdiction. A case in point is that of the control of immigration. Already Sidgwick noted that an absolute claim to exclude aliens could not be justified on the principle of mutual non-interference, and that in the case of territories greatly underpopulated a compromise would have to be found between the prescriptive rights of particular states and the general claims of humanity.[1] Since Sidgwick's day the control of immigration has been tightened, and in any case it is a matter which international law leaves to the decision of each country. Even the *Declaration of Human Rights*, though it asserts the right to emigrate,[2] says nothing about a right to immigrate. But clearly restrictions on immigration

1. op. cit., p. 255. 2. Art. 13 (2).

create difficulties for countries with a surplus of population. In justice, therefore, they ought not to be left to the unfettered will of each state, but should be dealt with by an international authority, capable of taking into consideration the needs of would-be migrants, the absorption capacity of different areas, the probable effect on the standards of life in the receiving country, and the possibility of providing alternative solutions where migration is not desirable. Similar considerations apply to international economic relations which, apart from concessions arranged by treaties, states claim to regulate as seems good to them, without regard to the effect of their regulations on other peoples. In these as in other matters the growing interdependence of peoples involves limitations of the right of independence which states are still loath to accept.

The problem that stands most in need of clarification is that concerning the equitable distribution of the means of well-being among peoples. In view of the fact that opinions differ widely about the principles of distributive justice within states, it is not surprising that their application to international relations has only recently begun to be explored. The process of decolonization has brought into prominence the problem of the 'underdeveloped' countries, and there is a growing feeling among the richer nations that the poverty and distress in which more than half of mankind is living are not only morally wrong, but a menace to their own security. The duty of promoting the economic and social advancement of peoples is explicitly recognized in the Charter of the United Nations. Its implementation, however, is left to specialized agencies such as the World Health Organization, the International Labour Organization, the United Nations Educational, Scientific and Cultural Organization, the Food and Agriculture Organization, the International Bank for Reconstruction and Development. These are autonomous, voluntary bodies established by agreements between governments, though the Economic and Social Council *may* enter into agreements with them and coordinate their activities.[1] On the practical results achieved by these organizations opinions differ. However this may be, there can be no doubt that they play and will continue to play an important role in providing a forum where the under-privileged peoples can air their grievances and express their demands for a more equitable distribution of the means of well-being. There is thus hope that they may be strengthened in various ways and prepare the ground for the establishment of a world authority capable of devising and assuring a more rational use and equitable distribution of the world's resources. Meanwhile the activities of the specialized agencies are limited by the willingness of the governments that provide the funds. They are hardly likely to make the vast increase in the contributions called for until they can free themselves from the burden of armaments and until they realize more clearly that political instability is largely conditioned by the persistency of gross economic inequalities among the peoples of the world.

There is good evidence to show that in recent decades the economic inequalities between the developed and under-developed countries have been increasing and that within the poorer countries the inequalities between individuals, classes, and regions are as great as they have ever been and that in many of them they are still growing.[2] What has so far been done to diminish these inequalities is pitifully small. Sixty per cent of the world's population are estimated to be in a chronic state of hunger or malnutrition and only a quarter enjoys adequate nutrition. The situation grows worse because the increase of population is greatest in areas where poverty is most acute. The injustice of this is plain enough, but efforts to deal with the economic and political problems involved have not so far proved effective. If the remedy is to

1. Articles 55 and 63 of the Charter.

2. See G. Myrdal, *Economic Theory and Under-developed Regions*, ch. 1.

be provided by the United Nations, the balance of power within it will have to be radically altered. There is indeed a growing demand that the Security Council should be enlarged from eighteen to twenty-seven, so as to obtain a more equitable geographical representation. But there seems little prospect of this proposal being accepted in the near future. Again, it is true that the voting strength of the 'Big Five' has waned under the influence of the African and Asian states who today constitute more than half of the 111 member states of the United Nations. Some of these, however, are split by internal dissensions and, in any case, really significant economic advances in many of the under-developed areas must depend on the efforts of the richer countries. Their governments are hardly likely to increase their financial commitments to international funds and at the same time abandon their power to control the institutions through which they are administered. No significant change in their attitude can be expected until the fear of war is removed. The problem of development is thus intimately linked with the problem of disarmament. Not only would disarmament make available large funds now used for military purposes, but it would help to create an atmosphere of mutual trust. This might make states less unwilling to accept serious limitations of their sovereignty and, what is perhaps equally important, enable non-governmental institutions to play a more effective role in the movements towards an equitable world order.

CHAPTER XII

Morality and Law

1

IN previous chapters I have frequently made use of the distinction between moral and legal rights and duties. This raises the more general question of the relation of law to morality. To this I now turn.

This subject has been greatly obscured by the use of highly ambiguous key terms like 'natural law' and 'positivism', and by a failure to distinguish between the question how law and morals have been and are in fact related and the question how in the opinion of philosophers they should be related. On the question of fact it is clear that the relations vary greatly. Systems of law which have grown up slowly in response to social needs embody relations between law and morals different from those in systems imposed from without at the command of a conqueror. Systems in which law, ethics, and religion are closely interwoven, as in the law of Islam, differ from secularized systems, and, in these again, the impact of moral opinion on law varies with the type of political structure and the influence of public opinion on legislation. Even within any one system and at any one time some parts of the law may be more deeply impregnated with moral or ethico-religious ideas than others. Historical investigation is often required to show how it comes about that acts hitherto left to moral or religious sanctions are brought within the criminal law, or, conversely, why acts condemned both morally and legally are removed from the list of crimes. Incest, for example, formerly not treated as a crime, was made punishable by death in 1650. Since the Restoration it had, as Blackstone notes, been left to the 'spiritual coercion of the spiritual courts'. Thereafter, bills to make it a criminal offence were at various times introduced in Parliament, but unsuccessfully. In 1908, however, an act was passed making incest punishable with penal servitude or imprisonment with or without hard labour. By an Act of 1956 the maximum punishment is seven years' imprisonment. The law relating to suicide may be cited to illustrate a change in the opposite direction. An act of 1961 abrogated the crime of suicide, and attempted suicide, punishable since 1854, thereby also ceased to be an offence. Neither morality nor law are closed systems. In the long run, though by no means uniformly, changes in moral outlook tend to be reflected in the interpretation of existing laws and in new legislation. On the other hand, moral ideas may themselves be clarified in the course of attempts to change the law, as can be seen in our own day in the movements for the reform of the criminal law or of the law of divorce.

There is a widely held view, by no means confined to legal Positivists, that law and morals are independent or, as it is sometimes put, that there is no necessary connexion between them. What precisely is meant by the claim to independence is, however, not very clear. That in fact law, or in earlier stages, custom, embodies moral ideas is not denied. True, we have no exact knowledge of the nature and extent of the connexion, yet on existing evidence there can be no doubt of its importance. Thus Professor Winfield in an examination of English case law, shows that, though judges do not attempt to make the law conform to any ideal ethical standard, they do appeal to the practical morality which they take to be for the time being prevalent in the community. And he quotes Lord Atkin: 'In dealings as between man and man the English Law does set up a high but not too high attainable standard of honest and fair dealing which to my mind is of the greatest value to the whole community and especially to the commercial community'.[1] Dowrick, in his study of *Justice According to the English Common Lawyers*, shows, it seems to me conclusively, that those who insist

1. *Legal Essays*, p. 287.

on the distinction between justice in the law and justice-according-to-law unwittingly assume a crypto-morality of their own. They attach value to certainty and its various beneficial consequences, to order and stability, personal liberty, impartiality and independence in adjudication, and equality of treatment.[1]

As against this, it will be argued that, though in modern societies legislation is, or may be, influenced by conceptions of well-being and though judges in applying the law are expected to show impartiality in surveying the alternatives, to be fair in balancing the claims of those affected, and to provide a reasoned basis for their decision, yet the connexion between law and justice is by no means always of this kind. Unjust laws are nevertheless laws and judges may be blind to changing social values. The answer to this argument is that, though often law lags behind morals, the link between them cannot be severed without endangering the very idea of a rule of law or of a *Rechtsstaat*. In this context Professor C. K. Allen's views are of great interest. He maintains that, while in the content of law there is no necessary relationship to morality, in the application of law 'justice is an absolute requirement'. The judge, in other words, in administering the law has to decide between rival claims, fairly and impartially, 'on a principle'[2] excluding personal prepossession or idiosyncrasy. I find it difficult to accept the implications of this distinction, if I have understood it rightly. There is no doubt moral value in decisions 'on principle', but I cannot see that we should or ought to continue valuing such decisions if the rules 'justly' applied are themselves unjust. It is true that it may be our duty to obey a particular law, though we think it unjust, and that judges may have to administer laws of which they disapprove. But this is so only because we think the legal system as a whole worth preserving and that our disobedience of a specific law may lead to disobedience of other laws which may be just, even though

1. op. cit., p. 189. 2. *Aspects of Justice*, p. 65.

we do not like them. The argument that unjust laws are still laws has its limits. A state dominated by a tyrannical legislator who rules by edicts and appoints judges to serve his will can hardly be considered a *Rechtsstaat*. Even the tyrant, if he is to retain his power, has, as Aristotle tells us, to appear in the light of the father of the state, the guardian of the citizens; to be, if not virtuous, at least 'half-virtuous'.[1]

The claim that law and morals are independent may take a more radical form. It may mean that law is a self-contained system, in the sense that we need not and ought not to go beyond law for a justification of law. This view is very widely held. I propose to discuss it here by reference to the work of Kelsen, who is perhaps the most ardent defender of the autonomy of law. His refusal to base law on ethics is traceable, in the last analysis, to his belief in the relativity of knowledge and of morals.[2] There is, he argues, no 'natural law', there are no immutable principles of justice to which the legislator or the judge can appeal. The validity of any particular rule of law is grounded in that of a wider or superior rule and, ultimately, of a *Grundnorm*, or a super – or initial – norm. For the acceptance of the initial norm no legal reason can be given, nor any other reason, so far as one can see, save historical fact. The actual content of the legal order, it seems, is the embodiment of a compromise reached in the struggle for power by competing groups. These succeed in concealing the nature of the struggle by pretending to act in the name of justice and the common good.[3] It is more consistent with human dignity, Kelsen insists, to abandon this pretence and to claim for law only hypothetical validity. Particular laws may be shown to be

1. *Politics*, V, XI.

2. *'Positivismus und (erkenntnistheoretischer) Relativismus gehören ebenso zussammen wie Naturrechtslehre und (metaphysischer) Absolutismus.'*
(*Die philosophischen Grundlagen der Naturrechtslehre und des Rechtspositivismus*, p. 14.)

3. op. cit., p. 68.

valid if they are consistent with the initial norm. The latter is morally indifferent, but, once accepted, the rest follows.

Kelsen's great contributions to the study of law have been widely recognized and they continue to be influential. As I am no lawyer I must confine myself to the philosophical issue. It seems to me that his ethical indifferentism is illusory, and cannot be maintained consistently with the distinction he takes as fundamental between facts and norms. To begin with, his appeal to 'human dignity' and the importance he attaches to what he calls a unitary legal order conceals an ethical commitment. Why insist on 'unity' or consistency in the law, if not out of respect for the moral imperative to pursue truth and to avoid unbalance between the different parts of the legal system?

Next, Kelsen's account of the relations between legal and moral obligation is far from clear. The legally obligatory defines what *shall* be and not what *is*. Up to a point, he explains, there must be a certain correspondence between the actual behaviour of people and what the law requires of them. On the other hand, there must be a possibility of acting against the law, since otherwise the law would lose its normative character and would merely describe what actually happens. What then makes the law binding, what gives it obligatory character? The answer, Kelsen stresses, is not to be found in the realm of fact, for example, in the pressure exerted by society on the individual, or in other forms of psychological constraint. To be binding is to be legally valid. A specific law is legally binding if it is in conformity with the initial norm. The validity of the initial norm has to be assumed. But once assumed, it is claimed, it transforms might into right. I find it difficult to see what the 'transformation' amounts to. Presumably 'right' here means 'legal right' and not ethical right, since the adoption of the initial norm is, as we have seen, ethically indifferent. If so, the transformation of might into right amounts to no more than the recognition of the fact that there is an effective legal order; that is, an authority in receipt of habitual obedience. In other words, the reduction of right to fact, a form of positivism which Kelsen repudiates, has not in fact been renounced.[1]

2

The independence of law and morals cannot be defended either as an account of the way in which law in fact works or of the way in which it ought to work. In fact the law of a society, and particularly the criminal law, embodies the moral attitudes prevalent in that society and cannot, in the long run, be made effective without appealing to these attitudes. Often, indeed, changes in moral outlook are not immediately reflected in the law. As already Sir Henry Maine noted, social opinion and social necessities are always more or less in advance of law. 'We may come infinitely near to the closing of the gap between them, but it has a perpetual tendency to reopen.'[2] But this makes the case for an ethically-based critical jurisprudence all the stronger. As Westermarck, himself an ethical relativist, pointed out:

> Philosophers and theorists of the law would do better service to humanity if they tried to persuade people not only that their moral ideas require improvement, but that their laws, so far as possible, ought to come up to the improved standard, than they do by wasting their ingenuity in sophisms about the sovereignty of law and its independence of the realm of justice.[3]

Granted that in fact positive morals and positive law are interconnected, though not always harmoniously; granted further that both are subject to revision in the

1. For further examination of Kelsen's view see H. Lauterpacht, in the collection *Modern Theories of Law*, 1933, ch. VII; M. Villey, *Leçons d'histoire de la philosophie du droit*, 1957, ch. XIX; M. Ginsberg, *Reason and Unreason in Society*, ch. XII.

2. *Ancient Law*, ch. II.

3. *Moral Ideas*, 1906, vol. I, p. 201.

light of a critical morality, the question remains how the line between them is to be drawn: the question, in other words, what acts or omissions should be legally enforced and what left to moral suasion and moral choice.

Before setting out my own views, I propose to consider two main approaches to this question, that of Kant and his Idealist derivatives and that followed by the Utilitarians. According to Kant legal coercion is justified to prevent interference with freedom, or, in other words, to assure equality in freedom.

When a certain use of freedom is a hindrance to freedom in accordance with universal laws, the compulsion which is opposed to it, as a hindering of a hindrance to freedom, itself agrees with freedom in accordance with universal laws.

The principle is intended to be purely formal; that is, independent of the ends of actions. As such it is, I think, too general to be really helpful in delimiting the sphere of legal coercion. Consider the case of property. Every man is free to appropriate objects for use. 'What is mine is that with which I am so bound up that the use which another should make of it without my consent would be a wrong one.' This leaves entirely untouched the question within what limits appropriation can be allowed without violating the law of equal freedom. Similarly, as we have seen, freedom of contract will not make for equal freedom without some limitation designed to equalize bargaining power. Kant's more general formula may perhaps be interpreted so as to meet this difficulty:

Legal right is the sum of the conditions (*der Inbegriff der Bedingungen*) in which the will of the one can be united with the will of another according to universal laws of freedom.[1]

If this is taken as implying that all the conditions of maximum freedom are to be considered, it would follow that, in deciding on the use of compulsion in a particular case, it would be necessary to take into account not only

1. *Einleitung in die Rechtslehre*. Werke. Cassirer edition: Band VII, p. 31.

the effects of universalizing the specific right in question, but of other relevant rights in the body of rights. The problem, in other words, would be to balance one freedom against other freedoms, but this could not be done without reference to the consequences of the policy adopted.

There are similar difficulties in Spencer's formula which closely resembles Kant's, though it was reached independently:

> Every man is free to do that which he wills provided he infringes not the equal freedom of any other.

He explains, as I have pointed out in a previous chapter,[1] that the formula is not to be stretched to justify aggression and counter aggression. It is intended to ensure mutual non-interference in activities conducive to life and its maintenance. In this, as in other respects, Spencer wavers between the principle of non-interference and the principle of assuring the greatest happiness. Despite these hesitations and ambiguities, the principle of equal freedom whether as formulated by Kant or Spencer retains its importance, provided freedom is interpreted concretely by reference to the various 'freedoms', defined by the body of rights, and to the conditions in which they can be satisfied so as to make possible greater freedom on the whole.

The British Idealists, especially Bosanquet and Green, adopted Kant's principle of the 'hindering of hindrances', and, like him, they maintained that law can only deal with outward behaviour and with intentions only to the extent needed to ensure compliance in terms of outward performance or abstention. Morality, on the other hand, is in its nature inward. It consists in the disinterested performance of self-imposed duties. The function of law, in so far as it uses compulsion, is to maintain the conditions which make morality possible, that is, to enforce rights, but it cannot and ought not to enforce righteousness, since it is not within its power to ensure that an action shall be performed from a moral motive. In so far as it relies on

1. See above, p. 57.

the hope of reward and the fear of punishment 'its value as an element in the best life is *ipso facto* destroyed'.[1] Bosanquet explains that his view coincides in principle with Green's principle that only such acts or omissions should be enforced by the public power as it is better should take place from the unworthy motives of the fear or hope of legal consequences than not take place at all.[2]

Both Bosanquet and Green stretch the formula limiting the use of compulsion by the state to the 'hindering of hindrances to freedom' to include positive acts. Thus illiteracy may be hindered by compulsory education and intemperance by municipalizing the liquor traffic. If we ask why not then hinder unemployment by assuring full employment, overcrowding by the public provision of houses, and immorality by punishing immoral and rewarding moral actions, the answer turns on the importance attached to moral growth as an inward process. Compulsion is only justified when we are able to show 'a definite tendency to growth or a definite reserve of capacity which is frustrated by a known impediment, the removal of which is a small matter compared to the capacities to be set free.'[3] That this could be very narrowly restrictive is shown in Bosanquet's early writings by his opposition to old age pensions, on the ground that to relieve men and women of the responsibility of planning for their old age would weaken their purpose, shorten their views, and make their lives more shiftless and thriftless. He was opposed even to providing free meals to children of poor families because to do so would take away from individuals already on the brink of demoralization

1. Bosanquet, *Philosophical Theory of the State*, p. 190.

2. 'Those acts only should be matter of legal injunction or prohibition of which the performance or omission, irrespectively of the motive from which it proceeds, is so necessary to the existence of a society in which the moral end stated can be realized that it is better for them to be done or omitted from that unworthy motive which consists in fear or hope of legal consequences than not to be done at all' – *Principles of Political Obligation*, para. 15.

3. op. cit., p. 193.

the last effective stimulus towards continuing the effort to meet their parental responsibilities. Green, on the whole, took a broader view. Thus he justified 'interference' with the freedom of contract on the ground that we must consider not only those who are interfered with, but also those whose freedom is increased by the interference. In particular, he urged that control was necessary in the sphere of health and housing, the growth of the population relatively to the means of subsistence, and the accumulation and distribution of landed property. He dealt with these problems, however, only in very general terms, and it is not clear how much he would leave to the initiative of individuals and how much to the state. The vagueness is specially marked in his treatment of the rights of property. In his view, inequality is inherent in property in so far as it is based on the free exercise of ability and energy of individuals, or on the functions they fulfil in society. But he does not inquire how great an inequality can be thus justified. He did, however, show greater concern than Bosanquet for the 'property-less proletariat', whose emergence he traces to inequality in the ownership of land. Presumably, the necessity of control which he allows in the case of land could in principle be extended to other forms of capital accumulation. But, in the end, the question as to the form which such control should take is left open. The argument throughout is dominated by the stress laid on inner freedom and spontaneous growth.[1]

3

In considering the Utilitarian approach to the problem of the relation of law to morals, I propose to deal mainly with the position adopted by Bentham and Mill. In Bentham's view 'private ethics' and the art of legislation have or ought to have the same end – the happiness of every member of the community. But the spheres of the two arts do not coincide. Every individual ought of his own

1. *Principles of Political Obligation*, paras. 209–10.

choice to do acts which promise to be beneficial on the whole and to refrain from acts likely to be pernicious. But it does not follow that he ought to be compelled by law to perform the one and to abstain from the other. Where then is the line to be drawn?

To answer this question Bentham refers back to his discussion of the cases 'unmeet for punishment'. These consisted, firstly, of cases where there was no ground for punishment; that is, where there was no evil in the act. Clearly in these cases there is no ground for ethical condemnation either. The second group of cases were those in which punishment was likely to be ineffective. These included cases of *ex post facto* law or of law insufficiently promulgated. It is possible that the acts involved ought to have come under coercive law earlier, and, if so, they come under private ethics. The other group of cases falling under this head are acts performed by agents incapable of being deterred by the threat of punishment: for example, infants, the insane, or those acting under threat of extreme physical compulsion. In these cases, 'if the thunders of the law prove impotent, the whispers of simple morality can have but little influence.' Next there is a group of cases in which punishment would be unprofitable; that is, in which the evils of punishment are greater than the evils of the offence. Thus there are offences for which the penalty to be at all effective has to be very severe to make up for the difficulties of detection. In Bentham's view, it is difficulties of this sort that account for the failure of the law to punish fornication or illicit sexual relations. Secondly, there are offences which cannot be defined with precision and in which the application of the law may easily result in innocent persons suffering penalties designed for the guilty. Hence the caution of legislators in prescribing legal penalties for such actions as come under the notion of rudeness or ingratitude.

To these considerations Bentham adds others based on his classification of the main branches of duty. There are first the rules of *prudence*; that is, those concerned with the individual's own interests. Bentham concedes that the individual may not know fully what these are. But it is not likely that the legislator will know them better. The law ought not therefore to interfere in this sphere except perhaps by doing what can be done indirectly by strengthening the moral sanction. To interfere directly would involve a degree of surveillance which could not succeed without 'spreading dismay through every family, tearing the bonds of sympathy asunder, and rooting out the influence of social motives.'

The rules concerning acts which affect the happiness of others Bentham groups under the heading of (a) *probity* forbidding acts likely to hurt others, and (b) *beneficence* enjoining acts likely to increase happiness. Of these the rules of probity stand most in need of the sanctions of the law. Bentham points out that in that branch of probity concerned with offences against property private ethics depends for its very existence on legislation. The law has first to determine what things are to be regarded as a man's property before the general rules of ethics can have any particular application. Similarly with offences against the state. In both cases the law may not be what it ought to be. What the individual ought to do in that case is a matter for private ethics.[1] Finally, as far as the rules of beneficence are concerned, legislation can do little. Their beneficial quality depends on their being performed from the motives of sympathy, love of amity, and love of reputation, and these cannot be brought into play by political coercion. These rules have therefore to be left in the main to private ethics.

Bentham's view of the difference between private ethics and the art of legislation turns upon the distinction between acts conducive to the individual's own happiness and acts conducive to the happiness of a community of individuals. The former should be left to such motives as

1. Bentham, *A Fragment of Government*, p. 150, London ed. 1776, and p. 114, ed. 1823.

appeal to the individual; the latter may come under legislative jurisdiction in so far as they can be affected by motives applied by the legislator. Private ethics and legislation ought to be directed to the same end, but whether particular acts should come under the one or the other depends upon what can and cannot be achieved by each in view of the motives to which they can effectively appeal.[1]

The main distinctions drawn by Bentham reappear in Mill but are given a deeper significance by a more positive conception of liberty as a condition of 'individual vigour and manifold diversity'. His position as defined in the essay on *Liberty* taken in conjunction with the chapter on 'The Limits of the Province of Government' in the *Principles of Political Economy* may be summed up in the following propositions:

1. Coercion as such is evil and the burden of proof lies with those who demand a limitation of freedom.

2. The only purposes for which an individual may be justly interfered with or coerced is (a) to prevent harm to others, and (b) to ensure that he contributes his fair share in the burdens incurred in the common defence of society and its members, or in any other work necessary in the interest of the society of which he is a member. In defining 'harm to others' a distinction must be drawn between the violation of interests which explicitly or implicitly constitute 'rights' and other hurtful acts which, though injurious or inconsiderate, do not violate rights. The former come under the sanctions of the law; the latter are punishable by opinion, though not by law. Elsewhere Mill distinguishes between legal and moral rights. But the ground of the distinction is not clear. It appears to turn partly on the difficulties inherent in the methods of enforcement available to the law.

3. The main stress is on a distinction between self-regarding acts – that is, acts which concern only the in-

1. *Principles of Morals and Legislation*, ch. XVII.

dividual – and other-regarding acts – that is, acts which affect others. As far as other-regarding acts are concerned, Mill agrees with Bentham that acts hurtful to others should be prohibited by law or opinion (Bentham's Rules of Probity), while beneficent or disinterested acts are best left to individual choice and persuasion and to methods other than 'whips and scourges, either of the literal or metaphorical sort'. As we have seen, however, the individual may also be obliged to contribute his share to what is needed for the defence and maintenance of society. On the other hand, acts which directly affect only the agent and need not affect others unless they like are 'the appropriate region of human liberty'. He allows that self-regarding acts may affect others. Thus the neglect of one's property or failure to develop one's faculties may adversely affect one's dependents or fellow creatures generally. Furthermore, vices may affect others by example. He insists, nevertheless, that, except in so far as an act involves direct and not merely contingent injury to others, society can afford to be tolerant. Three liberties are of fundamental importance: First, freedom of thought and expression. The latter indeed is clearly not purely self-regarding and hence might rightly be held to be subject to control. But thought and its expression are interdependent and the one cannot be free without the other. Next, liberty of taste and action, of doing and living as we like, providing only that we do no harm to others. Third, liberty of associating with others for any purpose involving no harm to others.

4. Governing all these principles is the general principle of 'utility in the largest sense, grounded in the permanent interests of man as a progressive being'.

Mill's examples and qualifications do not bear out his claim that the limits of social compulsion and control can be stated in terms of one very simple principle . . .

that the sole end for which mankind are warranted, individually or collectively, in interfering with the liberty of action of any of their number is self-protection. That the only purpose for which power can be rightfully exercised over any member of a civilian community, against his will, is to prevent harm to others.[1]

Consider his defence of liberty of thought and discussion. This is not based on the claim that thought is something that concerns only the individual; for clearly even the innermost thoughts and feelings of an individual may deeply affect society. That the expression of thought can do so is admitted by Mill himself. The real ground Mill has in mind is that freedom of thought and its expression are essential to the growth of knowledge, that knowledge and action based on it can only be advanced or at any rate can be best advanced through openness to new ideas and experiments in different ways of living.

Similarly, his objections to an inquisitorial 'moral police', inclined to 'invest mere likes and dislikes with the authority of moral law', do not depend on the distinction between self-regarding and other-regarding acts. The same applies to his other examples. Those who object to the private accumulation of property beyond a certain amount or to unearned incomes cannot be refuted on the ground that property is a matter of private concern. On the other hand, Mill concedes that other-regarding acts which might be injurious to others do not necessarily come within the class which calls for interference. Thus competition may involve benefit to some and loss or disappointment to others. But it is allowed on the ground that it is in the interests of society that persons should be able to pursue their objects undeterred by legal action, excluding only fraud, treachery, or force. Similarly, free trade is justified, despite the fact that trade is a social or other-regarding act, because it can be shown that interference will not achieve the desired results, such as the cheapness and good quality of commodities. The criterion is thus not derived from the distinction between acts which concern only the individual and those that concern

1. *On Liberty*, ch. I.

others, but from the principle of general happiness. To determine under what conditions this can be attained it is necessary to balance gains and losses and for this no simple formula will suffice.

In the *Principles of Political Economy* Mill allows several important exceptions to his general principle of non-interference. These are still worthy of attention. Firstly, there are things which cannot be left to spontaneous demand. Elementary education, for example, is something of which every child ought to be assured. Hence it is right to impose a legal obligation on parents to see to it that their children receive the necessary instruction and on governments to make such instruction accessible either gratuitously or at a trifling expense.

Next, there are a number of cases in which the person affected is not the best judge of the matter or even a competent judge. This applies in the first place to the mentally ill or the immature who are therefore entitled to protection by the state. Some restriction on the freedom of contract may be necessary. For example, the hours of work by children cannot be left to the decision of employers and should be limited by law. 'Freedom of contract, in the case of children, is but another word for freedom of coercion.'

A second exception is the case of contracts or engagements in perpetuity. The law should be chary of sanctioning such contracts, and, where allowed, should ensure that they are entered into only after due deliberation. In certain unforeseen and unforeseeable circumstances it should, however, be possible for the parties, not indeed to revoke their engagements at will, but to obtain release from them on a sufficient case being made out before an impartial authority. These considerations are highly relevant to the marriage contract, the most important of all cases of engagements for life.

Thirdly, control may be justified in cases in which individuals do not act directly for themselves but through delegated agency as, for example, in joint-stock associations. In these circumstances, self-interest is not a sufficient guide. 'Private management in such cases is hardly better entitled to be called management by the persons interested than administration by a public officer.' The state may therefore have to intervene to protect the public from the dangers of monopolistic power or to ensure fit performance of the service in question.

A fourth exception arises where individuals are unable to obtain their object except in concert and when concerted action is liable to be defeated by individual recalcitrance. Mill instances hours of work where a minority willing to work longer hours could defeat the collective desire of a whole class of persons for shorter hours.

A fifth exception relates to acts which individuals do, not for their own interest, but for that of others. The most important example that Mill discusses is that of public charity. In his view, the certainty of subsistence should be guaranteed by law to the destitute able-bodied and should not be allowed to depend on voluntary charity. Subject to the principle of 'less eligibility', the relief of the indigent is a social duty.

Finally, the objection to government interference does not apply to the undertaking of services of importance to present or future generations which individuals or associations of individuals would not normally undertake. Mill instances, among other things, scientific research or exploration. The question to be asked is whether the work deemed beneficial is likely to be done by individuals and, if so, whether it is likely to be done better or more effectively by government agencies.

Bringing these various points together we may sum up Mill's view of the functions of government acting through law as follows:

1. Compulsion as such is evil and its use has to be justified.
2. It is rightly used in prohibiting and punishing acts

which are clearly injurious to other persons, whether the case be one of force, fraud, or negligence.

3. On the positive side, intervention which may involve compulsion is justified: (i) to achieve common purposes which cannot be left to the forces of supply and demand – such as education; (ii) to protect the immature and helpless; (iii) to control the power of associations, managed not by the persons directly interested but by delegated agencies; (iv) to protect individuals acting in concert in cases where such action cannot be effective without legal sanctions; (v) to achieve objects of importance to society, present and future, which are beyond the powers of individuals or voluntary associations or which, if within their powers, would not normally be undertaken by them.

Since Mill wrote, of course, the forms of state action have multiplied in ways unheard of a hundred years ago. But in so far as the use of coercion is concerned, it is arguable that changes in the law in free societies can generally be shown to fall within one or other of the types of exceptions to the principle of non-interference enumerated by Mill. What remains as of abiding value is the principle that every limitation of freedom has to be rationally justified. This justification cannot be compressed, as Mill sometimes claims, into a single formula, and it follows from his own exceptions that it cannot be based on any clear-cut division between a public and a private sphere of action. The problem is to balance one freedom against other freedoms, one constraint against other constraints, bearing in mind the conditions inherent in the tools available to the law.

4

The problem of the scope of legal compulsion has recently been raised afresh in connexion with the Wolfenden *Report on Homosexuality and Prostitution*. The authors lay down the following principles:

> The function of the criminal law in so far as it concerns the subject of this inquiry ... is to preserve public order and decency, to protect the citizen from what is offensive or injurious, and to provide sufficient safeguard against exploitation and corruption of others, particularly those who are specially vulnerable because they are young, weak in body or mind, inexperienced, or in a state of special physical, official, or economic dependence.
>
> It is not, in our view, the function of the law to intervene in the private lives of citizens, or to seek to enforce any particular pattern of behaviour, further than is necessary to carry out the purposes we have outlined.

In commenting on the *Report* in his lecture on the *Enforcement of Morals* Lord Devlin has taken these passages to imply what he takes to be a fundamental error in jurisprudence, namely the separation of law from morals. I doubt whether in this form the criticism is justified. The issue has been confused by the introduction of a very ambiguous distinction between a 'private morality' and a 'public morality'. This distinction may be intended, firstly, to mark off acts done in private from acts done in public, and to stress the principle that both in legislation and in methods of detection the law should respect privacy. This, however, is not disputed by anyone in this debate. It may be intended, secondly, to coincide with the distinction drawn by Mill between rules relating to acts which affect others and acts which concern only the agent or need not affect others unless they like. If so, it will be widely agreed, as I have argued above, that it will not suffice to define the limits within which the law may use coercion. The principle that the only ground for compulsion is 'to prevent harm to others' is clearly inadequate, for it remains to define what constitutes harm or what is offensive or injurious, and this cannot be done, as Sidgwick has shown, without reference to a conception of well-being, such as the general happiness. The terms 'public' and 'private' may, thirdly, point to a much deeper distinction. By 'public' morality may be meant what older writers called positive morality; that is, the working code to which people are normally expected to conform. 'Private' morality, on the other hand, may stand for the morality accepted by the individual conscience, which may differ from the public morality in approving acts conventionally condemned and condemning others conventionally approved. This has nothing to do with the distinction between self-regarding and other-regarding acts. For the public morality includes duties to self as well as duties to others, and freedom of conscience may be pleaded in relation to acts which undoubtedly affect others; as, for example, conscientious objection to military service.

If these different meanings of the distinction between public and private morality be borne in mind, the issues raised by the Wolfenden *Report* will, I think, be seen in clearer light. Firstly, the *Report* does not commit itself to a separation of law and morals. The preservation of public order and decency, the protection of citizens from what is offensive or injurious, the provision of safeguards against abuse of power over those who are particularly vulnerable, which they take to be the function of the law, do not fall outside the scope of morality. On the contrary, they are minimal conditions of life in society and as such come under the elementary rules of justice. Their exclusion from the sphere of morals only makes sense if the terms moral and immoral are confined, as is often done in popular writings, to the relations between the sexes.

Second, granted the link between law and morals, two questions remain. (a) What is to be done in considering a change in the law when moral opinion is divided? Are there criteria other than individual likes and dislikes to which appeal can be made? This is the fundamental problem of social ethics. (b) How are we to draw the line between that part of morality or immorality which needs legal enforcement and that which the law ought to leave alone? As to (a), neither the *Report* nor its critic is very illuminating. Lord Devlin allows that the standard 'does not depend on the counting of the heads'. He appeals instead to the 'reasonable man'. But the reasonable man is not the reasoning man: 'he is not expected to reason about anything and his judgement may be largely a matter of feeling.' Yet the feeling has to be a 'genuine feeling', one that would still be strongly felt after the matter had been considered 'calmly and dispassionately'. Lord Devlin tells us that it is in determining what 'right-minded' persons feel that investigations such as those made by the Wolfenden Committee are of value. But in fact the Committee admit that they found great difficulty in discovering what standards people appeal to in forming their opinion about what is offensive or injurious or inimical to the common good.[1] They in their turn do not explain how they hope to arrive at 'a just and equitable law' in the matter with which they are concerned. Their task does not extend, they say, 'to assessing the teaching of theology, sociology, or psychology', and nothing is said of moral philosophy. But this is what has to be done in any serious effort to deal with proposed changes in the law in matters about which moral opinion is divided. A double inquiry is needed; a critique of the moral principles and assumptions and an inquiry into the relevant facts and tendencies. We cannot assume that public or positive morality is unchangeable or beyond criticism, or that we know enough of the forms of social adjustment that are possible. If law and morals are to be linked we need to reach agreement on the procedure to be followed in bridging the gap between them. This I take to be the task of a critical jurisprudence, and a study of recent work on controversial issues – as, for example, capital and corporal punishment, birth-control, euthanasia, divorce – will show that such a jurisprudence must make increasing use of the social sciences combined with philosophical analysis of the extent and nature of any disagreements there may be on matters of moral principles.

1. Paras. 15 and 16.

On the dividing line between law and morals the Wolfenden Committee based their view mainly on the distinction between private and public morals.

> Unless a deliberate attempt is made by society acting through the agency of the law to equate the sphere of crime with that of sin, there must remain a realm of private morality and immorality which is, in brief and crude terms, not the law's business.[1]

This, as we have seen, is open to the objection that it confuses the various senses in which the terms 'private' and 'public' morality may be used. Nor is the reference to the notion of sin helpful. Sin is moral evil considered as an offence against God. But I take it that this means that it is an offence against God because it is morally evil but not that it is morally evil because it offends God. What is morally evil has therefore to be first determined, and in the matters at issue religious views in fact change as moral ideas change. The reference to sin is thus logically a detour which may be theologically important but which does not obviate the need for independent rational examination. On the particular issue involved, I understand that in the Roman Catholic view, as in that of the Church of England, 'penal sanctions are not justified for the purpose of attempting to restrain the sins against sexual morality committed in private by responsible adults.'[2] It seems, then, that even if crime is equated with sin there would still remain the problem of discriminating between the sins that are and the sins that are not the concern of the law.

Lord Devlin is no doubt right in stressing the point that the law must keep close to what is taken to be the moral sense of the community. But he does not allow for the part that the law may play in shaping the moral sense of the community. A balance of conflicting considerations is thus involved. If the law is out of touch with the pre-

1. Paras. 13 and 61.
2. Cited, *Journal of Delinquency*, July 1958, p. 8.

vailing opinion it will be brought into contempt. On the other hand, the law can do much to influence moral opinion. It is at this point that the 'conservative' and the 'radical' differ, the latter being prepared to take greater risks in advocating changes in advance of what is taken to be, sometimes erroneously, the prevailing opinion. A comparison of the history of the Prohibition Laws in the U.S.A. with the current laws of desegregation is instructive in this context. It may well turn out that the desegregation laws, if persistently enforced, may help to bring about a change in attitude, in behaviour, and eventually in moral convictions.

The root of the matter is a certain ambiguity in the principle defining the limits of freedom by reference to what is and what is not 'consistent with the integrity of society'. How is this to be ascertained? As we have seen, the decision is not left to the voice of the majority, but to the feelings of the 'reasonable man'. But if the concept of the 'reasonable man' is to apply not only to the man in the jury box or to the judge but also to the legislator, then surely guidance other than feelings are required in reaching a decision on the merits of a proposed enactment or repeal. In such matters as homosexuality, for example, a good deal of scientific evidence is available, as the Wolfenden Committee found, and more is assuredly obtainable by further research. If the voice of the majority is not accepted as decisive, neither should the dogmatic assertions of the 'reasonable man' if unsupported by the available evidence on the facts and philosophical analysis of the moral issues involved.

5

I must now try to bring together the principal conclusions suggested by my survey.

On the question how law and morals are *in fact* related no general answer can be given. There is a moral element in all law as soon as the notion emerges that no one ought to be a judge in his own cause, and methods are provided for settling disputes by reference to general rules without the use of force by the parties concerned. But the extent to which the rules are in fact impartially applied, and still more the extent to which the rules themselves command the moral assent of those subject to them, vary enormously in different societies. We have no way of estimating with any precision the part played by arbitrary domination in the growth and maintenance of the law, or for determining the limits at which discontent, sharpened by a feeling of injustice, results in open resistance and revolt. Furthermore, conceptions of what constitutes arbitrary power and general well-being are themselves shaped or influenced by existing inequalities of power, political or economic. Nevertheless, moral factors gain in strength in the course of social development and as legislation comes more and more to rely on fact-finding inquiries and scrutiny of the ends which the law ought to serve.

On the question how law and morals *ought* to be related writers on jurisprudence still differ very widely. But the view that they are independent is very obscure and I think indefensible. The ultimate justification of law is that it serves moral ends. The science of positive law and the theory of legislation are distinguishable, but both are impoverished by separation. I know of no attempt to free law from morals which does not in the long run, consciously or unconsciously, reintroduce ethical principles. I have referred to the difficulties involved in Kelsen's defence of the autonomy of law. Similar difficulties recur in other attempts, such as that made by Duguit to establish an 'objective' theory of law independent of morals. Duguit professes to replace ethical categories by the notion of solidarity or interdependence. But interdependence is not in fact used by him in an ethically neutral sense. For in one sense all societies which manage to cohere somehow are based on some kind of interdependence. We are offered no criteria for distinguishing between societies resting on domination and societies relying on free cooperation. How are we to effect the transition from the one kind of solidarity or interdependence to the other? In the end, Duguit appeals to a sense of justice which he appears to reduce to a sense of proportion and a desire for equality. His argument thus goes beyond what can be deduced from the bare idea of social equilibrium and unwittingly assumes a standard in the light of which different types of society can be evaluated.[1]

But the dependence of law on morals must not be taken to imply that there is a set of moral principles which can be laid down once and for all and to which the legislators can appeal for guidance. What is implied is, I think, that both positive law and positive morals are open to criticism and to mutual correction. Thus there are deep-rooted differences of opinion about distributive and corrective justice and about the ethics of property or the family, and these differences are reflected in the movements for social reform. It is important to determine how far these differences depend on a fundamental divergence of moral outlook and how far they are due to obscurities arising from insufficient knowledge of the relevant facts and social tendencies and to confusions between judgements of value and judgements of fact.

The tendency of liberal as contrasted with totalitarian societies has been to avoid both the separation and the complete fusion of law and morality. While changes in the law have been increasingly influenced by conceptions of well-being, there has at the same time been a recognition that there are certain things in life which depend for their value upon inner choice and spontaneity and which the law in so far as it uses coercion should leave alone.

We can, I think, elicit a number of principles which in

1. *Traité de droit constitutionel*, 2nd ed., vol. I, p. 54. On Duguit's theories reference may be made to G. Gurvitch, *L'idée du droit social*, and to G. Davy, *Eléments de sociologie – sociologie politique*; Ginsberg, *Reason and Unreason in Society*, ch. XII.

free societies are coming to be more or less consistently applied in drawing the line between law and morals. These depend partly on the limitations inherent in the *modus operandi* of the law and partly on the end to which social policy is directed.

Thus (a) the law ought only to deal with what can be ascertained on reliable evidence and with acts which can be precisely defined. This is specially applicable to the criminal law, whose sanctions must be confined to overt acts or omissions which inflict definite evils on specific persons or the community at large. As Fitzjames Stephen pointed out, in language reminiscent of Mill's rejection of an inquisitorial moral police, if the criminal law were not thus restricted it would be entirely intolerable. 'All mankind would be criminals and most of their time would be passed in trying and punishing each other for offences which could never be proved.'[1] (b) The law deals primarily with overt or externally observable acts. This does not mean that it can ignore intentions, for it distinguishes between acts done with intent and acts done unintentionally. It is true, however, that the law does not punish a person for intentions which do not issue in deeds, though it may punish incomplete acts which constitute a potential danger. Furthermore, law can prescribe what is to be done or not done, but it cannot enforce states of mind. It can enforce outward obedience but not respect for authority. It cannot ensure good will or gratitude or restore alienated affection. (c) The law must as far as possible respect privacy. Only such breaches of the law ought to be dealt with as can be proved without interfering with the private lives of individuals to an extent that greater evils would result than the evils it is sought to prevent.

These are principles of demarcation arising from the limitations inherent in the machinery of the law. Other principles follow from the nature of the ends which morally the law ought to serve.

(a) There are certain minimal conditions of an ordered

1. *History of the Criminal Law in England*, vol. 2, p. 78.

social life the ensuring of which cannot be left to the good will of individuals. What these minimal conditions are depends on the level of social development. It is clear that in all societies the individual has to be protected against violence; that is, against attacks on his life and safety. Again, in all societies the individual must have reasonable security against interferences with property in *personalia*; that is, things directly used by the possessor. Rights in other kinds of property vary greatly in different societies and, as Bentham saw, the law has first to determine what things are to be regarded as a man's property before we can determine what constitutes interference with his rights in them. In our own society the ethical basis of the institutions of property is under attack, but, so long as they remain unchanged, the law has to use its sanctions to protect them. In all societies the relations of the sexes are regulated. In western societies there is a fair amount of agreement on the ethics of monogamous marriage. But the relations between law and morals in this sphere are far from clear. Premarital and nonmarital relations are not crimes. Positive morality condemns them, but the ethical basis of the condemnation is increasingly challenged. On the other hand homosexual relations are considered criminal as such by some codes, while others bring them under rules protecting dependents and the immature, or under rules of public decency.

The function of sex morals is to maintain a form of family life believed to be most conducive to the continuity and well-being of the human race and to give full scope to the affections and emotions vital to happiness and self-fulfilment. The rules of positive law and morals are gropings to attain these ends, but we must admit that the sociological assumptions on which they rest are still, as Sidgwick argued, in his time, a mere *anticipatio mentis*, awaiting empirical verification. We are not in possession of the data which would be required to establish generalizations concerning the effect of various degrees of sexual freedom or forms of marriage on the quantity and quality of the population. Nor do we know how far in the individual merely 'sensual' relations interfere with the higher forms of the love relationship or with the full development of personality. The inconsistencies in the law and in the working moral code dealing with relations between the sexes are thus not very surprising.

Among the conditions of an ordered social life are the provisions made by the civil law for giving effect to voluntary transactions, for settling disputes when voluntary efforts have failed, and for ensuring restitution or compensation for wrongs inflicted. In detail, the provisions may appear to be morally indifferent. For example, it is morally indifferent whether motorists should keep to the right or to the left, but it is not indifferent that there should be a rule to which all should conform. In this case the moral end is clear, the safety of persons. In other cases, the law may have to select one of a number of rules in themselves morally indifferent, in order to assure the smooth working of social life and to eliminate sources of friction.

(b) With the growth of the idea of social responsibility replacing earlier more individualist notions, it has come to be realized that there are certain ends which are best secured by an inclusive unit with compulsory powers; for example, health and education. In western societies it is widely recognized that the state, without necessarily taking over the direct management of the economic structure, ought nevertheless to have sufficient control over it to assure to all its members the minimum conditions of mental and physical well-being and to prevent abuses arising from inequalities of power. But, of course, there are wide differences of opinion, partly based on divergent views of social justice, but to a greater extent on economic and sociological grounds, about the areas of social organization to which such conduct should be extended and the manner in which it should be exercised. It should be remembered that the state's action in these matters is by no means necessarily coercive. It can do much by providing the machinery for collective bargaining and perhaps giving legal force to the agreements thus reached.

(c) When uniform or concerted action is necessary to attain common ends great difficulties arise when individuals abstain on grounds of conscience; as, for example, in conscientious objection to military service. In the World Wars the state in this country and in some others in fact made provision for exemption. I take it this was partly based on the belief that concessions to the conscientious objector would not seriously hamper the general working of the Military Service Acts and would not endanger the safety of the nation. But this, of course, does not dispose of the problem in principle. Imagine a situation in which the governing power is convinced that a certain type of action is necessary for the common well-being and in which the individual can by his refusal effectively hinder the governing power in its efforts. Then, assuming conscientiousness on both sides, we have a tragic situation in which right clashes with right. The community must then take action against the recalcitrant individual and he, in resisting, must be prepared to take the consequences.

(d) Finally, there are certain ends which from their very nature can flourish best in freedom. Such are religion, learning and science, philosophy and art. The state acting through law can and, in certain circumstances, ought to help by providing the external conditions these ends require, but it must avoid anything like direct control.

In sum, there is no single principle for determining when liberty may be restricted. In general, restraint is justified when it is necessary in order to secure greater freedom on the whole. What we call freedom consists of a body of rights or liberties. The problem is to balance the various freedoms when they conflict, and to discover the conditions in which the values involved may be attained in harmony. This is not too remote from the formula of equal freedom. But instead of saying that liberty is limited by the like liberty of others, we should say limited by any one of a system of liberties and by the relative importance of the ends sought. The formula of the hindering of hindrances retains its importance, but it does not adequately cover the coercive powers of the law in promoting positive ends. For the distinction between self-regarding and other-regarding acts we substitute the distinction between ends which can and ends which cannot be attained by compulsion. Broadly, then, three questions have to be asked: (a) Is the use of force necessary or can the end aimed at be secured by suasion or voluntary agreement? (b) Will the liberty which is furthered by restraint in one sphere interfere with equal or more important liberties in other spheres; or, again, is the interference with some individuals necessary in order to equalize freedom or to increase the freedom of others? (c) Can the end in question be attained by compulsion or does its value depend on its being freely or spontaneously pursued? These questions have to be faced in any effort to distinguish between the rights and duties which require and permit of legal enforcement and the rights and duties which are best assured by moral means; that is, by inner conviction and free acceptance.

Index of Names and Subjects

Index of Names

Index of Subjects

Some Pelican books on allied subjects are described on the remaining pages

PERSONAL VALUES IN THE MODERN WORLD

M. V. C. Jeffreys

The future of our civilization depends on the extent to which we can rescue and promote personal values. The Professor of Education at Birmingham University discusses in this book the need for the rediscovery of a coherent view of life, the achievement of intelligent and effective communication between people and groups of people, and the encouragement of voluntary action both alongside and within public administration. The undermining of individual responsibility and mutual human respect by the impersonal mass-production of a 'faceless' culture is essentially an educational problem, and the main aspects of education are therefore discussed at some length.

PRIMITIVE GOVERNMENT

Lucy Mair

We take so much for granted the familiar forms of government – parliament, cabinet, ministries, law courts, and local authorities – that we are apt to forget which features constitute the essential elements of rule. These become clearer when we study how government has evolved to suit the needs of family, tribe, nation, and even empire.

Dr Mair has carried out field work on various widely differing systems which, in spite of the imposition of colonial rule, still in part obtain in East Africa. In these primitive societies it would appear that concepts of law and government were already understood and developed. In fact Dr Mair contends, contrary to some previous opinions, that no known society exists without them, even though their forms may be rudimentary.

Some such systems are quite outside the experience of western readers. For instance, an apparent anarchy may prove, on examination, to be in reality a well-ordered kind of government. In one society political responsibility is diffused throughout the whole; in another men have built up a kingdom which could be compared with those of medieval Europe.

In this survey of the way in which government is conducted without modern technical equipment, Dr Mair throws much new light on its historical evolution.

THE RISE OF THE MERITOCRACY

Michael Young

Dr Michael Young has christened the oligarchy of the future 'Meritocracy' – and the word is now part of the language. For it would appear that the formula I.Q.+effort=MERIT may well constitute the basic belief of the ruling class of the next century. Projecting himself into the year 2034, the author of this telling satire shows how present decisions and practices may re-mould our society.

Already today it is no longer enough to be somebody's nephew to obtain a responsible post in the civil service, in teaching, in science, or in commerce. Experts in education and selection apply scientific principles to sift out the leaders of tomorrow. You need intelligence rating, qualification, experience, application, and a certain calibre to achieve status – in a word, you must show 'merit'. Is this an undivided blessing?

'Its wit, its style, and its continuous fountain-gush of new ideas make it compulsively enjoyable reading from cover to cover' – *Time and Tide*

'Brilliant essay' – *Guardian*

FREEDOM, THE INDIVIDUAL AND THE LAW

Harry Street

Civil Liberties are very much in the news. At the heart of every incident that concerns the rights and obligations of the individual lies a conflict, sometimes muted, sometimes violent, between competing interests: freedom of speech *v.* security of the state, freedom of movement *v.* public order, the right to privacy *v.* professional integrity. Every day brings fresh reports of 'punch-up' politics, banning of controversial posters, curious corners of theatre censorship, abuse of telephone tapping, contempt of Parliament . . . the headlines never stop.

Yet Professor Street's *Freedom, the Individual and the Law* is the first comprehensive survey of the way English law deals with the many sides of Civil Liberty. After an introductory description of the powers of the police, Professor Street addresses himself in detail to the main areas of freedom of expression, freedom of association, and freedom of movement.

'For anyone who values his liberty this book is a must' – *Tribune*

'Imaginative, fresh, and compelling, his book brings alive the liberties we enjoy and those we are in danger of losing . . . minor masterpiece' – *Observer*

JOHN CITIZEN AND THE LAW

Ronald Rubinstein

'The best "popular" account of everyday law that has ever appeared at the price . . . will delight and instruct John Citizens in their thousands' – *New Statesman*

This fifth edition of *John Citizen and the Law* has been thoroughly revised and enlarged to over four hundred pages by the author's son, Christopher Rubinstein. There are new chapters on Civil Liberties and ownership of land, and major changes in the chapter on betting and gaming. Information on hire-purchase, the Rent Act of 1957, and many other important adjustments in English law are included to bring the book right up to date.

THE CRIMINAL LAW

F. T. Giles

The object of this book is to give a short, readable account of the English criminal law. The first part is devoted to a detailed account of a trial for murder as seen from the legal point of view. An outline of the powers and procedure of the criminal courts is given in the second section. The last part deals with the offences most commonly occupying the attention of the courts, such as murder, manslaughter, theft, and fraud.

This third edition of *The Criminal Law* has been brought completely up to date.

THE QUEEN'S COURTS

Peter Archer

English law embodies generations of experience, but it is constantly adapting itself to new situations, and the twentieth century has witnessed the birth of numerous tribunals which have taken their place alongside the ancient courts.

Of all these, their work, and their place in English life, *The Queen's Courts*, now completely revised and brought up to date, sets out to tell. It concludes with a comparison between the legal institutions of this country and those which function in different settings for different ways of life.

THE LAW IN PELICANS

Considering how often the ordinary citizen, as householder, parent, businessman, or traveller, is involved in the law, it is remarkable how little has been done to explain to him what the law is; how it has come to be what it is; and how it might be improved.

Pelicans have embarked, therefore, on a bold, new attempt to explore for the general reader a variety of legal topics of wide public interest.

In addition to the books described on the two previous pages, the titles which have already been published are:

THE ART OF THE ADVOCATE
Richard Du Cann

THE CONSUMER, SOCIETY AND THE LAW
Gordon Borrie and Aubrey L. Diamond

THE FAMILY AND THE LAW
Margaret Puxton

THE IDEA OF THE LAW
Dennis Lloyd

LAW IN A CHANGING SOCIETY
(Abridged edition) W. Friedmann

Future titles will include:

A SHORT HISTORY OF ENGLISH LAW
Alan Harding

THE WORKER AND THE LAW
K. W. Wedderburn